DARK HEART

By the same author

Blood on the Thistle
Frightener (with Lisa Brownlie)
No Final Solution
A Time to Kill
Devil's Gallop
Deadlier Than the Male
Bloody Valentine
Indian Peter
Scotland's Most Wanted

DARK HEART

Tales from Edinburgh's Town Jail

DOUGLAS SKELTON

MAINSTREAM
PUBLISHING

EDINBURGH AND LONDON

First published in Great Britain in 2008 by
MAINSTREAM PUBLISHING COMPANY
(EDINBURGH) LTD
7 Albany Street
Edinburgh EH1 3UG

ISBN 9781845963095

A catalogue record for this book is available
from the British Library

Typeset in Bembo

Printed in Great Britain by
Cox & Wyman Ltd, Reading

This book is dedicated to the memories of those writers who understood the allure of the subject and who have influenced what follows: to Sir Walter Scott, who provided the sense of romance; to Robert Louis Stevenson, who explored the dark side; to Samuel Rutherford Crockett, who furnished the blood and thunder (not to mention the tendency towards purple prose); to William Roughead, who knew that crime was part of history; to Robert Chambers, who knew the power of a well-turned phrase; and to John Prebble, who was a far better writer than I could ever hope to be.

CONTENTS

INTRODUCTION

August 2007

The area around St Giles' Cathedral in Edinburgh's High Street is choked with people. Predominantly young, they have come from all parts of the globe to enjoy – as performers or spectators – the excitement of the annual Festival and Fringe. The sky above is overcast but it is warm and dry, which is a godsend in a summer that has proved more soggy than sultry. On this, the first Friday of the three-week-long arts binge, the ancient street is awash with colour and thrumming with noise. Clowns in bright costumes are sent in, jugglers toss and catch a variety of implements, acrobats tumble and caper to the amazement of the crowd. The cobbles are carpeted with a layer of colourful flyers discarded by uninterested passers-by. But that does not matter, for there are thousands more to be dished out by young theatricals hoping to lure an audience. Not everyone appreciates the fun and the colour, though, for a man in a white van leans impatiently on his vehicle's horn, snarling at the crowd blocking his way that 'this is a street, no a playground'.

Two hundred years ago, this part of the street was certainly no playground but nobody here today seems to know or care. Today, it is all about art and entertainment. Back then, it was a different matter. In the early part of the nineteenth century, and for more than 250 years prior to that, the High Street beside the cathedral was the site of Edinburgh's Tolbooth, the town jail, the famous – or infamous – Heart of Midlothian. Now, on this day in the early part of the twenty-first century, only a solitary blues singer, strumming a guitar and croaking his lyrics as he sits against the cathedral wall, invokes in some small way the spirit of that dark place. For the blues is the music of loss, of pain, of suffering – and the Tolbooth was acquainted with all three.

I first became aware of it some years ago when a friend asked me why people spit on the heart-shaped mosaic of stones on the ground near the cathedral entrance. Being a Glaswegian, I did not have a clue. However, at the time I was writing a true-crime book which featured some historical murders and, of course, the Edinburgh Tolbooth loomed into my consciousness. Later, I wrote *Indian Peter*, the story of Peter Williamson. On his return from adventures in North America, Peter settled in Edinburgh. Again, the Tolbooth thrust itself into my mind, for it stood opposite Peter's lodgings in Byres' Close. I began to notice more and more references to the building in my research materials and, even though my next book detailed more modern horrors, my mind continued to return to the dark, stone-built 'grave for men alive' in Edinburgh's High Street.

In many ways, it is a shame that nothing of it has survived, apart from an arched doorway, which was incorporated in Sir Walter Scott's house at Abbotsford. He, at least, understood the value of retaining something tangible of history. Of course, it was impractical to have one of the main thoroughfares of a growing city blocked by such a building. However, when the decision to remove it was made in 1817, the failure to consider its place in history was an act of municipal vandalism. It had been, in its day, home to both the town council and the Scottish Parliament. Noble lords had massed here during times of national emergency. Mary, Queen of Scots, held court here and its door was decorated at night by notices calling her 'whore' and 'murderer' following the death of her husband. When a new Tolbooth was built a few feet away, Mary's son, James VI, sat in judgement within its walls – and used them to shield himself from rebellious nobles and turbulent preachers. The courts heard cases of theft and treason and murder in this new structure, while the rooms of the old building became cells, their walls echoing to the groans of prisoners doomed to die on the scaffold.

Apart from the Abbotsford doorway, the only physical links to the Tolbooth are the warding, liberation and relief books. There are 39 of them in total, stretching from 1657 to 1817, and in them are listed the thousands of souls who came through the doors of what Sir Walter Scott called the Heart of Midlothian. The ink with which they were written is fading now and the thick sheets of paper are yellowing. Some leaves are encased in plastic to shield them from the ravages of time and the destructive touch of modern fingers. The ornate script is often impossible to read to the untrained eye – in fact, some sections appear to be in either Arabic or Cyrillic script. Luckily, there are printed extracts from the early records from which details can be drawn.

Some years are missing. Some names that I expected to find are absent. In certain cases, entries have been excised. A sharp blade has sliced chunks from the paper, sometimes complete pages, removing names from the prying eyes of posterity. Were they removed under official sanction, in order to distance the authorities from unpopular decisions? Or had a memento-hunting researcher ripped off the archive and the nation? The period around the incarceration of radical lawyer Thomas Muir is just one example of this historical tweaking or hooliganism.

These incomplete volumes remain our only bridge across time to the Tolbooth. We can visit the site on the High Street and seek out the marks in the ground that purport to show its dimensions (not nearly big enough to my mind, although I am no surveyor) but that is not enough. The warding books, plus letters and other documents, were in existence then and they still exist now. When you touch them, you touch history. It takes a bit of imagination but the terse entries in these books help bring the past to life. Finding the 1664 note instructing the keeper of the Tolbooth to remove the head of the Marquis of Argyll from the spike on which it had rested for three years can transport the mind back through the centuries. The keeper becomes real again and his voice, ordering a servant to fetch wrights and slaters to repair any roof damage, is clear. There are scribbled computations on the front pages of the books and these conjure up the image of a jailer sitting in guttering candlelight, scratching away with a quill in a bid to make the books balance – or calculate how much he is owed for warding his prisoners.

I do not apologise for my flights of fancy, for I am a storyteller, not an academic. The tales I include here are all linked in some way to the Tolbooth 'complex' – the jail, the council buildings which held the courts and the cathedral, which on occasion acted as city chambers, justice building and prison. For a few of the stories, tradition rather than documentary evidence tells us that the men and women involved were held in the Heart of Midlothian. As ever before, I fall back on the advice of John Ford in *The Man Who Shot Liberty Valance* (itself a Scottish name, if derived from the Norman): 'When the legend becomes fact, print the legend.'

CHAPTER ONE

A PLACE IN HISTORY

It was a powerful building, even as it stood cheek-by-jowl with the magnificence that was St Giles' Church. Tall and turreted, dark and imposing, it blocked Edinburgh's High Street like a massive stone sentinel, leaving a gap of between 14 and 20 feet for the populace to go about their business. The high tenements, or 'lands', as they were known, rose up around it as if, in the words of one commentator, 'the antique fabric had been dropped whole and complete in the midst of the pent-up city'. Its walls had been blackened by decades of smoking chimneys, its windows so grimy they were almost opaque, although now and then a white face could be glimpsed peering out. One look would be enough to tell even the most casual observer what this place was – the town jail. One of Edinburgh's best-known landmarks, it was also one of the most hated. Even today, the spittle of good burghers covers the heart-shaped arrangement of cobblestones that marks the site of its entranceway. Some will know why they are expectorating on that particular spot; others will do it merely because it's the thing to do.

It became known as the Tolbooth, or Tolbuith, but it was not an office for the taking of roadway tolls, as we would understand the term today. Rather, it was originally the building to which the people came to pay their taxes, as well as acting as a headquarters for the growing civic bureaucracy. King David I (reigned 1124–53) gave the monks of Holyrood Abbey the rights to the revenues of the town. However, the town was expanding and, as the monks' influence waned, albeit only slightly, the burgeoning band of burgesses grew in influence and the throne recognised that some sort of permanent centre was needed in which the people could pay their dues. Also, according to a nineteenth-century architectural report on the history of the Tolbooth, the town had been 'burned and pillaged a little more thoroughly than usual' during an incursion by the English. Some rebuilding work proved necessary, so, in 1386, Robert II, the grandson of Robert the Bruce and the first Stewart king, granted the town a charter, the 'Carta Fundi de le Belhous', that proclaimed:

> Know ye, that we have given, granted and by this our present charter have conferred to our beloved and faithful, the burgesses and communities of Edinburgh, and their successors in time to come, 60 feet in length and 30 in breadth of land lying in the market place of the said burgh, on the north side of the street thereof; given and granted to them, and their foresaid successors, a special license to construct and erect houses and buildings, on the foresaid land, for the ornament of the said burgh, and for their necessary use.

There were 'belhouses' in other parts of Scotland and they were, exactly as the name suggests, houses with a bell. The bell was a very important part of the civic life of Edinburgh, not to mention the need for an alarm during incursions by enemies both foreign (the English) and domestic (rebellious nobles). The aldermen of the burgh used it to call the 'guild brethren together for the transaction of business'. For this, smaller bells would peal through the town, with three strikes of the Belhous bell ending the call. If the guild brethren did not drop what they were doing and come running, they could be fined twelve pennies. In addition, no one was allowed to buy fish, cheese or any other commodity until the bell was rung to signal that the day's trading could begin. The bells also became a handy source of income, as charges were levied to ring them to mark birthdays, marriages or funerals.

Perhaps this belhous is the earlier building on the site referred to by author and publisher Robert Chambers in his *Traditions of Edinburgh*. He believed this older structure, later subsumed into the fabric of the Tolbooth, was 'a kind of peel or house of defence, required for public purposes by the citizens of Edinburgh when liable to predatory invasions'.

The building became the 'pretorium burgi de Edinburgi' mentioned in early Acts of the Scottish Parliament. It appears for the first time in an official document of 1403. The great and the good massed here on a regular basis to form the Parliament. They met on the upper floor of the building, with royalty in full dress regalia sweeping across a platform extended from a house opposite to receive the fealty of the 'loyal' burghers or to listen to their gripes. While affairs of state were heard in the upper chambers, commerce raged in the collection of small shops beneath them, providing rents that helped swell the city coffers. So, while the lords sat above swathed in fine cloths and velvets, the tradesmen beavered away below making and selling them. There was commerce all around the building, for the area surrounding St Giles' was the marketplace. The famous luckenbooths, more substantial than stalls, grew out of the Buithraw, a row of booths used by lawyers and public officers. Merchants saw the benefits of such property and so the idea grew until the luckenbooths lined the High Street and the land around the church building itself. Their successors can be seen today in the small stores enticing tourists with their tartan trinkets and mementos of Scotland.

A variety of theories have been put forward as to the derivation of the name luckenbooths. Chambers says that the word 'lucken' signified 'closed', reflecting the fact that these shops were enclosed rather than being open stalls. Others say that the name came from a woollen cloth sold there, made in the Dutch town of Lacken. The root of the term may well have grown from the Celtic word for cheek, '*leacan*', because the booths stood at the side – or cheek – of the church.

The site of the Tolbooth, beside the marketplace and the principal church, reflected how integral it was to the business and administration of the town. The building also became very important in the affairs of the nation. Chambers believed it was likely here that Parliament gathered to debate the future following the murder of James I in Perth in 1437. While his queen slaked her thirst for revenge with the blood of the main conspirators – and in so doing gave the people of Edinburgh a grisly spectacle to enjoy – the Lords of Parliament pondered the state of the kingdom under a boy king. James II had been crowned at Holyrood Abbey – the first time a Scottish king had been proclaimed monarch in Edinburgh, breaking the tradition of being so anointed at Scone. Others hold that the first General Council after James's death was held in the Great Hall of Edinburgh Castle, where the Queen had lodged her six-year-old son for safety.

What is certain, however, is that in November 1438 Parliament did meet in the pretorium burgi de Edinburgi, and again in 1449. By 1451, the name by which the building was to become better known appeared for the first time in an Act of 'the parleament of ane richt hie and excellent prince, and our soverane lorde, James the Secunde, by the grace of Gode, King of Scotts, haldyn at Edinburgh the begunyn in the Tolbuth of the samyn'. By this time, the King, known as 'James of the Fiery Face' because of a livid birthmark, was entrenched in struggles with the Douglas clan. Scottish history is stained with the blood of men slaughtered in the pursuit of power and, like all Stewart monarchs, young James was no stranger to treachery and death. At ten, he had been present when his childhood friend William Douglas was lured along with his brother to a dinner in Edinburgh Castle and butchered by the Livingston/Crichton faction. The boy James may have wept for his friend murdered at the 'Black Dinner' but at 21 he displayed his own ruthlessness, personally stabbing a Douglas lord in the neck during a supper in Stirling. The 1451 parliament was designed to curb the power of the Douglas family by enforcing Acts 'against the encroachments on the royal prerogative'. James II ruled until he was 29, dying when a cannon exploded during an assault on Roxburgh, then in English hands.

His son, again James, was of an artistic bent but still displayed the treacherous nature that marked many a Stewart monarch. He surrounded himself with advisers whom the Scottish barons viewed with contempt. When he refused to dismiss them, the barons seized a half-dozen and hanged them without trial from a bridge in the Borders town of Lauder. The King was then taken prisoner and imprisoned, comfortably, in Edinburgh Castle. James had already appealed to England for aid against his rebellious nobles, and a force of 10,000 men under the command of the Duke of Gloucester marched on Edinburgh in 1482, arriving just as the barons were in council within the Tolbooth. It was here that the King's brother, the slippery Duke of Albany, convinced them to make him regent. The English returned home but kept the prosperous town of Berwick for their trouble, while James was released from captivity and returned to the throne by his brother. An early chronicle by Robert Lindsay of Pitscottie states that the King refused to mount a horse to take him to Holyrood Abbey until his brother climbed on behind him. Perhaps he feared an attempt on his life or perhaps he was adhering to the old adage of keeping friends close but enemies closer. Together, they rode to the abbey 'quhair they remained ane long tyme in great mirrines [merryness]'.

Following the English incursion, the provost of Edinburgh, William Bertraham, told his burgesses and merchants gathered in the Tolbooth that they would pay the English king 6,000 merks sterling, repaying a debt owed by the King. In return James made him and his baillies sheriffs, entitling them to certain privileges. Importantly, the following year, he recognised the efforts made on his behalf by the city's craftsmen. They had sided with him during the struggle with the barons and had taken to the streets when Albany came to rescue him. He conferred on them a blue banner to be used by the artisans of Edinburgh as a call to arms during times of war, which were often, and acts of civil disobedience, which were even more often. According to one unlikely history, written by an eighteenth-century Freemason, the famed Blue Blanket, which over the centuries became both a Masonic symbol and an emblem of Edinburgh, was first created by the Pope around 1200 and was carried to the Crusades by members of the Scottish brotherhood.

Parliaments continued to be convened in the Tolbooth, though this king favoured Stirling as a home. His barons still conspired against his rule, including his erstwhile saviour, his brother the Duke of Albany, who finally fled to England from where he staged a minor incursion that was beaten back at Lochmaben by a local force. He died one year later, in 1485, in France. James III hung on to his throne until 1488, when he was killed at Sauchieburn, near Stirling, by a rebel army that included his own son.

Although racked with guilt over his involvement in the murder of his father, James IV became the nation's best-loved Stewart king. His death fighting the English at Flodden, where the flower of Scottish nobility died with him, left Edinburgh in mourning and its town council, based in the Tolbooth, decimated. As news reached them of the disaster in the south, the remaining officials issued a proclamation demanding that the townspeople 'have reddy their fencible gear and wapponis [weapons] . . . for the keeping and defens of the toun against thame that wald invade . . .' Meanwhile, the authorities exhorted the city's women not to be seen in the street mourning the dead but instead to take to the church and offer up prayers for the salvation of the nation from the English threat. It was during these uneasy days that a standing watch was created out of a force of 24 men. This was the forerunner of the Town Guard, which from the seventeenth century to the early nineteenth was the closest Edinburgh had to a police force.

The proclamation was heeded, the town and buildings, including the Tolbooth, duly fortified with the considerable aid of Lothian farmers and their workhorses. An enclosing wall, which became known as the Flodden Wall, was built around the city and the citizenry held their breath in anticipation of an attack that never came. Henry VIII, busy fighting the French, ignored the troublesome gnat that was Scotland – at least on this occasion. The people's grief for the lost king was allowed to flow uninterrupted by military matters. In Edinburgh, a rumour began to gain currency that James was not dead but had been carried to safety from the carnage of the battlefield by four of his loyal noblemen. But dead he was, his body remaining unburied by the English for some years. It was moved from place to place before the head, which had been cut off by workmen for fun, was finally buried in an anonymous grave in London during the reign of Elizabeth I.

The High Street around the Tolbooth now became the restless battleground for control of the Scottish throne as powerful nobles vied for the regency. Armed men paraded from Castle to Palace and dirks were drawn at the slightest provocation. On one side was the Earl of Angus, who positioned himself in line by marrying the Queen. On the other was the Earl of Arran, who claimed right by blood. The prize was possession of the boy king James V and dominion over all. Parliament favoured neither of their lordships and secretly approached the Duke of Albany, the son of James III's treacherous brother, to take the regency. The French-speaking duke appeased the warring factions and urged the Queen – Margaret Tudor, the sister of Henry VIII – to behave like 'ane guid Scottish woman'.

Albany also turned on the man who had aided him to power, the powerful Border noble Lord Home, who had fought at Flodden but had refused to ride to the beleaguered king's aid. 'He does well that does for himself,' he was reported to have said. 'We have fought our vanguard already, let others do as well as we.' This decision to look to himself eventually led to the popular belief that he had murdered

James on the battlefield. Lord Home and his brother William were arrested on the orders of Albany, who had heeded the poisonous words of his new adviser John Hepburn, an enemy of their blood. The Border noblemen were swiftly tried, found guilty and executed. Their heads were duly fixed on the Tolbooth tower for all in the city to see. These were not the first noble heads to adorn the building – and they would not be the last.

Albany visited France in 1517 to negotiate a new treaty with the French king but found himself the victim of royal duplicity and political expediency. France and England had long snarled at each other across the Channel and English kings had often sallied forth to war but at this time the two superpowers were uneasy friends. When Henry demanded that Albany be prevented from returning to Scotland, King Francis I agreed. The much-vaunted Auld Alliance was always more of a guideline than a code and this was one of the occasions when the French proved it. Albany's four-month visit became four years and during his time away the grasping Scottish nobles spilled blood on the moors, fields and streets of home. The most famous skirmish was the so-called 'Cleanse the Causeway' street battle in Edinburgh's High Street in April 1520. A reiving pack of Home family warriors thundered into the city and reclaimed the heads of their kinsmen from the spikes on which they had languished for nigh on five years. The remains were buried with all due reverence in the kirk at Blackfriars.

When the flimsy peace between Henry and Francis predictably fell apart, Albany was allowed to return with a French force to pacify the still-seething Scotland and also to strike a blow at England from the north. However, memories of Flodden remained alive in the collective mind of Parliament and they refused to back any form of invasion, so, in 1524, Albany renounced the regency and returned to France in disgust. James V, although only 12, was displayed to the people of Edinburgh at his investiture. Angus had now seized control and he opposed a motion that Parliament be held in the

Castle, insisting that it be kept in the accustomed place – the Tolbooth – 'and that the King be conveyed along the High Street, and in triumph shown to his own people'. In the end, Angus won his point – although, this being Scotland, not without some show of force – and Parliament duly assembled in their old home in the Tolbooth.

James V, when he finally took control, was to become known as 'the poor man's king' and often wandered his realm in the guise of a common farmer, 'the Goodman of Ballengeich'. He took the first steps to make Edinburgh the legal capital with the instatement in the Tolbooth of a College of Justice, later better known as the Court of Session. The idea was to make justice more readily available to the common man, with 15 clerics and laymen acting as a supreme civil court. The King received permission from the Pope to draw the cash for the new court from the Church, which promptly raised the rents of its tenants to meet the sum agreed, thus exacerbating the growing hostility the commoners had for the established religion. Within 20 years, the corrupt and dissolute old Church would be rent asunder by the reforming zeal of John Knox and his fellow Protestants. Whether or not life improved much for the common people under the pursed-lipped, Bible-thumping Presbyterians depends on your point of view.

And so life went on in and around the hulking building, which continued to play an important role in the town's affairs. Parliament met less and less in the upstairs rooms and eventually had its own premises in Parliament Close nearby, but the town council still used the old building as a meeting place, while the Court of Session continued to hear cases. The town's magistrates dealt with flashes of lawlessness not just among the ever-warring nobles but also among common desperadoes. In 1554, the council register records that following frequent assaults and robberies in the streets, lanterns were to be hung in streets and closes and to remain lit from five in the evening until nine, when all decent people were deemed to be at home and in their beds. It has been noted that this was the earliest form of public street lighting in the city.

In 1558, the country was again in the hands of a regent – in this case Mary of Guise, the mother of Mary, Queen of Scots – and in the throes of religious upheaval. Knox and his reformers had attacked ecclesiastical buildings and fears were expressed for the safety of similar sites in Edinburgh. The capital's populace was leaning heavily towards the new religion and the city's magistrates pleaded with Protestant leaders to spare the magnificent churches and houses of worship. To save St Giles' Church, 60 men were posted there and the ornately carved stalls, used during services by the high clergy and nobles and as such prime targets for the axe-wielding reformers, were removed to the security of the neighbouring Tolbooth. The mob attacked the monasteries of Black Friars and Grey Friars, leaving nothing standing but a few walls. Other churches were also targeted – including St Giles', despite the armed guard – with altars trashed and religious images destroyed.

One year later, the reforming movement had pushed on even further and all-out war was on the horizon, with the Protestants backed by Queen Elizabeth of England and led by a group of nobles styling themselves the Lords of the Congregation. The French Mary of Guise was supported by troops from her own country. The Protestant lords massed in the Tolbooth, where Lord Ruthven and the preachers declared their wish that Mary be removed from the regency as an obstinate idolatress. They wanted all foreign troops removed from Leith, where they were stationed, and an order was sent to that effect. Naturally, the French forces ignored the decree and, back in their High Street headquarters, the lords prepared to send in the grandly named Army of the Congregation of Christ. However, they did not factor in the ferocious religious ardour of the ministers, who were outraged by the use of St Giles' as a workshop for scaling ladders and, because of this blasphemy, prophesied the campaign's failure. Whether by divine will or superstitious soldiers rattled by their clergy's fiery words, the prediction proved correct and the French forces pursued the retreating Scots army into the Canongate, slaughtering and pillaging as they advanced, much to the delight of the old queen.

The new religion eventually overcame the old and in 1560 Parliament decided to disestablish the Roman Catholic Church in Scotland. Protestant leaders, the stench of martyrs executed for their faith still burning in their nostrils, set about stamping out any trace of the Church of Rome. Whatever the new ways promised for the future, tolerance was not to be one of them. The arrival of the young, and devoutly Roman Catholic, Mary, Queen of Scots from France did nothing for the peace of the nation. The magistrates of Edinburgh issued an order that attendance at the Sunday kirk was expected of all subjects, even priests of the old faith. Some who did so seized the opportunity to attempt to wean the populace away from the followers of Knox and were promptly ordered to leave the city within 48 hours. Mary protested this high-handed treatment of her subjects but the staunch magistrates merely thumbed their noses at her and repeated their order. Mary then wrote to the council and demanded that they convene in the Tolbooth and choose themselves a new set of magistrates. The council acquiesced to the royal demand but did not take the trouble to find out exactly whom she would have preferred to see enforcing the laws. Mary, being a Stewart (or rather a Stuart, for she had adopted the French spelling of her dynastic name), was none too pleased, for she ended up with magistrates who were no more interested in her religious views than the first bunch.

Nevertheless, when she made a triumphal entry to the capital on 2 September 1561, she found the streets gaily decorated and the public buildings the scene of pageants and allegories, some designed to subtly warn her against any opposition of her subjects' chosen faith. It all started off well. At the head of the Lawnmarket was an arch with children singing and a suspended cloud, which opened to reveal 'ane bonnie bairn'. The child was lowered and gave the young queen the keys to the town, a Bible and a psalter covered in the finest purple velvet. Other scenes met her at the Tolbooth and the Mercat Cross – angels and virgins – but at the Tron there was a none too subtle warning of the fire awaiting idolaters.

By this time, the old Tolbooth had fallen into some disrepair and was in a state quite unfitting to its noble office. Much of the business of the council had been transferred to St Giles' Church – part of which was being used as a prison for adulterers (this eventually became known as 'Haddo's Hole' because Royalist Sir John Gordon of Haddo was imprisoned there before his execution). Mary either noticed the dilapidated state of the Tolbooth herself or it was brought to her attention – or perhaps she found the idea of municipal business being conducted on holy ground too distasteful. At any rate, on 6 February 1561, she sent a letter to the town council stating:

> The Queiny's Majestie, understanding that the tolbuith of the Burgh of Edinburgh is ruinous and abill haistielie to dekay and fall doun, quhilk will be warray dampnable and skaythfull to the pepill dwelland thairabout . . . Thairfor her Heines ordinis ane masser to pass and charge of the provest, baillies, and counsale, to caus put workmen to the taking doun of the said tolbuith, with all possible deligence.

It was also ordered that alternative accommodation be found for the Lords of Session as well as for other members of the town's expanding legal industry. As time progressed, the council was warned that the entire court system would be transplanted to St Andrews unless something was done to accommodate them. The council continued to meet in the Holy Blood aisle of St Giles' Church while work progressed. Throughout the project, the provost and his baillies were faced with the problem of scraping up the cash to finance the building of a new Tolbooth and, as is the case today, corners were found that could be cut in order to save them some 'siller'. The master of works was ordered to use as much of the timber from the old building as possible, which prompted the tenants in the shops to complain that he was making off with material that they had paid for out of their own pockets. The council promised that any losses would be reimbursed but failed to mention exactly when.

Although the council wanted to preserve the old building as much as possible, the master of works continued to cannibalise it for materials to save money. Stones from the cast-down Chapel of the Holy Rood, which stood between what would eventually be Parliament House and the Cowgate, were also recycled for the New Tolbooth. But still money was short, despite additional taxation. The master of works threatened to walk away from the job unless further capital was forthcoming.

At length, the New Tolbooth was completed, standing side by side with its still crumbling predecessor and St Giles' Church. The new building was to act as the meeting place for both Parliament and the council, as well as the courts and the magistrates. In May 1563, Mary presided for the first time over Parliament, riding in procession to the new hall and graciously accepting the loyal greetings of her subjects along the High Street.

Things, of course, changed. The Belhous had become the Tolbooth, which was superseded by the New Tolbooth, or Session House, and, ultimately, power gravitated away from the Tolbooth buildings. In 1639, the seat of government moved to the new Parliament House. The Court of Session and Privy Council went with it. Only the High Court of Justiciary, formed in 1672, remained in the New Tolbooth, or Session House, and did not move until as late as 1809. The ever-spreading mass of local government meant the town council became too big for the Session House. It sprawled first into rooms in other buildings around the church and finally transplanted into new premises on the north side of the marketplace, the Royal Exchange. The New Tolbooth was pulled down in 1809. Its predecessor outlived it by eight years.

In the seventeenth century, though, it was still crumbling and in 1610 a cash-flush council decided to repair it. The rubble of the previous century was finally removed and that section rebuilt. When it was finally demolished 200 years later, it was noted that the later workmanship was not as fine as the old. Three krames, or small shops, were built into the west gable but were eventually replaced by a two-storey extension to the five-storey Tolbooth. This platform would eventually fulfil a dread purpose.

Since 1560, the council had had a new use for what was left of the old building. In the past, the Belhous had been used as a lock-up or a 'thieves' hole'; in around 1480 it was noted that of the booths on the ground floor, the sixth 'is made a presoun'. The dark towers of the Tolbooth were no stranger to the miseries of malefactors, with heads and other body parts often adorning its spikes and walls. Now it would act solely as home to the criminals, traitors and debtors of the town. Its noble past was well and truly behind it. From then on, the Old Tolbooth was used as the 'tyne gaol'.

Ahead was only darkness.

CHAPTER TWO

JAIL TIME

The dark heart of Midlothian was ideally placed for its new function. Crooks and malefactors were found guilty in the New Tolbooth and later in the courts in what was to become Parliament Square. From there, it was a short walk to their new lodgings. For some, it was not so very long before they were faced with the ministrations of the headsman's axe or the Maiden, a beheading machine that was in operation long before its more notorious French counterpart was a steely glint in Dr Guillotin's eye. And if decapitation was not their fate, there was always the prospect of being burned at the stake or of a long drop on a short rope. Again in these cases, the condemned did not have to travel very far to meet their doom, for many sentences were carried out at the Mercat Cross, on Castle Hill, in the Grassmarket and, eventually, on the two-storey extension to the Tolbooth gable.

The art of hanging was not in the early days of the Tolbooth the near science of later, more enlightened years, with its carefully computed drop lengths. For centuries, death by hanging was little more than a lynching, with the victim standing on a cart, the noose around the neck, the rope over a branch of the 'dule tree' (hanging tree) and the end coming with a sharp slap on the horse's behind. If no cart or horse was available, then a group of strong men simply hauled the condemned up by the neck until dead. Later, the gallows replaced the dule tree and the doomed were required to climb a ladder and were duly 'turned off' to be slowly strangled. Later still, around the eighteenth century, the trapdoor was devised but the offender was still more often than not throttled to death as he or she swung on the rope. Finally, the short drop intended to snap the neck came into play, although it was not unknown for the hangman to miscalculate the length needed.

After a hanging, the body would be left for a period of time before being taken down and either mutilated as part of the sentence or given to anatomists for dissection. Sometimes the corpse was hung to rot in chains as a deterrent to others. The first such Scottish criminal recorded to have been displayed in this way was pirate John Davidson, who was executed on 6 May 1551, within the floodmarks on the sands of Leith, as tradition demanded for his crime.

Of course, not every criminal was put to death. For many, the Tolbooth was home for a considerable period. Good King James V may have wanted justice for his people but it was a long time coming for many. Scottish justice was a corrupt institution, easily undermined by those with the money, power or might to enforce their will. From the Middle Ages, Scottish barons held hereditary jurisdictions over their lands, the right of *fossa et furca* – pit and gallows. They could condemn a man for the slightest crime – or no crime at all – and claim a portion of his assets. If the widow of an executed felon had no assets, then they could take her only blanket. This system continued until hereditary jurisdictions were abolished in 1748, when sheriffs and justices of the peace took over enforcement of law. The lords of the manor, however, simply ensured that they were granted these posts and business continued more or less as usual.

Magistrates and judges were easily bought or blackmailed and many a man and woman rotted in the Tolbooth, forgotten, because they had not bribed a judge to buy their freedom, even though they had served their sentence. Others could wait for years before being tried because they had not paid the authorities to have their case heard.

Of course, even then, there were those in authority who deplored such travesties of justice. In March 1661, the ranking members of the justiciary realised that 'severall persons ar imprisoned in the tolbuith of Edinburgh upon aledged crymes comitted by them'. These poor souls had been 'lyen in prisson of a long tyme without any lybell or sumonds of accusation against them'. Accordingly, the magistrates of the town were told to bring them to trial within eight days or set them free.

Convicted felons, including the many imprisoned for debt, could appeal to the nobility to bring influence to bear to have their time in the Tolbooth cut short. In 1711, Robert Fliming, 'a forgerer', wrote to Mr Alexander Findlater, 'minister of the gospell at Hamilton', enclosing a plea to the Duchess of Hamilton. Sentenced to die for his crimes, Fliming had received a brief reprieve but was, naturally, anxious to avoid the death penalty altogether. He told the minister, presumably of his parish, that he had been moved by the preaching of Mr James Webster in the Tolbooth (for it was the duty of the keeper to ensure that prisoners attended Sunday services). The minister, he said, had read from the 118th Psalm and its message had struck home. 'The Lord hath chastised me sore but not given me over to death. I shall not die but live and declare the works of the Lord,' Fliming wrote, quoting the psalm. He went on, 'From the consideration of which I was made to conclude that God seemed to say I should not die this death. Yet this does not give any encouragement to security for death is certainly coming and may be sooner than reported.' He wanted the minister to present 'Hir Grace the Duches of Hamilton' with the plea he had enclosed, in the hope that she would intercede for his life or prevail upon her husband to do so. 'I humbly begg and suplycat your Grace's compassion and pitie, for bringing to perfection salvation to poor guilty me,' he wrote in his appeal to the Duchess. He hoped that he would be given either a sentence or a reprieve that would allow him to live until his 'brath be otherways cut' – by natural means.

Whether the nobles stepped in or not, Fliming was granted a stay of execution but not set at liberty, so the spectre of death still hung over him. Three years later, he was writing again, this time to the country's most senior law officer, Lord Justice Clerk James Erskine of Grange, hoping that he would 'forever be freed from that shamefull and publick death which by my atrocious crime I had made myself lyable to'. He went on:

> Therfor, I humbly supplicat and begg your Lordships Gracious and compassionat bowells may be moved with pity towards sinfull and miserable me, in condescending to write to the Honourable Earl of Marr, your Lordship's brother, who is Her Majesties principall Secretarie of state for this Nation, to interceed at Her Majesties Mercyfull hands for a liberation whereby I may be set at liberty, and not be left to ly pyning away in such a long and unexpressably miserable confinement, which being so great an act of charity will draw down Heaven's reward, for which your lordships poor petitioner shall pray, and in hope of your Lordships pity and help.

Two months later, matters had still not been resolved, for he was once again in correspondence with Lord Grange:

> O My lord
>
> It is reported that your Lordship is speaking of allowing the sentence passed upon me to [be reduced to] banishment, if your Lordships could be secured that way from being further troubled with poor sinfull me. And therfor that your lordships may be secured I shall not only consent to, but also subscribe my oun banishment out of Scotland. And I hope that the Lord has so sanctified this long and sore afflicting dispensation to me, as thereby I shall be made to see the according will of sin, and so to watch and pray that I may be kept from iniquity, by grace strengthening me. Let me therfor find Grace in your Lordships sight, for the Lords sake, that I may be freed from this long and most lamentable confinement, this way,

before your Lordships leave this city, and I only took so much time aloued me as I may easily transport myself, and so by the Grace of God, strengthening me, I hope I shall never more be troublesome to your Lordships.

I shall not multiplie words but rest in hope waiting with patience for your Lordships Gracious answer.

There appears to be no record of whether Fliming was banished or freed, but after crawling of such monumental proportions it is to be fervently hoped that he was. However, we must bear in mind that Lord Grange, whom Robert Chambers described as a 'scandal to his profession', was not the type of man much moved to pity or mercy. Considering he had his own wife kidnapped and held prisoner for years, whether Fliming's case is likely to have inspired compassion in him is open to some doubt. However, he did, on taking office, make moves to clear the jails of Scotland of men and women imprisoned without trial, so perhaps he was not as black as he was painted.

The punishment meted out did not necessarily reflect the crime, for there was no 'set tariff' and felons could be hanged even for minor infringements. If death was not demanded, then flesh could be whipped and branded, eyes gouged, tongues bored, hands and ears sliced off, bones crushed or, if the judge was not feeling particularly bloodthirsty, there was banishment, deportation, slavery and, of course, incarceration. This does not mean that everyone accused of a crime was dealt with brutally. The Tolbooth warding and liberation books reveal that many an accused person was released by order of the sheriff or the Lords of Justiciary within days or weeks of being incarcerated there. Early records show that prisoners were set at liberty, albeit temporarily, to deal with urgent personal matters and during the plague years they might be freed if close relatives were taken ill. For instance, in 1624, John Hamilton was released from the Tolbooth to care for his wife, who was not only pregnant but stricken with fever.

Felons could also gain their freedom by agreeing to military service, for Britain was seldom at peace and there was always a need for fresh recruits. In July 1792, James Gow, accused of theft, 'was liberate and went to be a soldier'. An entry in the warding book for 31 December that same year, regarding the case of John Muirhead, servant to Robert Wight, farmer at Kingsknowes, shows that even then there was some concern for animal cruelty, even if that concern was more a matter of property than humanity. Mr Wight had seen three of his horses stabbed 'under night' while they were in his stables. Two of them had died and the wounds of the third were 'in such a manner and apparently with design [that its] life is in danger'. Subsequently, all his servants and workers were examined and it was felt that Muirhead was guilty 'art and part of the aforesaid crimes'. He was locked in the Tolbooth but allowed to enlist 'and was therefore liberated by the magistrates'.

Six smugglers were warded in the Tolbooth on 8 December that same year after firing on the excise yacht the *Royal George* 'within four or five leagues of the shore . . . in the firth of Forth'. The excisemen had put a shot across their bows and they had retaliated, killing one seaman and wounding another two. They could easily have been executed but the courts must have been feeling merciful, for later that month they were placed on the man-of-war *Thebes* for active service.

Corporal and capital punishments, though, were meted out not only with sickening regularity but also with quite stunning speed, so there was little need for the large prisons we know today. However, in 1425 an Act was passed to deal with cases of 'Forethought Fellonie and Chaud-mella [sudden malice]'. It declared that if malice aforethought was established, 'the life and the gudes of the trespassoure are to be in the Kingis wills to [which] prisson hee sall bee held'. Clearly, then, there was prison provision on a relatively large scale even then.

Theoretically, felons needed to be held for only a short period of time before sentence was carried out. Sometimes the accused was kept in his own home, under guard, until his court appearance. Sometimes other houses were used: in Edinburgh, Robert Gourlay's house in Old Bank Close (removed in the nineteenth century to make way for George IV Bridge) was one such place. It was felt to be so secure that James VI took shelter here when Francis Stewart, Earl of Bothwell, proved a threat. In addition, castles had dungeons and many had pits. In Inverness, criminals were kept in a room under a bridge, which regularly filled with water. But mainly it was the town tolbooths that became the local prisons.

In the warding and liberation books of the Tolbooth, there are many examples of crime and punishment being dealt with at what to modern eyes is alarming speed. On 3 April 1792, one John Boyd, 'designing himself wright, late from Haddington but sometimes passing by the name of John Wallace and a native of North Berwick', was imprisoned 'for stealing a variety of cloaths, blankets, sheets and other articles from sundry persons in and about Edinburgh'. The following day, he was sentenced to be 'whipit on the platform [at the] west end of the Tolbooth the 18th April current and to receive on his naked shoulders fifty lashes by the hands of the common hangman'. After this sentence was carried out, he was 'to be set at liberty and banished the city . . . for the space of ten years'. If the man was caught inside the city limits within that time, he was to be 'apprehendit and committed to Bridewell or house of correction of this city at hard labour for twelve months'. He was also, for good measure, to be whipped again and once more banished.

As Britain grew as a colonial power, it began to offload many of its undesirable citizens on the New World. The West Indies and the American colonies were such dumping grounds, as was Australia. In 1793, grocer John Stirling was found guilty of housebreaking at the Masonhouse of Mellfield in the parish of Liberton: 'the greatest part of furniture therein was stole and carried off.' He was to be 'banished beyond the seas during all the days of his life' and on 20 April he was put on board a ship travelling south with the 57th Regiment and sent to the prison hulks on the Thames for a time before being sent to Australia. His co-accused, Peter Campbell, was also sent to the hulks but died on 25 August, before he could be transported.

The Edinburgh Tolbooth was also used as a staging post for prisoners from other jails. On 6 December 1793, John Reid and Abraham Sherwood 'were carried from the prison at Ayr and incarcerated in the Tolbooth for the purpose of being conveyed to the hulks on the river Thames'. The Heart of Midlothian had other felons within its walls at that particular time awaiting transfer and they were all duly shipped off.

The Old Tolbooth was the epitome of what Scots law called *squalor carceris*, literally 'dirty prison', the principle that the awfulness of jail was an intrinsic aspect of the punishment. Essentially, a prison's denizens were not just punished, they were also seen to be punished, and there was no hint of anything like comfort – unless the inmate could pay for it, of course.

Author and publisher Robert Chambers saw inside the jail before it was demolished in 1817. 'There was something about the Old Tolbooth which would have enabled a blindfolded person led into it to say that it was a jail,' he wrote. 'It was not merely odorous from the ordinary causes of imperfect drainage, but it had poverty's own smell – the odour of human misery.'

Lord Cockburn, who during his time as Advocate Depute sent many a man to its noxious embrace, also remarked on the stench – and cast doubt on the efficacy of the *squalor carceris* policy. In *Memorials of his Time*, published posthumously in 1856, he wrote:

A most atrocious jail it was, the very breath of which almost struck down any stranger who entered its dismal door; and as ill-placed as possible, without one inch of ground beyond its black and horrid walls. And these walls were very small; the entire hole being filled with little dark cells; heavy manacles the only security; airless, waterless, drainless; a living grave. One week of that dirty, fetid, cruel torture-house was a severer punishment than a year of our worst modern prison – more dreadful in its sufferings, more certain in its corruption, overwhelming the innocent with a more tremendous sense of despair, provoking the guilty to more audacious defiance.

The stench to which Chambers and Cockburn refer rose in defiance of official statute, for the keeper, known as the 'gudeman' or 'guidman', of the Tolbooth was duty-bound to keep the prison and its environs clean. In both the 1728 and 1810 Acts of Council for the regulation of the Edinburgh jail, it is stated that whoever held the post had to pay particular attention to the hygiene of his charges, for cleanliness was next to godliness. The regulations dictated that the walls of the jail were to be scrubbed down twice a year with strong limewater and the stairs were to be swept and scraped twice a week and washed once in the same period. In addition, 'all dung, filth and ashes' were to be emptied from each cell by ten in the morning and a fresh supply of water carried up to each room by the same time. It was also the keeper's responsibility to ensure the street around the prison was swept and washed regularly. It was recognised that some prisoners were committed 'in a state of great filth, without any change of clothes' so the jailer was obliged to have in store at all times one dozen coarse linen shirts. These would be taken back when prisoners were liberated. There was no statute regarding how often these clothes were to be changed and it was regularly the case that a prisoner wore the same garments throughout his stay.

The gudeman himself, according to articles issued in the year 1606, must be 'of a good name, credit and estimation', he could not be a drunkard, slanderer or backbiter and could not be 'injurious to any man by word or deed, privately or openly'. Also – unsurprisingly, considering that they formulated these articles – he was ordered to be obedient to the magistrates. The keeper's post was much sought after because it brought the holder a certain position in life. He could also make a comfortable living, for although neither the council nor the Crown paid him, he did have the right to levy fees on the prisoners. There was, of course, a sliding scale of dues. For instance, freemen of the town or burgh paid less in fees than 'unfreemen or strangers'. The bulk of his income came from debtors, although there were regulations in force that prevented them from being too heavily penalised. Society understood that a person who failed to meet his or her financial responsibilities could be incarcerated. When that happened, the creditor who had had them jailed – the incarcerator – paid the jailer a fee based on how much was owed, a fee that the debtor would be expected to reimburse. The prisoner also had to pay for every night he or she spent behind bars. The irony was, of course, that the financial straits that might have led to the imprisonment in the first place were exacerbated by the growing debt incurred while inside.

This all sounds as if the keeper exploited the dire situation in which debtors found themselves but that was not necessarily so. There would almost certainly have been cases in which the gudemen were not as gude as all that but it must be remembered that anyone running into financial trouble was fully aware of the possibility of a jail sentence. It was an accepted part of life. No prisoner was allowed to extort cash from another and, of course, the jailer had to ensure that no bodily harm befell an inmate at the hands of another. This did not prevent the jailers from lending cash and the jailed could often run up a considerable debt. This would be due to be repaid at the end of the sentence and if funds were not forthcoming, the newly liberated individual could find himself back in the lock-up at the instigation of the jailer.

There is one recorded case of a keeper helping a debtor out of trouble – and then having to go to court to get his money back. James Walsh helped carter and gilder John Begbie out of jail by assisting in obtaining from his creditor a deed of consent for his liberty. He also made a small loan to Begbie 'to satisfy his incarcerating creditor for the expense of writing' the deed. In addition, Begbie was freed without paying some of his jail fees. After struggling for

16 months to get his money back, Walsh took Begbie to court in 1806. The debtor claimed that it was wrong for a jail to claim fees but Walsh hit back, saying that the prison fees were his only means of income and pointing out the variety of expenses he incurred in running the institution. The fees, he added, were based on the limits set in 1728 and, with inflation, were comparatively low. To rub salt into his financial wounds, Walsh knew that Begbie had received a considerable sum of cash from foreign interests and had failed to pay his debts. Walsh won his case and four years later the town council increased the fees.

Sought after it may have been but the life of a jailer was not all beer and skittles. He stood to make a nice income but in return he had to engage 'servants' to help him run the prison. He was also liable for the supply of coal, oil and candles. If any inmate should escape – and that seems to have been a fairly common occurrence – it was the jailer's responsibility to see to it that he was caught within 24 hours. If he was apprehended during this period, the prisoner would be fined £40 sterling. If he remained at liberty, the jailer would be liable to pay the fine – and settle the prisoner's debt, if that was why he had been incarcerated in the first place.

To prevent any escapes, the keeper was ordered personally to visit each and every cell (or 'apartment' as they were delicately called) twice a day to ensure that the inmates had not made any attempts to cut through the iron bars or break through the walls, roof, joists or floor. He was also to take particular care that 'no instruments of any kind be conveyed to, or be in the possession of, the prisoners, whereby they may effect their escape'. Naturally, weapons and armour were not allowed within the precincts of the jail but if any weapons were discovered, the guilty party was to be refused meat and drink. (Given that many complaints were lodged over the food, that may not have been as much of a punishment as the authorities thought.) However, bearing in mind the violent natures of many of the inmates, trouble did flare up. The Privy Council recorded on 8 November 1610 that 'misreule' was 'daylie committit be the wardouris [prisoners]' who made 'commotions and trouble amongin thamselfies'. They also resisted the efforts of officers to control the tumults and often threatened their lives. Anyone who caused such disturbances was to be 'immediately layed in yrnis [irons]'. In addition, the keeper was to 'at all times keep the male and female prisoners separate, and . . . prevent all intercourse between them'. Meanwhile, prisoners accused or convicted of capital crimes or waiting to be transported, banished, pilloried or subjected to corporal punishment were to be locked in their rooms at all times, except when ordered otherwise by a magistrate or for health reasons.

Keepers were also warned 'to beware of giving up the person of any prisoner upon the verbal order of a magistrate or other judge. He is at all times to require a written order.' The jailer neglected this rule – an oblique reference to the corruptibility of the judiciary – 'at his peril'.

In his *Traditions*, Robert Chambers provides a superb description of the building's interior:

> The principal entrance to the Tolbooth, and the only one used in later days, was at the bottom of the turret next the church. The gateway was of tolerably good carved stone-work, and occupied by a door of ponderous massiness and strength, having, besides the lock, a flap-padlock, which, however, was generally kept unlocked during the day. In front of the door there always paraded, or rather loitered, a private of the town-guard, with his rusty red clothes, and Lochaber axe or musket.

The Town Guard, or City Guard, were the descendants of those 24 watchmen appointed in the panic after Flodden, although the force came fully into being in 1682, when a body of 108 men was raised to keep the townsfolk under control during civil unrest. However, according to Edinburgh legend they were a much older force and had been in existence when the Romans pushed into Scotland.

The myth stated that some of the Guard joined the invading army and that three stalwarts formed part of Pilate's personal guard at the Crucifixion of Christ. In fact, the Town Guard were a military command under the order of the magistrates. Chambers writes that by the beginning of the nineteenth century they had become a largely useless body of men and an object of ridicule to the general public, who nicknamed them 'the Town Rats' because their once red greatcoats, waistcoats and breeches, faded to a dull brown with age. At their height, during the eighteenth century, they consisted of three large companies of men, each under the command of a lieutenant, who, by custom, was called 'captain'. They were called out when the Edinburgh mob raged and, at least in those days, were quite a fearsome body of men, more than capable (as we shall see) of using deadly force. Up until 1785, they had a guard post in the High Street but when the street was being levelled they transferred their headquarters to the ground floor of the Tolbooth. Here, Chambers writes, 'a few of them might constantly be seen on duty, endeavouring to look as formidable as possible to the little boys who might be passing by'. Often, they merely lounged drunkenly on a bench outside. Made up almost entirely of Highlanders who were grateful for the sixpence-a-day pay they received, latterly the Town Guard came into their own only when called out to special occasions, like meetings of the General Assembly, public executions or even the races at Leith. 'But, in general,' writes Chambers, 'they could hardly be considered as of any practical utility.' Superseded in law-enforcement duties in 1805, when an unarmed police force was established in Edinburgh, the Guard was finally disbanded in 1817.

Lord Cockburn was sorry to see them go, although he acknowledged that the advent of the police force 'made them useless'. He wished, though, that 'they had been perpetuated, though it had been only as curiosities'. He went on:

They were all old, hard-featured, red-nosed veterans; whose general history was, that after being mauled in the wars, commonly in a Highland regiment, they brought their broken iron bodies home, and thought themselves fortunate if they got into this fragment of our old burgher militia, where the pay was better than nothing, and the discipline not quite inconsistent with whisky, while the service was limited to keeping the peace within the city.

Cockburn, like Chambers, noted their use of the Lochaber axe, a long, vicious-looking weapon, of which he wrote that it was 'a delightful implement. One saw Bannockburn in it.' He recalled, 'One of these stern half-dotard warriors' sitting on either side of prisoners facing trial,

his huge hat on his old battered head, and his drawn bayonet in his large gnarled hand. They sat so immoveably, and looked so severe, with their rugged weather-beaten visages, and hard muscular trunks, that they were no unfit emblems of the janitors of the region to which those they guarded were so often consigned. The disappearance of those picturesque old fellows was a great loss.

The 'region' he referred to was, of course, the town jail. The guardhouse of the 'Town Rats' on the north side of the Tolbooth had formerly been occupied by shops, which brought some revenue to the magistrates. A one-time thieves' hole next to the main entrance way was to become, towards the end of the prison's life, a shoe shop. Beside that, wrote Chambers, lived the turnkey in 'a dismal, unlighted den, where the grey old man was always to be found, when not engaged in unlocking or closing the door'. He continued:

On passing the outer door . . . the keeper instantly involved the entrant in darkness, by reclosing the gloomy portal. A flight of about twenty steps then led to an inner door, which, being duly knocked at, was opened by a bottle-nosed personage denominated

Peter, who, like his sainted namesake, always carried two or three large keys. You then entered *the Hall*, which, being free to all the prisoners except those of the *East End*, was usually filled with a crowd of shabby-looking but very merry loungers. A small rail here served as an additional security, no prisoner being permitted to come within its pale. Here also a sentinel of the city-guard was always walking, having a bayonet or ramrod in his hand. The *Hall*, being also the chapel of the jail, contained an old pulpit of singular fashion – such a pulpit as one could imagine John Knox to have preached from; which, indeed, he was traditionally said to have actually done. At the right-hand side of the pulpit was a door leading up the large turnpike to the apartments occupied by the criminals, one of which was of plate iron. The door was always shut, except when food was taken up to the prisoners.

The 'very merry loungers' would be the low-category prisoners – the petty crooks and debtors. Visitors were allowed into the jail from 9 a.m. to 3 p.m. and then again from 4.30 p.m. to 9 p.m. Doctors and lawyers, though, could gain access at any time. During lock-down periods, the keeper was ordered to have the keys of the prison on his person and that they were 'not to be entrusted to servants'. Visitors could bring prisoners 'victuals but no spiritous liquor'. Beer and porter were exempt from this rule and, until 1810, wine was allowed. If any spirits were required, they could be purchased from the in-house sutlery. Of course, the turnkey could be paid to turn a blind eye to anything short of escape (and perhaps even that).

But if anyone needed a reminder of where they were, they had only to look at the board fixed to the far wall. On it were etched a few lines from a poem which first appeared in 1618 in a book called *Essayes and Characters of a Prison and Prisoners* by a lawyer named Geffray Mynshul. Although the lines originally described the King's Bench Prison in London, they were particularly apposite in Edinburgh's jail:

A prison is a house of care,
A place where none can thrive,
A touchstone true to try a friend,
A grave for men alive.

Sometimes a place of right,
Sometimes a place of wrong,
Sometimes a place for jades and thieves,
And honest men among.

The hall was 27 feet long and 20 wide, with the ceiling 12 feet high. One part of the hall was partitioned off into two rooms, both given over to whoever the captain of the day was. One was used as his pantry, the other as his counting-room and arsenal, although in later years the weaponry available to the Town Guard was limited indeed. Chambers tells us in his pen portrait that it contained 'an old musket or two, a pair of obsolete bandoleers, and a sheath of a bayonet, intended, as one might suppose, for his defence against a mutiny of the prisoners'. Inside the captain's rooms was a double window that was, according to tradition, once the door through which the King would have entered the Tolbooth to attend Parliament, having crossed a special 'bridge' constructed between the building and a house opposite.

Another window at the other end of the hall overlooked the main doorway and was used by the inner turnkey to let the doorman below know that visitors were on their way out. The window was thrown open, he would bellow, 'Turn your hand,' and his colleague below would unlock the door and let the visitors out into the open air and freedom.

On the two floors above the hall, there were two rooms occupied solely by more serious felons, who were manacled in irons to a bar along the floor. Thus shackled, the prisoners had limited room in which to move, eat and sleep. Many were freed only in order to keep a date with the executioner. Access to the various floors was gained by a spiral staircase with 'a greasy rope' as a handrail, 'which, some one was sure to inform [the visitor] afterwards, had been employed in hanging a criminal'. Chambers recorded that the western part of the Tolbooth was of 'more modern construction' and that its four storeys were given over entirely to housing debtors 'except a part of the lowest one, where a middle-aged woman kept a tavern for the sale of malt liquors'. This small store, the aforementioned sutlery, no doubt came in handy for keeping the loungers in their merry state and was yet another means of income for the gudeman, who claimed a percentage of the profits. On the second floor of this newer part was a doorway that led out to the platform on which felons were hanged. On the floor above, there was 'an ill-plastered part of the wall, covering the aperture through which the gallows was projected'.

Such, then, was the squalid 'tyne gaol' of Edinburgh. There was no exercise yard save the main hall where the prisoners milled about, no open area to cleanse the lungs and few windows through which the felons could gaze at Oscar Wilde's 'little tent of blue'. It was a fetid, often plague-ridden hellhole. In 1645, debtors were freed during an attack of 'the pest', as plague was known. In the same year, the Marquis of Montrose demanded the release of 150 Royalist prisoners being held there; plague had ravaged the city and decimated the jailers and prisoners alike. Those who survived such epidemics found themselves at the mercy of the building's considerable rat population – George Wishart, Montrose's biographer and later Bishop of Edinburgh, carried the scars left by rodent teeth for the rest of his life.

Montrose experienced the hospitality of the jail himself, while awaiting execution. We cannot know if the words of Dante's famed *Inferno* crossed the marquis's mind as he scratched his own epitaph on a Tolbooth window with a diamond. Sir Daniel Wilson, in his *Memorials of Edinburgh in the Olden Time*, certainly did think of them, however. He wrote: '[Dante's] memorable inscription for the gates of hell might have found a scarcely less appropriate place over its gloomy portal – All hope abandon, ye who enter here!'

Chapter Three

Heads You Lose

It is the year 1637 and Edinburgh is in tumult. There has been disruption in St Giles' Church and the ever-present mob is rioting in the streets. The city council has taken refuge in its Tolbooth fortress and is waiting for the storm to abate. But this was a fury that would never die – and the ripples it caused can still be felt today.

It was religion that caused it, or rather the power and even the money that come with it. There were two things that caused a Scot's blood to boil in those days: one was an attack on his pocket, the other an assault on his faith. Charles Stuart's attempt to foist episcopacy on his northern kingdom amounted to both. The Scottish Kirk had waded through blood to emerge victorious over Roman Catholicism the century before and now the King in London had decreed, among other things, that a new prayer book must be used during devotions. Charles I was the son of James VI and grandson of Mary and, like them, he was a staunch Stuart with a belief in absolute monarchy. As with his father, this extended to a wish that the Church be unified under his control, as God's anointed on earth. He wanted to appoint bishops, who would be answerable to him, and he wanted a Book of Common Prayer. He also wanted the considerable revenues that the Church could command. The Scottish Presbyterians were proud of their independence from the monarchy and viewed his edicts as popery with a crown. To them, his moves were but a short step away from the return of idolatry, which they deemed tantamount to devil-worship. The plans were met with resentment and even violence as those few ministers who supported them were chased from their pulpits.

And so we come to that day in 1637 when an attempt to read from the new Book of Common Prayer in St Giles' sparked a riot. The congregation, already peeved that a new altar said to be idolatrous was under construction, reacted violently. There was a cry of 'Dost thou say Mass in my lug?' and the fabled Jenny Geddes threw her three-legged 'creepie-stool' at the minister, whose quick duck saved him from a nasty bump. The resultant riot was no doubt preordained, for it was reported that some of the 'women' in the vanguard of the protest were, in fact, recognisable Kirk ministers in dresses. The bedlam, cross-dressers amongst it, spilled onto the street outside and the city's provost and his magistrates found themselves besieged in their chambers within the New Tolbooth. As was often the case with the Edinburgh mob, the authorities had to negotiate for peace as if it were an invading army. A committee was formed from among those opposed to the growth of episcopalianism and it demanded the abolition of the new services. The King refused to accede to these demands and ordered that the committee and the mob, including the nobles and clergy who supported it, be deemed traitors. This, predictably, prompted more rioting.

In Edinburgh, a young Scots nobleman stood at the Mercat Cross and cheered the rioters on. He was an enthusiastic supporter of his Church's independence, so he leaped onto a barrel and spurred them on with word and gesture. An older friend watched him and observed that the young man would not be happy until he was raised even higher, 'by three fathoms of rope'. It proved a highly prophetic statement, for that young man was James Graham, Marquis of Montrose. He would die not far from that spot, high on a gallows, before his body was butchered by fanatics of the very Kirk he was on that day in 1637 defending. And his head would lie spiked on the Old Tolbooth for many a year.

The Tolbooth was no stranger to heads of state, either in a political or a literal sense. A notable building in the centre of the growing city, it was an ideal site on which to place the body parts of those deemed traitors, and for centuries this was the custom of authorities bent on discouraging anyone from challenging the might of King, Parliament or, as we shall see, the Kirk. The heads of the Border nobles who had fallen foul of the regent Albany and the dangerous power games that forever raged in Scotland's palaces and castles had adorned the jail. Over 60 years later, though, another regent found the situation reversed.

The Earl of Morton took control of the throne when James VI was still an infant and the boy's mother, Mary, was in the hands of Queen Elizabeth. As James grew older, he learned to dislike and mistrust the foxy old earl, no doubt influenced by the constant jealous whispers of rivals that echo through Scottish history. So when the regent was denounced as being one of the conspirators in the murder of James's father, Lord Darnley, his fate was sealed. In 1581, he was brought to Edinburgh from Dumbarton Castle, where he had been held. He was imprisoned not in the Tolbooth but in the house of Robert Gourlay nearby, and there he was kept under the watchful eye of 'waged men'. On 1 June, the High Street rattled with swords and armour as soldiers took their stations at the Cross and the Tolbooth, for this was the day when the former regent was to be taken in convoy to meet his accusers. Morton denied all the charges. His trial, like many another in Scotland then and now, was a farce and he was found guilty and sentenced to be 'headed, quartered and drawn' the very next day – for justice then was swift, if far from sure. In a letter, Morton pleaded with the 15-year-old king for mercy but James refused even to read it.

Legend has it that Morton himself brought the idea of a beheading device back to Scotland after a visit to Halifax, where such a contraption had been in operation for generations. If that is true, he may well have regretted his decision as he lay in his cell that night.

On 2 June 1581, the wily regent stepped onto the execution platform where stood the dreaded Maiden, the Scottish beheading machine. At around 4 p.m. on that black Friday, he went bravely to his death, speaking to the crowd from the four corners of the platform, as was the custom, before laying his head on the block and waiting for the blade to fall. Onlookers heard the old man repeating 'Lord Jesus, receive my soul' over and over before the blade scythed down and separated his head from his shoulders. Legend, again, tells us that he was the first to feel the sting of the Maiden's blade, but that honour belongs to Thomas Scott, accused of complicity in the murder of Queen Mary's secretary David Rizzio. Morton's body lay on the platform for four hours, while the head was taken to the highest point of the Tolbooth and placed firmly on an iron spike. It remained there for 18 months before finally being removed by permission of the King and buried in Greyfriars kirkyard. The regent's body was thrown into a common grave on the Burgh Muir, a walled area near what was once the South Loch (and is now the Meadows) set aside for the bodies of convicted felons and excommunicates. Here would also be thrown the torso of the Marquis of Montrose.

Like most romantic heroes of history, James Graham, Marquis of Montrose, was probably not as fine as he has been painted. The idea of him that has come down through the centuries is of an idealistic, passionate and loyal warrior with a poetic streak, whose magic touch failed him only when he was betrayed by others less steadfast than he. That popular image has him forever in armour, his long brown hair tumbling to his shoulders. His handsome face is either fleshy and weak or, as in a later portrait, slimmer and more resolute. He was a man of honour or a traitorous spawn of the Devil, depending on which side of the battlefield you stood.

He had attracted the ire of the godly crew known as Covenanters by apparently changing sides during their struggles with the Stuart kings over who would control religion. He had been a fervent supporter of the Presbyterian cause, signing the National Covenant that gave the movement its name. Notably, he coerced the Royalist council of Aberdeen into submission. He also played a central role in the betrayal of the Marquis of Huntly, a supporter of the King, leading to his imprisonment in the Castle in 1639. Montrose's part in this has been described by one historian as 'mean and shabby' and Huntly never forgave him, although they would later fight on the same side. When it seemed that Charles I had agreed to the Kirk's demands – though the King had no real intention of bowing down to the surly Scots ministers – Montrose placed himself firmly in the royal camp. Montrose did not like Charles's attack on his faith but neither did he agree with the extremes to which the Covenanter leaders wished to push matters. Many of these men were not fighting for religious freedom. Faith can be a wonderful thing but fanaticism is dangerous, and they wished their version of religion to be adopted across the kingdom, by force and by blood if necessary.

The two Bishops Wars fought on Scots soil between 1639 and 1640 may have been limited in scope but they were precursors to the so-called English Civil War, which, in fact, raged on both sides of the border. The opposing sides each appealed to the Scottish Covenanters for help, and in the end support was granted to Cromwell's Parliamentarians, who also resisted the threat of episcopacy. For Montrose, it was a case of 'thus far and no further'. Apparently a genuine man of conscience – his lapse of good taste, if not judgement, over the Huntly affair and later accusations of war crimes apart – the gallant marquis had now set himself on a path to glory and, ultimately, an excruciating death. He should have heeded the maxim 'put not your faith in princes', for the two kings he championed were not worthy of such loyalty, while the men he antagonised proved themselves capable of exacting a fierce revenge.

He promised to win Scotland for his king and raised an army in the Highlands, an act that did nothing to endear him to his former Covenanter colleagues. Many in his army were Irish Catholics attached to the Donald clan, while others were Scots clansmen who were loyal to the King – or at least willing to fight for a chance to strike hard at the Marquis of Argyll, who had sided with the Covenanters. In this tale, if Montrose is the hero, then Argyll is the villain. But this being Scottish history, such matters are never black and white; the complex natures of Montrose and Argyll can be painted only in the grey cast of both men's eyes.

Argyll was a powerful, accomplished politician who may have been sincere in his religious beliefs but who may also, as was the way with Scots nobles, have recognised an opportunity to increase his power base. He was described by contemporaries as 'the most dangerous man in Scotland' and 'the most crafty, subtle and overreaching politician that this age could produce'. Yet he was a loving husband and family man, who was said to have 'a large and understanding heart'. The Royalists' image of the man seems to be captured in a 1652 portrait: stark, dark robes, long brown hair tucked under a dark skullcap and a disapproving glare towards the viewer from eyes with the faintest suggestion of a squint. There is a considerable difference between the Argyll of this portrait and one of a few years earlier, in which he is every inch the Cavalier, with fine cloth at his throat, his hair long and flowing, his face adorned by a carefully cultivated moustache and Vandyke beard.

Montrose, through his undoubted charisma, held his small force together and they won a momentous victory at Tippermuir in 1644. Outnumbered and outgunned, the Highland army, equipped with only a few muskets and one bullet apiece, supplemented with swords and even stones, decimated the Covenanter force. The scale of the killing was immense: it was said that if the bodies had been laid side by side, a man could have walked on the dead from the scene of the battle to Perth, several miles distant, without touching firm ground. This slaughter and claims of atrocities committed elsewhere, some undoubtedly the wicked imaginings of Covenanter spin doctors, served to demonise the marquis in the minds of his foes. Even so, Tippermuir marked the start of his

'Year of Miracles', a period during which he seemed unbeatable, despite the odds. As the war went against Charles in the south, news came from Scotland of victory after victory. But the joy was cut short in 1645 at Philiphaugh, near Selkirk, when Montrose's army, depleted after many of his Highland allies had returned home with booty collected during the campaign, was defeated in a bloody rout. The forces of the godly slaughtered all before them, citing as justification the alleged atrocities committed elsewhere in Scotland by Montrose's troops. Even women and children – camp-followers and servants – were cut down. Montrose escaped but the King's cause in Scotland was lost.

The Marquis of Huntly, who had continued to oppose the Covenanters in the north, was captured in December 1647 and imprisoned in the Tolbooth. Although removed to the Castle, he developed dysentery and there was a chance his ill health would claim him before the hangman. Moves were made to save him from the death penalty but the Covenanting Marquis of Argyll said there was nothing that could be done. On 22 March 1649, Huntly went to his death dressed in mourning black. Sick and weary, he was defiant to the last. As he had told his jailers when he was imprisoned a decade earlier, 'You may take my head from my shoulders, but not my heart from my sovereign.' On the heading platform, he showed these were not mere words.

When Cromwell's forces had Charles executed, even the Scottish Covenanters were horrified, for although they opposed the King's policies, they always deemed themselves loyal to the Crown. They proclaimed the Prince of Wales to be King Charles II, but the tall, dark-eyed young man refused to return to his country to take his throne. He had not forgiven the Covenanters for siding with the men who had murdered his father and so he sent Montrose back from exile to wage further war against them. The poet in Montrose expressed his grief over the death of the King.

Great, good, and just, could I but rate
My grief and thy too rigid fate,
I'd weep the world to such a strain
That it should deluge once again.
But since thy loud-tongued blood demands supplies
More from Briareus' hands than Argus' eyes,
I'll sing thy obsequies with trumpet sounds,
And write thy epitaph in blood and wounds.

His words were brave and heartfelt but in the end their reach exceeded their grasp for this new campaign ended in defeat at Carbisdale. The brave marquis, on the run in the Highlands, was eventually betrayed by a MacLeod lord – or his wife, depending on what you believe – in return for a reward that was made up partly in oatmeal. Meanwhile, Charles had begun to negotiate with the Covenanters over his return to power, if only in Scotland.

And so, James Graham, 1st Marquis of Montrose, was brought to Edinburgh already a condemned man. The marquis's final days have been well documented, by Wishart, by John Buchan, in contemporary accounts and letters, and in Ronald Williams' masterful *Montrose: Cavalier in Mourning*. On 18 May 1650, he entered the city by the Watergate, at the foot of the Canongate, where the magistrates waited to greet him along with the hangman, driving a common cart. He was strapped into the vehicle and led through the streets to the Tolbooth, where he was to spend the final few days of his life. According to reports, he accepted this ignominy with good grace and with the courage that he had shown throughout his campaigns. The zealots had ensured that the widows and children of men who had died opposing him thronged the streets. The intention was that the mob would stone him, perhaps even kill him, but when the crowds saw how well he comported himself, they stayed their hands – and were lambasted by their ministers for it.

There were many lords and ladies who watched him go by. Lady Jean Gordon, Countess of Haddington, laughed at his plight and insulted him, prompting one man in the crowd to tell her that 'it became her better to sit upon the cart for her adulteries'. Montrose's old enemy, the Marquis of Argyll (his power base still strong, although that would soon change) sat in the shadows of a balcony at Moray House, his wife at his side. The Royalist forces had harried him around his own lands and he had escaped with his life only through luck and, some said, a strong streak of cowardice. Montrose somehow sensed they were watching him. When his crude carriage halted momentarily underneath, he looked up, expecting to be berated by the man whom he had led a merry dance round the Highlands. Also in Argyll's company was the Covenanter lawyer Archibald Johnston of Warriston, whose hand had been most forceful in the drafting of the 1638 National Covenant that Montrose had signed. The two men were said to have withered under the calm gaze and slipped quietly into the house. Only the Countess of Argyll showed her true colours, spitting at Montrose as he waited below.

Finally, this particular ordeal was over and Montrose arrived at the Tolbooth. He handed the hangman some gold with the words 'Fellow, there is drink money for driving the cart' before being taken to his cell.

The men of God were not yet finished, for they visited him in his new lodgings and began to question him. He asked them to let him be but the following day, Sunday, they were back to continue their exhortations. He dismissed them again, saying that if they thought they had affronted him the day before then they were very much mistaken 'for he thought it the most honourable and joyful journey that he had ever made'. His demeanour merely outraged the Covenanter fanatics and on the Monday they were back. This time, their number included a powerful little preacher from Stirling, James Guthrie, who berated him for his morals – the marquis was something of a ladies' man – and for using Irish Catholics in his campaign against the Covenant. Montrose hit back at any suggestion that he had betrayed his Kirk, saying, 'The Covenant I took, I adhere to it. Bishops, I care not for them. I never intended to advance their interests.' He in turn accused the men before him of rebelling against the King. Guthrie, being a Royalist who would seven years later argue with Cromwell over the rights of King Charles II, felt duty bound to deny that charge, stating that it was a 'sectarian party that rose up and carried things beyond the true and first intent of them'.

Still they harangued him, trying to get him to repent in order that he would avoid the terrors of hell he could expect for being an excommunicate. Montrose told them sadly, 'I am very sorry that any actions of mine have been offensive to the Church of Scotland, and I would, with all my heart, be reconciled with the same. But since I cannot obtain it on any other terms – unless I call that my sin which I account to have been my duty – I cannot, for all the reason and conscience in the world.'

After the ministers took their leave, Montrose was allowed to prepare to meet his accusers in Parliament – a mere formality, for he had been condemned to die years before. He had a breakfast of bread dipped in ale and then attempted to spruce himself up, although he was not allowed a blade in order to shave lest he take his own life. He told the jailer, 'You need not be at so much pains. Before I was taken, I had a prospect of this cruel treatment and, if my conscience would have allowed me, I could have dispatched myself.' He was even refused the services of a barber and so, dressed in a black suit and knee-length scarlet coat, the magistrates led him unshaven and unwashed from his cell to Parliament House. Here he was accused of being 'a person most infamous, perjured and treacherous, and of all that ever this land brought forth, the most cruel and inhuman butcher and murderer of his nation, a sworn enemy to the Covenant and peace of his country'.

Archibald Johnston then read the foregone conclusion that was the sentence and Montrose was formally condemned to death. Told beforehand to drop to his knees, Montrose looked up as the pronouncement of doom was made. Perhaps he had expected some clemency, for he knew that Parliament had reached a limited agreement with the new king, and everything he had done was in service of the throne. He had answered accusations of the alleged atrocities committed by his troops by saying that 'even the greatest of generals have rarely succeeded on all occasions in preventing the licence of their soldiers'. However, he said, when he heard of any crimes he ensured that the guilty party was punished at once. 'Never was any man's blood spilt but in battle and even then many thousands of lives have I preserved. And I dare here avow in the presence of God that never a hair of a Scotsman's head that I could save fell to the ground.'

Still the religious zealots would not let Montrose rest. As he lay in his Tolbooth cell awaiting death on the high gallows, they came to him with their psalms and their prayers and their promise that the fires of hell awaited him. Montrose had already dismissed them with the words, 'It becomes them rather to be hangmen than me to be hanged.' Now he thanked them for the glory of his death. 'I think it a greater honour to have my head standing on the ports of this town than to have my portrait in the King's bedchamber,' he said. Finally, he tired of their exhortations and pleaded, 'I pray you, gentlemen, let me die in peace.'

So they left him, but hardly in peace, for his final hours were disrupted by his jailers, who had been instructed to make him as uncomfortable as possible. Proving himself a man ahead of his time, Montrose was known to detest the smell of tobacco smoke, and so they made a point of puffing on their pipes nearby and exhaling their fumes in his direction. According to legend, Montrose spent the longest, darkest night of his life in scratching a verse on the gloomy window of his cell with a diamond:

> Let them bestow on every airth a limb,
> Then open all my veins, that I may swim
> To thee, my Maker, in that crimson lake;
> Then place my par-boil'd head upon a stake,

Scatter my ashes, strew them in the air;
Lord! Since thou knowest where all these atoms are,
I'm hopeful thou'lt recover once my dust,
And confident thou'lt raise me with the just.

The morning of 21 May arrived amid a rattling of drums and blaring of trumpets, for the Town Guard and the garrison of the Castle had been alerted to the threat of a possible rescue attempt by men still loyal to the condemned. Montrose, on being told of this, was suitably sarcastic: 'Do I, who have been such a terror to these worthies during my life, continue still so formidable to them now, when about to die? But let them look to themselves; for even after I am dead, I will be continually present to their wicked consciences, and become more dreadful to them than when in life.'

As he waited for them to take him on his final walk, Montrose set to combing out his long brown hair. Archibald Johnston came to his cell and could not hold his tongue; he made a barbed comment about the marquis's vanity. 'While my head is my own, I dress and arrange it,' the marquis retorted. 'Tomorrow, when it is yours, you may treat it as you please.'

They came for him at two in the afternoon and escorted him to the place of his death at the Mercat Cross. Although he had been denied the right to visits from friends, they had managed to provide him with a suit of clothing so that he could meet death in some style. He had dressed himself in a scarlet suit with silver lace, delicate white gloves, silk stockings and shoes with ribbons. His hat glittered with a golden band. According to one observer, he was 'more beseeming a bridegroom than a criminal going to the gallows'.

Years before, it had been prophesied that he would dangle on three fathoms of rope. Now he would hang on a gallows an amazing 30 feet high – all the better for the assembled multitude to see this enemy of God and Kirk meet his doom. As friend and enemy alike watched, he climbed the steps to the platform. There, literally in the shadow of the noose, he told the crowd, 'Doth it not often happen to the righteous according to the way of the unrighteous? Doth not sometimes a just man perish in his righteousness, and a wicked man prosper in his wickedness and malice?'

His arms were pinioned and he was led to the ladder. He paid the hangman, as was the custom, and as he was pushed off the gallows, his final words were: 'May almighty God have mercy on this afflicted country.' One observer wrote in what is clearly an early form of reportage:

> It is absolutely believed that he hath overcome more now by his death in Scotland, than he would have done if he had lived, for I never saw more sweeter carriage in a man in all my life. I would write more largely if I had time, but he is just now a-turning off from the ladder: but his countenance changes not.

The crowd groaned as the body plummeted and the rope snapped back. The hangman wept, as did some of the audience. But Argyll revelled in the death of his nemesis, staying for the bloody spectacle that was to come. The body hung on the rope for three hours before it was cut down and the dismemberment began. Montrose's head was chopped off and spiked on the Tolbooth, while the arms and legs were removed and sent to be nailed up in public places at Glasgow, Dundee, Aberdeen and Perth. What was left of his body was thrown into a grave on the Burgh Muir. Argyll, it was said, 'triumphed at every stroke which was bestowed on his mangled body'.

Two days later, Lady Elizabeth Napier, married to Montrose's nephew, saw to it that the body was found. The heart was removed and carefully wrapped in the finest lace. The organ was preserved and placed in a steel box made from the blade of the dead man's own broadsword. This was then placed in a golden box, which in turn was kept in a silver urn. It was eventually given to Montrose's son, the 2nd Marquis, and, after passing through many hands, finally ended up in the possession of an Indian prince, who gallantly returned it to a Scottish family on learning of its tragic story. On his own violent death, executed after an uprising by the British, he wished that his family would treat his heart in the same way as the Scots had that of the heroic Montrose. The urn made its way to revolutionary France, where it was entrusted to an Englishwoman who promised that she would hide it from the authorities, who were then commandeering all gold and silver, before ensuring it was returned home. The woman died before she could make good her pledge and the heart of the hero vanished from history.

Meanwhile, as Montrose had predicted, his ghost haunted the men who had helped torment him.

Two weeks before Montrose died, the young king he had defended so earnestly reached an agreement with the Scottish authorities to claim his throne. Perhaps the King could have saved the marquis with a word, perhaps not. Whatever the case, it appeared it was not politically expedient for him to try. However, he did not forget the price Montrose had paid in defending his right to rule. Although Argyll placed the crown on Charles II's head at Scone on 1 January 1651, his days were numbered. Charles still had Cromwell to deal with, so he bided his time before moving against the powerful noble and his Covenanter friends – friends, however, who were already deserting him. In 1660, with Charles now restored to the throne, Argyll made one final attempt to re-establish his power. But he had gone too far: an ill-advised alliance with Cromwell in 1652 and his betrayal of an uprising that same year had not gone down too well with the King. That, his Covenanting past and his involvement in the execution of Montrose sealed his fate. Unlike Montrose, Argyll was allowed representation at his trial for treason before the Scottish Parliament. Even so, the outcome was a foregone conclusion: he was to be executed, his arms struck from his body and his head spiked on the Tolbooth.

Earlier that year, the King had decreed that Montrose's body be retrieved from its common grave on the Burgh Muir and what was left of his limbs returned to Edinburgh from the towns to which they had been sent. The head was to be removed from the Tolbooth spike on which it had weathered for more than ten long years. Montrose's kinsman Mungo Graham took the grim remnant down and kissed it before placing upon it a coronet. The various parts of the body were brought together again and laid in state at Holyrood Palace. Under the dark-grey skies of a threatening thunderstorm, the remains were carried with solemn majesty to St Giles', where they were laid to rest – although, in the late nineteenth century, when a search was made for those relics none could be found.

Argyll lay in his cell in the Castle listening to the bells pealing and knew that his cause was lost. He had resigned himself to his fate, knowing that his trial was, like that of Montrose, a mere formality, even though he was to be defended by a brilliant advocate, Sir George Mackenzie. As he listened to the cheers in the streets, he must have known his head would shortly take the place of his old enemy's on the Tolbooth spike. After he was condemned, he found his wife waiting for him in his cell. 'They have given me till Monday to be with you, my dear,' he told her. She appealed for clemency but there was none forthcoming. She even tried to help him escape, by changing clothes with him in his prison cell so that he could leave the castle in her sedan chair. Argyll, though, declined to go through with it. He had never been a noticeably brave man but in his final hours he found his courage. Transferred to the common jail that was the Tolbooth to await execution, he wrote: 'I am as content to be here as in the Castle, and I was as content in the Castle as in the Tower of London, and there I was as content as when at liberty; and I hope to be as content on the scaffold as in any of them all.'

As they took him from the Tolbooth, he stated, 'I could die like a Roman but choose rather to die as a Christian. Come away, gentlemen – he that goes first goes cleanliest.' He called to James Guthrie – also imprisoned in the Tolbooth – and the two old allies embraced. 'Such is my respect for your lordship that, if I were not under sentence of death myself, I could cheerfully die for your lordship,' said the fiery little minister.

On the afternoon of 27 May 1661, the Marquis of Argyll died on the Maiden. 'I had the honour to place the crown upon the King's brow,' he had told his judges, 'now he hastens me away to a better crown than his own.' He laid his head on the block and lifted his hand. The blade fell – and one marquis met the fate of the other. The King did not sign his death warrant until the following day. Argyll's head was fixed to the west end spike of the Tolbooth, where it rotted for three years before Charles allowed it to be taken down. In the Tolbooth records for 7 June 1664, there is the following instruction:

> Thes ar ordering you with all heast to taike down the marquess of argylls heid & give it to the laird of Arbruchell the bearer heiroff, ffor I have instantlie recevit his majestis comand for the same. Taik wreights and sletters helpe as ye shall have neid. Let it be done wit quyetness.
>
> Andrew Ramsay, provost, to the gudman of the tolbuith.

Underneath the note is another, signed by C. Campbell, acknowledging receipt of the head.

Guthrie, the powerful little man who had preached at Montrose in his cell, was next to suffer the ire of the King. Although he was a Royalist, his Church came first and he wished the new King to keep the reformed faith. He was arrested and tried on treason charges – twice. He proved adept at defending himself but as the proceedings dragged on he decided they must be drawn to a close. 'My Lord, my conscience I cannot submit; but this old crazy body and mortal flesh I do submit, to do with it whatsoever you will, whether by death or banishment or imprisonment or anything else.' He then went on to warn, 'If you put me to death, you shall bring innocent blood upon yourselves and upon the inhabitants of the city.' But death it was. He told his wife he was luckier than his old friend Argyll, who had been beheaded: 'I am to be hanged on a Tree as my Saviour was.'

On 1 June 1661, he was taken to the gallows at the Mercat Cross, defying the Stuart devotion to episcopacy to the last. 'I take God to record upon my soul, I would not exchange this scaffold for the palace and mitre of the greatest prelate in the land.' The minister in him refused to die, for he preached to the crowd for an hour before he was turned off the ladder. Guthrie's head was hacked off and placed not on the Tolbooth but on the Netherbow Port, a fortified city gate between the High Street and the Canongate, where it stood for 27 years, his son often running out into the street to stare at it. According to legend, the King's commissioner, the Earl of Middleton – whom Guthrie had excommunicated years before – passed under the Port and blood from the head dripped into his carriage. They said that no amount of scrubbing could remove the stain.

That left only Archibald Johnston of Warriston, the canny lawyer turned principal scribe of the National Covenant. The Kirk had split itself over the return of Charles II to the throne and, like his patron Argyll, Johnston found himself out of favour and lacking in power. His rabid fervour had helped weaken the Scottish army against Cromwell – his was among the voices demanding the purging of the less holy from the ranks – and his involvement in Montrose's death and other acts only served to turn the King against him. Bankrupt, he grudgingly accepted Cromwell's shilling and even became a member of the English Parliament. But the times they were a-changing, and with the Restoration Johnston's fortunes again waned. He fled Scotland just ahead of an arrest warrant and the furious authorities had him denounced as a traitor at the Mercat Cross. He travelled the Continent, an increasingly ill and frightened old man.

In 1663, Johnston's wife was recognised in France by an English spy. The authorities in Scotland moved fast and had him extradited, first to the Tower in London and then to the less celebrated but no less austere surroundings of the Tolbooth. Dragged to the council rooms in the Session House, he threw himself to his knees and begged for mercy. He claimed he had lost his memory through repeated bleedings during his illness and could not even recall his Scripture. The council was prone to mercy but Parliament was not as understanding. Warriston again begged for mercy on bended knee but the sentence of death levied in absentia was to stand.

As he awaited his final hour in the Tolbooth, he at least had something he and his friends had denied Montrose: company. The Tolbooth warding books record that on 8 June 1663, the keeper was ordered to 'permitt Rachell Johnstoune and Margaret Johnstoune, to go within the tolbuith and stay with their father until 10 of the clock att night'. A servant, William Johnston, was allowed to stay all night with his employer. Covenanter literature tells us that the youngest daughter had bravely asked to remain with him while he had spent six months in the Tower of London and that she subsequently did the same in the Edinburgh jail. Perhaps her presence helped him stiffen what resolve he had left. His Covenanting courage had deserted him before Parliament, now he was concerned that he did not 'faint in the hour of trial'. As for Montrose twelve years before, they built his gallows high at the Cross. Despite his earlier display of terror, he died bravely, talking to the crowds from the platform in a clear, steady voice, although some say his words were 'unintelligible nonsense'. Then he gave the signal and he was turned off, his head joining Guthrie's on the Netherbow Port.

There was one man involved in the destruction of Montrose who escaped a bloody death. The marquis had been betrayed to the Covenanters by Neil MacLeod of Assynt for a reward of 25,000 Scots pounds, a fifth of which was paid in 'sour meal'. He later denied being anywhere near his castle when Montrose arrived there and was subsequently captured. But in 1660, MacLeod was arrested for his part in Montrose's capture and carried to the Tolbooth to face trial. He spent two years in the Edinburgh jail before being released on the orders of a surprisingly magnanimous king, his guilt or innocence never established in court. He was back in court 14 years later, charged with piracy and rebellion. He was released on a not proven verdict.

Montrose had been avenged. The Church had been brought firmly back into line, at least for the moment. It was, though, only the beginning of Charles II's attack on the Reformed Kirk. There was more blood yet to be shed – and the Tolbooth would be splashed with much of it.

CHAPTER FOUR

ALTAR EGO

The pain was intense.

They had thrust his leg into what they called 'the boot'; in reality it was merely a wooden box or an iron case around the limb and a series of wedges around the knee. When he declined to answer a query put to him, his torturer hammered in another wedge. A surgeon stood by, a finger on the victim's pulse to monitor his strength. Again the mallet struck home and the man screamed but his questioner merely nodded to the torturer and demanded 'one touch more'. Another question, another denial and then 'one touch more' until the bones of the knee were shattered into kindling. Eleven hammer blows in total there were before they were sated with their cruelty, eleven touches before they called a halt. He was dragged back to his Tolbooth dungeon, his leg useless, his body racked with agony.

'I protest solemnly in the sight of God,' the victim had cried, 'I can say no more, though all the joints in my body were in as great anguish as my leg.'

The prisoner was Hugh McKail and he was a man of God. But he was also a Covenanter and he had taken part in an uprising that had ended bloodily for the rebels in hills near Edinburgh. The return of a Stuart to the throne was made possible in large part by the Scots and the Covenanters who had been horrified at their part in the killing of the new king's father. They had turned against their ally Cromwell, who had at least paid lip-service to their demands that their brand of Christianity be adopted across the nation. 'I beseech you, in the bowels of Christ, think it possible you may be mistaken,' the Protector had pleaded with them, but to no avail. They believed the best way to honour their faith and their National Covenant was through the throne. So they waged war against Cromwell with an army stripped of anyone deemed ungodly by their zealot ministers, not realising that in battle you need the atheist's sword as well as that of the believer. At Dunbar, Cromwell told his forces to trust in God but keep their powder dry and won a momentous victory, killing 3,000 of the Scots and taking 10,000 prisoner.

When the Protector died in 1658, the way was left open for the return of the Stuarts. Charles had been crowned King years before at Scone and in 1660 he returned to a London glad to see the back of Puritan strictures. In Edinburgh, bells pealed, cannons roared, wine streamed from a fountain at the Mercat Cross and the people celebrated from the Tolbooth all the way to Holyrood. For many of his Scottish subjects, the joy was short-lived. Charles had, like Cromwell, nodded in the direction of the National Covenant when it suited him but he was in power now – and for a Stuart that meant absolute authority. His grandfather, James VI of Scotland and later James I of the unified nation, had first butted heads with the Church over who would control it; his father, Charles I, had brought the two countries to war because of his desire to install episcopalianism; now the black-haired young monarch wanted to continue that holy work. The Covenanters would kneel, both physically and spiritually, before him as God's lieutenant on earth.

So began the period of guerrilla warfare, terrorism (on both sides) and attacks on freedom that were known as the Killing Time. Across central and Lowland Scotland, ministers were ejected from their pulpits for refusing to bow to royal authority, lists were compiled of those who failed to attend the new services and fines levied.

Ordinary folk were killed in the fields for failing to take an oath that effectively placed King before Church. The Presbyterian faithful, meanwhile, flocked to open-air services, or conventicles, in defiance of legislation.

And in the Tolbooth, business was booming.

James Guthrie went to his death for his adherence to the Covenant, so too did Argyll and Warriston, although their executions carried a whiff of vengeance for their part in the killing of Montrose. In 1666, a minor rebellion rose in Galloway and, at least in the eyes of the authorities, threatened the capital. It led to the anguished cries of the God-fearing echoing around the dingy corridors and damp rooms of the Tolbooth and other places of confinement across the country before many were stilled by the jerk of a hangman's rope.

In November 1666, a party of troops was attacked in Galloway by a band of men outlawed for their non-adherence to the new Church. It is said the troops were in the process of torturing an old man over an open flame, and there is little reason to doubt it. There was a brief moment of violence – and the Pentland Rising had begun. It began with that old man's whimper and ended with a musket bang in the snow-dusted hills near Edinburgh. Men had rallied to the call to arms and marched towards the city, taking prisoner King's man Sir James Turner along the way. Their numbers rose as they made their way north-east, claiming loyalty to the King but not to his new Church, but decreased as time passed and courage waned. At their height they numbered around 3,000 but by the time they reached Edinburgh little more than a third remained.

Among them was Hugh McKail, a young preacher who had fled to the Netherlands following an inflammatory sermon in St Giles', during which he had denounced Arch.' ishop James Sharp, a former Presbyterian who had taken the King's episcopalian shilling, as a 'Judas in the Church'. Once back in Scotland, McKail joined the rebels in Ayr and rode with them to Edinburgh through the cold and wet weather. He was not a strong man – although under torture he showed considerable grit – and his health was so frail that it was noted that he would have 'fallen off his horse, if one had not laid hold of him and held him up'. His weakened condition kept him from travelling any further than Colinton, on the outskirts of the city, and he left the marchers to go to his father's home. He was arrested near Liberton and sent to the Tolbooth.

It was here that he was tortured. The adventure had ended in blood and death in the snow at Rullion Green in the Pentland Hills and the authorities wanted to know who had fomented the rebellion. The Earl of Rothes led the interrogation and it was he who supervised the use of the boot. However, the brave little preacher refused to tell them anything. He was sentenced to death for his part in the insurrection – he had been spotted among the marchers in Ayr, Ochiltree and Lanark, and when caught was found to be armed. His defence was that he had not taken part in the battle, but his conscience plagued him over that stance, for he knew he would have fought had his health not failed. Covenanter literature tells us that his constitution may have been weak but his spirit was not. Although in agony because of his shattered knee, he told one man on the eve of his execution, 'Fear of my neck makes me forget my leg.' He also quipped, 'I am not so cumbered about dying as I have often been about preaching a sermon.'

He shared a cell in the Tolbooth with another Covenanter, Glasgow man John Wodrow, who had been taken at Rullion Green. On the morning of their execution McKail roused his cellmate with the words, 'Up, John – you and I look not like men going this day to be hanged, seeing we lie so long.' It was five in the morning.

On the afternoon of 22 December 1666, Hugh McKail died at the Mercat Cross along with Wodrow and four other men taken in the Pentland Hills. From the platform, he delivered an impassioned sermon to the assembled multitude; the address would be the precursor and indeed template for many a dying speech in the years to come.

'Now I leave to speak any more to creatures, and turn my speech to Thee, oh Lord. Now I begin my intercourse with God, which shall never be broken off. Farewell, father and mother, friends and relations. Farewell, the world and all delights. Farewell, meat and drink. Farewell, sun, moon and stars. Welcome, God and Father. Welcome, sweet Jesus, the mediator of the New Covenant. Welcome, blessed spirit of Grace, God of all consolation. Welcome, glory! Welcome, eternal life! Welcome, death!'

Those six men were the last of their faith to be executed in Edinburgh for twelve years, although many others met their maker at the hands of the executioner elsewhere. When he died, Hugh McKail was only 26 years of age.

One man who escaped the bloodletting at Rullion Green was Captain John Paton. He would not, however, escape a term in the Tolbooth and death on the gibbet. His story is perhaps one of the most rousing tales of the Killing Time. An Ayrshire mercenary who fought on the Protestant side in the Thirty Years War, he returned home so changed by his experiences in the bloody Continental conflict that his parents did not recognise him. He was a fierce and able warrior, despite suffering from an asthmatic condition, who reputedly killed 18 men in a single action. Fighting for the Covenant against Cromwell, and surviving the purging of the ungodly from the ranks by the godly, he impressed General Tam Dalyell of the Binns with his prowess. Later, they would be on opposing sides on the snow-covered slopes of the Pentlands – for Dalyell, loyal to his King, was in command of the government dragoons who cut the rebel force to pieces at Rullion Green. Paton, who had joined the rebels in Ayrshire, tried to shoot the white-haired general but the ball deflected off the old warrior's iron breastplate. The captain then refilled his pistol with a silver bullet – not because, as Covenanter myth-makers would have their followers believe, Dalyell was in league with the Devil but because silver could pierce the armour. However, luck was with the old warhorse that day, for just as Paton fired a soldier moved in the way and took the bullet instead. The captain battled his way through a knot of dragoons and galloped across the hill. Three followed and Paton swung his sword, cutting off the head of one before leaping across a wide, muddy ditch and turning to the others to say, 'My compliments to your master, and tell him I shall not be with him tonight.'

For the next 17 years, Paton was a hunted man. He was among the Covenanters defeated at Bothwell Bridge in 1679 and escaped from the clutches of the authorities many times. Finally, he was captured near Kilmarnock, age and his medical condition making him frail and, for once, easy to control. However, the dragoons who found him had no idea what a prize they had – until a farmer inadvertently called him by his name. In the Tolbooth, where he was taken on 14 April 1684, he once again came face to face with his old commander and nemesis Tam Dalyell. The old general clearly bore no grudge for Paton's attempts to kill him all those years before, for he said, 'John, I am both glad and sorry to see you. If I had met you in the way before you came hither, I should have set you at liberty; but now it is too late. But be not afraid, I will write to his Majesty for your life.' However, Paton was considered too much of a renegade. He was condemned to death for his part in the battles at Rullion Green and Bothwell Bridge. His execution was twice delayed, the second time thanks to Dalyell's intervention. In the court records on this occasion, it is noted, 'John Paton, in Meadowhead, sentenced to die for rebellion, and thereafter remaining in mosses and moors to the high contempt of authority, reprieved till Friday come sen'night, and to have a room by himself, that he may prepare more conveniently for death.'

On Friday, 9 May, Captain John Paton went to that death for which he had prepared in his solitary cell in the Tolbooth. It was said later that the King had pardoned him, perhaps as a result of Dalyell's pleas, but a bishop held the paperwork back until the sentence was passed.

Another famed Covenanter had passed through the Tolbooth seven years earlier. The Reverend Alexander Peden was with the insurrection of 1666 but dropped out at Lanark. He was declared a rebel with a price on his head. Already proscribed from preaching for refusing to follow the new ways, he took to the moors, holding conventicles across south-west Scotland. He was captured in June 1673 and held in the Ayr Tolbooth before an order was raised by the Earl of Rothes – Hugh McKail's torturer – instructing a Major Cockburn to take a command of six horsemen to Ayr where they were to 'receive ye person of Mr Alexander Pedine, a rebell, in ye tolbuth there, and bring him in saiffe custodie to the tolbuthe of Edinburgh'. Peden was fortunate in that he was not executed but merely imprisoned on Bass Rock, an island in the Firth of Forth – although conditions there might have made him long for death. On the rock, he and fellow Covenanters were kept in close confinement night and day, not permitted to see or talk to one another and hearing, he wrote, 'only the sighs and groans of our fellow prisoners'. Peden himself said they 'envied the birds their freedom' during their periods of exercise. The island is now a bird sanctuary.

After more than four years on the rock, he was brought back to the Tolbooth, remaining there for fifteen months before being told he was to be sent with other prisoners to the plantations of the Americas, where they would be sold as slaves. Peden and others regained their liberty in England when they convinced the captain of a ship due to take them across the Atlantic to set them free. He never again enjoyed the dubious comforts of the Tolbooth, nor did he feel the weight of the hangman's rope on his neck. He died a hunted man on his brother's farm in Ayrshire. He was interred in Auchinleck kirkyard but soldiers removed the body with the intention of hanging it from the gibbet in Cumnock. Prevented from doing so by a local landowner, they contented themselves with burying his body at the foot of the gallows.

In life, Peden had hoped he would be buried beside Covenanter

Richard Cameron on the moorland known as Airds Moss near Muirkirk in Ayrshire. Fife-born Cameron, known as 'the Lion of the Covenant', had been declared an outlaw after his Sanquhar Declaration, which called the King 'a tyrant and usurper' and an enemy of Jesus Christ. On 22 July 1680, he and others were on Airds Moss when they were spotted by a group of soldiers. According to Covenanter legend, Cameron washed his hands and face that morning, saying, 'This is their last washing. I have need to make them clean, for there are many to see them.' It would prove a prophetic statement – and one in which the Tolbooth, so far away in Edinburgh, would figure.

As rain fell from a leaden sky, the two forces clashed on this bare piece of land. Nine Covenanters died, including Richard Cameron, whose head and hands were hacked from his body to enable an officer to claim a reward. What was left of the preacher's corpse was buried with the bodies of eight of his comrades on the stark moorland where they fell. The body parts were carried to Edinburgh, where they were shown to the Privy Council with the words, 'There's the head and hands that lived praying and preaching, and died praying and fighting.' The grisly artefacts were also brought to the Tolbooth, where they were shown to Cameron's father, Allan, a prisoner thanks to his work in organising conventicles in Fife. He was asked if he knew them and the old merchant took them, kissed them and said, 'I know them! I know them! They are my son's, my dear son's.'

Five Covenanters were taken alive that day and brought to Edinburgh. Two – a Mr Manual from Shotts and John Vallance of Auchinleck – died of their wounds. Galloway men Archibald Allison and John Malcolm were kept for over a month before they were hanged in the Grassmarket. Allison was allowed to tell the crowd, 'I declare here, where I stand, before Him who will be my judge within a little, my design in coming forth with arms was to hear the Gospel preached truly and forcefully.' It does raise the point that when the Bible states, 'Thou shalt not kill,' it does not follow that up with 'unless your Church is under threat'.

But the grisliest fate awaited David Hackston of Rathillet. He was a man the authorities very much wanted to see dance the hangman's jig. He had been with the band of men who brutally murdered former Presbyterian turned tormentor of Covenanters Archbishop James Sharp on a lonely stretch of countryside above St Andrews known as Magus Muir, although he had not raised a sword in anger. He had also fought at Drumclog and Bothwell Bridge. He battled bravely at Airds Moss but was wounded, captured and eventually brought to Edinburgh. While in the Tolbooth, he wrote an account of the Airds Moss battle in which he praised his own men and applauded his enemies for recognising the Covenanters as 'brave, resolute men'. It would have been better for him if he had died on that wet and misty day in Ayrshire, for his execution on 30 July was particularly dreadful. The sentence read that he be:

> drawn backward on a hurdle to the Mercat Cross; that there be an high scaffold erected a little above the Cross, where, in the first place, his right hand is to be struck off, and, after some time, his left hand; then he is to be hanged up, and cut down alive, his bowels to be taken out, and his heart shown to the people by the hangman; then his heart and his bowels to be burned in a fire prepared for that purpose on the scaffold; that afterwards his head be cut off, and his body divided into four quarters; his head to be fixed on the Netherbow; one of his quarters with both his hands to be affixed at St Andrews, another quarter at Glasgow, a third at Leith, a fourth at Burntisland; that none presume to be in mourning for him, or any coffin brought; that no person be suffered to be on the scaffold with him, save the two bailies, the executioner and his servants; that he be allowed to pray to God Almighty, but not to speak to the people; that Hackston's and Cameron's heads be fixed on higher poles than the rest.

Later that year, in December, another four veterans of the Airds Moss battle were executed.

The first Sunday after the deaths at Airds Moss, the Reverend Donald Cargill, preaching to a Shotts conventicle, asked the congregation, 'Know ye not that there is a prince and a great man fallen this day in Israel?' The great man, of course, was Richard Cameron, for whom the Cameronian regiment was later named, and the much older Cargill knew him from the time, not long before, when together they had eluded pursuing troops in the Galloway heather. Cargill had been denounced as a rebel with a price placed on his head for preaching sedition and even going to the lengths of excommunicating the King and his advisers, an act unlikely to have endeared him to Charles. Many of his friends and followers were caught and executed but he managed to evade capture for some time. He was eventually arrested at Covington Mill in Lanarkshire and brought to the Tolbooth. The Privy Council took a ballot to decide Cargill's sentence; he was condemned to death by a margin of just one vote. He and two men caught with him were executed on 27 July 1681 – just a few days over a year since his friend Richard Cameron fell at Airds Moss.

In August 1684, three men – Thomas Harkness, Andrew Clerk and Samuel McEwen – were hanged in the Grassmarket for their part in an attempt to free nine captured Covenanters at the Enterkin Pass in Galloway. They ambushed the patrol escorting the men to Edinburgh, killed three soldiers and saved all the prisoners but two. John MacKechnie was wounded and taken to the Tolbooth, where he died 13 weeks later when his wound turned gangrenous. William Grierson was blinded by a bullet in the face. He was found near death on the hillside and tended to by friends but was soon recaptured by soldiers combing the land for the ambushers. He was held in the Tolbooth for a period but, surprisingly, the authorities showed mercy and set him free, deeming him no longer a threat due to his blindness.

The last Covenanter to be executed in Edinburgh was James Renwick, a native of Moniaive in Dumfries and Galloway. Like

Hugh McKail, he was of a weak constitution, and he was given to fainting fits as the stresses and terrors of being a hunted rebel took their toll. An early interest in religion soon gave way to a questioning of his faith, but then, on 27 July 1681, he received a blinding flash. Renwick's road to Damascus was the Grassmarket and the vision that had the scales dropping from his eyes was not of God but of Donald Cargill being executed for his beliefs and his non-adherence. The 19-year-old Renwick forgot his doubts and resolved to follow in the old preacher's footsteps. Refusing his MA from Edinburgh University because he could not accept the King's authority over his Church, he travelled to Holland to study further. Two years later, he was back in Scotland and preaching at proscribed conventicles. Leading the life of a hunted man, Renwick dodged dragoons while he held services for hundreds of hatches, matches and dispatches – baptisms, marriages and funerals. Within one year, some figures claim, he had brought as many as 600 children into the faith, and he was seen as a very real danger by the authorities. In September 1684, the Privy Council issued a strongly worded edict that commanded and charged:

> all and sundry our lieges and subjects that they nor none of them presume, nor take upon hand to reset, supply, or intercommune with the said Mr James Renwick, rebel aforesaid; nor furnish him with meat, drink, house, harbour, victual, nor no other thing useful or comfortable to him; or to have intelligence with him by word, writ, or message, or any other manner of way whatsoever, under the pain of being esteemed art and part with him in the crimes foresaid, and pursued therefor with all rigour to the terror of others. And we hereby require all our sheriffs and other officers to apprehend and commit to prison the person of the said Mr James Renwick wherever they can find him.

Despite such dire warnings, Renwick was shielded by friends and believers for a further three years, during which time he published the 'Apologetic Declaration and Admonitory Vindication', which showed that the Covenanters were just as capable of tough talk as the authorities. Rejecting Charles II's claims of superiority all over again, it also threatened dire repercussions on anyone who should inform on the faithful or 'whosoever stretch forth their hands against us'. The document was, in part, a response to the King's Abjuration Oath, which required people to denounce Covenanting principles and accept the Church as an instrument of the state. Anyone who refused to take the oath could be shot on the spot.

In February 1685, Charles died, leaving his brother James to take the throne. James was a Roman Catholic and his behaviour in Scotland had given the people there no cause to love him, so resolve stiffened even further in the Presbyterian ranks. In May 1685, James Renwick thundered into Sanquhar with 200 horsemen, like his hero Richard Cameron, to pin the second declaration to the town's market cross. This denounced James VII as an idolater and murderer and in turn made Renwick even more of a 'seditious villain' than before. Even so, he remained at liberty for a further three years before being caught during a clandestine visit to Edinburgh. It was not dragoons but excisemen who finally trapped him, in the home of a known smuggler. The preacher was not going to go down easily, however. He might have been praying when they heard and discovered him but he also had a pistol to hand. During the subsequent struggle, he managed to escape from the house on Castle Hill and bolted down Castle Wynd, pursued by the customs officers, who battered him about the head until he collapsed. When the prisoner was taken to the Tolbooth, an incredulous captain of the Town Guard commented, 'Is this boy the Mr Renwick that the nation hath been so much troubled with?' James Renwick was only 26 years of age.

He pled guilty to charges of refusing to accept the King's authority, failing to pay taxes and persuading believers to bear arms at conventicles. The date of his execution was set for 8 February 1688, but his death was postponed for a week, during which various friends tried to convince the young man that he should at least partly accept the King's authority; he refused. Clearly, there was little appetite left for the death of such men and renewed efforts were made to make him change his mind but Renwick seemed to welcome the idea of martyrdom. On the day of his death, his mother and sister were allowed into his cell to make their goodbyes and then he was led out to the Grassmarket to preach his final sermon. However, few in the huge crowd heard his words, for the drummers were ordered to beat a loud tattoo. Renwick sang the 103rd Psalm, read from the 19th chapter of the Book of Revelation (which tells of a Christian avenger with flames of fire for eyes) and prayed. Clouds crowded on the thin winter sun and Renwick cried, 'I shall soon be above these clouds.' Then, finally, it was all over.

Although Renwick was the last Covenanter to be executed in Edinburgh, he was not the last to die at the hands of the authorities. That dubious honour fell to innocent Ayrshire boy George Wood. The 16-year-old was unfortunate to be in the fields near Sorn on the night soldiers were searching for Covenanters who had helped free an Irish minister being transported to Edinburgh to face trial. A trooper gunned Wood down without warning in June 1688.

James VII tried to appear more tolerant than his brother and in 1687 he repealed 'all penal and sanguinary laws made against nonconformity to the religion established by law'. However, he still adhered to a belief in the divine right of kings and his moves were seen by the Protestants as a means to help further his own religion rather than any genuine show of tolerance. He removed Protestants from public office and replaced them with Roman Catholics, conventicles were still prohibited and death meted out to anyone who attended them. On the other hand, many ministers who had been banned from their pulpits or put in prison were allowed to return to their vocation. In December 1688, James's reign collapsed and he fled the country. His daughter, Mary, took the throne with her husband, William of Orange, and finally the Killing Time was over.

In *The Scots Worthies*, eighteenth-century historian John Howie estimated that 18,000 Scots were punished, banished or killed for their adherence to the Presbyterian cause. Even Covenanter literature acknowledges that to be an exaggeration. However, when you factor in the number of men killed in battle – including the thousands who fell at Dunbar and those marched to death and slavery in the aftermath – then the figure may not be so wide of the mark.

And on hillsides and moors across Lowland Scotland, there are solitary stone markers reminding us where men and women fell for their beliefs. They stand as stark reminders of the horrors that can be committed when men talk of the supremacy of one religion over another. Yet we cannot shake our heads and say times have changed; there is little to separate the twenty-first century from the Killing Time. The dogs of war still bark today and innocent blood continues to be shed in the name of God or the twin deities of Democracy and Profit.

Robert Louis Stevenson was fascinated by the tales of the Covenanters, and his famous poem 'To S.R. Crockett', also known as 'Blows the Wind Today', is a fitting way to remember the horror of those far-off events that still resonate today.

> Blows the wind today, and the sun and the rain are flying,
> Blows the wind on the moors today and now,
> Where about the graves of the martyrs the whaups are crying,
> My heart remembers how!
>
> Grey recumbent tombs of the dead in desert places,
> Standing-stones on the vacant wine-red moor,
> Hills of sheep, and the howes of the silent vanished races,
> And winds, austere and pure.

Be it granted me to behold you again in dying,
Hills of home! and to hear again the call;
Hear about the graves of the martyrs the peewees crying,
And hear no more at all.

CHAPTER FIVE

SCRATCHING WITCHES

To the Devil a Doctor

In the late fifteenth century, the Church of Rome was becoming increasingly alarmed by the growth of heresy and so a bull was issued by Pope Innocent VIII in order to stem what was believed to be a flood of souls being seduced by the dark side – witchcraft and Satanism. This authorised the Holy Office, or the Inquisition, as it is more popularly known, to prosecute witches. Innocent VIII was a great supporter of both the Roman Inquisition and the recently established Spanish Inquisition, set up by Ferdinand and Isabella and overseen by the ruthless Dominican friar Tomás de Torquemada.

The book used by the holy men of the Inquisition as a guide to rooting out those who had fallen under the glamour of the Devil and all his works was the 1486 bestseller *Malleus Maleficarum*, the 'Hammer of the Evildoers' or 'Hammer of the Witches'. Its authors, Jacob Sprenger and Heinrich Kramer, were a pair of German friars who had grown concerned about the high level of heresy in their own country. This hefty volume – running close on a quarter of a million words – taught would-be witch-hunters how to spot dabblers in the black arts and how to put them to the question.

Fear of witchcraft reached the shores of Scotland, although many of the earliest recorded cases seem to have been motivated more by a love of money or power than a love of Christ. A popular theme was an accusation of threats against the King, as in 1479 when John Stewart, Earl of Mar, was accused of trying to harm James III by melting a waxen image. The fact that the earl was the King's brother did not help him, for he bled to death in prison when overly enthusiastic doctors applied leeches to combat a fever. The King's other brother, Alexander, Duke of Albany, was also accused but he showed just how slippery he could be when he escaped from Edinburgh Castle, killing his guards and dropping down the rock face on a rope made out of bed-sheets. A pageboy who escaped with him broke his legs in a fall and Albany carried him to Leith, from where the duke escaped to France. He did not return until James was imprisoned by the barons in the rebellion of 1482. Meanwhile, the man who had made the allegations, Robert Cochrane, became Earl of Mar, which was no doubt his plan all along, and received his comeuppance during the rebellion: he was among the King's advisers hanged from Lauder Bridge.

In 1535, Lady Jane Douglas was accused of conspiring by means of sorcery to poison King James V. The accusation was levelled by William Lyon – a relative of her first husband, Lord Glamis – who had quite fancied becoming her second husband. However, she had rejected his suit and married another kinsman, Lord Lyon. The accusation was taken seriously and Lady Jane, her husband, her son and the family priest were brought to Edinburgh to face trial. There were some misgivings about the whole proceedings but William Lyon seems to have had considerable pull, for he convinced the courts to torture the accused on the rack until they confessed. Lady Glamis was then carried to Castle Hill, where she was chained to the stake and burned alive, barrels of tar and rags dripping in oil piled up around her as an accelerant. Like Albany more than 50 years before, her husband attempted a daring escape from his cell in the Castle but, unlike Albany, fell to his death. Later, William Lyon's conscience moved him to confess that his accusations had been false.

In the second half of the sixteenth century, the Inquisition in

Europe was at the height of its power. Calvinist Scotland, of course, would have no truck with such Papist hocus-pocus but that did not mean that it denied the existence of witches. For, as we have seen, the Presbyterians were not slow to unleash the wrath of God on anyone who did not follow their path. During the reign of Mary, Queen of Scots, the first laws were introduced to curtail witchcraft. An Act of Parliament passed on 4 June 1563 stated that 'nae person [should] take upon hand to use ony manner of witchcrafts, sorcery or necromancy, or give themselves forth to have ony sic craft or knowledge thereof, there-through abusing the people'. It also stated that no person should 'seek ony help, response or consolation at ony sic users or abusers of witchcrafts'. Of course, it ended with the customary admonition 'on pain of death'.

And there was a great deal of pain and death awaiting anyone accused of being in league with the Devil. Torture was commonplace and it was used with some glee in trying to extract confessions from the accused. The authorities believed that traffickers with Satan did not act in isolation and so they felt it their duty to subject any person suspected of being a witch or wizard to the direst of tortures to loosen their tongues and get them to name names. Women had their heads shaved, were stripped naked and thrown into the coldest cell of the Tolbooth, where the jailers delighted in beating them, starving them, depriving them of sleep and tormenting them by applying lit candles to their flesh. They could be 'thrawed', having a rope wrapped around their heads and tightened. Their nails could be wrenched off with pincers, or needles pushed under them. They could be whipped and branded. A leg could be encased in an iron brace, the brace placed into a fire and the fire stoked until the metal grew white hot and roasted the skin. They could be thrown into deep water to sink or swim. If they sank and drowned, they were deemed innocent; if they did not, then they were guilty. In Edinburgh, the Nor' Loch (now the site of Princes Street Gardens and Waverley Station) was the favourite spot for this punishment. It was also, incidentally, a handy spot to exact swift punishment on less occult malefactors found guilty at special night courts: they were carted off to the loch and drowned. Finally, whether or not the witches had confessed – although generally they had – and whether or not they had implicated others, they would be burned at the stake, just like Lady Jane Douglas. Some were lucky to be first 'wirreit' – strangled – but others were 'burnt quick' which often meant being put in a tar barrel and burned alive.

It may well have been in the time of Mary's son, James VI, when what was to become known as the Authorised Version was being written, that the line 'Thou shalt not suffer a witch to live' was inserted into the Bible. He might have been 'the wisest fool in Christendom', but Jamie the Saxt was obsessed with the black arts, the practice of which he deemed 'a synne most odious', and that Old Testament line gave the holy just cause to stamp out anything deemed unholy. Intelligent he might have been, but James was a paranoid, suspicious man, often with good cause, and the machinations of witches and warlocks were yet another threat to his well-being. He even wrote a tract on the subject, *Daemonologie*, which, along with the *Malleus Maleficarum*, became something of a 'how to' handbook for the growing body of witch-hunters.

Superstition, jealousy, greed and religious fervour could all come into play during witch-hunts. A woman might be accused of being a witch simply because she was unmarried and lived alone. If a woman used natural remedies – the old ways – to heal human or animal, she could be accused of being a witch. If she was attractive and turned the heads of married men, she could be accused of being a witch. However, despite feminist arguments that the witch crazes were entirely a masculine conspiracy to keep women in their place, some of the accused probably did believe themselves to be in league with the Devil, whether through insanity, substance abuse or mass hysteria. Then, of course, they might actually have been witches or at least adherents to ways older than the Christian Church. Like many a religion, Christianity has often shown itself less than keen to tolerate older beliefs. While it welcomed some traditions into the embrace of its own customs (for instance, Hallowe'en, Easter and even Christmas), the rest it declared anathema and resolved to root out.

In 1590, in Tranent, East Lothian, a local baillie and landowner suspected a servant-girl of being a witch – and set in motion one of the most infamous and far-reaching witch-hunts in Scottish history. Before it ended, over 70 people were accused of being part of a coven that threatened the life of the King, his new wife and, by extension, the security of the nation. Before it ended, blood was shed in the Tolbooth and screams heard on Castle Hill as those found guilty were throttled by the executioner's rope or roasted over an open flame. Politics once again reared its ugly head as a powerful nobleman who scared the little king was accused of being at the centre of the plot.

Serving-girl Geillis Duncan was young, she was pretty and she had one particular skill: she could heal the sick. Her ability to bring comfort to the ailing, and her habit of sneaking out at night, aroused the suspicion of her master, David Seaton. He felt duty-bound to investigate the notion that her arts were more occult than Hippocratic, although why the Devil would give his followers the ability to relieve suffering is a bit of a puzzler. So pretty young Geillis was put to the question. Seaton had her arrested and interrogated about her alleged involvement in sorcery. The girl denied the charge but that was not enough for the good men of Tranent and so the pilniewinks were brought into play. This device, bastard kin to the thumbscrews, saw the girl's fingers wedged between two plates of iron which were then tightened by means of a screw until the flesh ruptured and the bones fractured. It was, as was noted at the time, 'a most grievous torture' but still the girl would not break. Then a search was made of her body for a Devil's mark: a spot that was impervious to pain and did not bleed. It could be something as simple, not to mention commonplace, as a birthmark or even a mole. Unsurprisingly, such a spot was found on Geillis's neck. She was thrown into a Tolbooth cell, where she was further tormented until her spirit was broken and she freely admitted being in league with the Devil. In addition, she named others as being members of her coven.

So began the North Berwick witch trials. In the weeks and months that followed, around 70 people, mostly women, were rounded up and questioned. The best-known case is that of Agnes Sampson, a local midwife. Like Geillis before her, this seemingly respectable woman stoically denied all the charges against her. Only at first, though, for it was ordered that she be taken to the Tolbooth, where she was to 'receive such torture as hath lately beene provided for witches'. She was thrawed, deprived of sleep and forced to wear the witch's bridle, a special version of the branks, or scold's bridle, which was reserved for nagging, gossiping or blaspheming women. An iron frame was fitted over the head and a spiked metal gag that could pierce the cheeks, tongue and palate thrust into the mouth. Agnes was denied food and water, and led around by a chain attached to the branks, each tug of which would have been agony. When a search was made of her naked body, a Devil's mark was found on her private parts and she finally confessed all. She was found guilty of 53 counts of witchcraft, including healing the sick. She was to be bound to a stake and strangled until she was dead and thereafter her body burned to ashes; all her moveable goods were forfeit and brought 'in to the use of our sovereign lord'. So James not only got rid of a cadre of demonic plotters but also topped up the royal coffers.

Membership of the North Berwick coven was truly republican in nature, for the group not only included serving-girls and midwives but also reached into some of the highest echelons of local society. Barbara Napier was the widow of the Earl of Douglas, who held the imposing Tantallon Castle near North Berwick. She was accused of having used her black arts to murder her husband by mysterious means in 1588. She was acquitted of that charge but was found guilty of consulting with witches. Her pregnancy ensured that she avoided the direst punishment. Leniency was shown and she was released, although James was sharply criticised for sanctioning this by ministers who said that he and his council were not assisted by God in reaching the decision. The reason God had withheld the wise counsel of killing the woman, apparently, was 'because [the King] had not repented sufficiently for his former sinnes'.

Another accused, Euphame Mackallean, or Maclean, was the daughter of dead Court of Session judge Thomas Mackallean. This did not help her in the end, for she was found guilty of nine counts, including using sorcery to murder a child and treason. She tried to escape the stake by claiming she was also with child, but she was either lying or not high-born enough, for she burned, screaming her innocence, on 25 June 1591.

It was not just women who were accused. Men were also named and no leniency was shown. According to the testimonies elicited from the tortured women, one of the principal warlocks of the coven was Prestonpans schoolteacher Dr John Fian (often spelled Fean, Fain, Fane or Feanne), sometimes called Cunningham. Little is known of his early years – but his death is well documented. He managed to escape shortly after his arrest, which was a mistake, for when he was recaptured he was taken to the Tolbooth, where he was subjected to what an English witness described as 'a most straunge torment'. Needles were driven under his fingernails 'even up to the heads'. The nails were then pulled off using the 'torkas', a set of pincers peculiar to the Scottish torture chamber. He refused, even then, to confess to being part of the coven and so they resorted to the 'bootes'. They hammered in the wedges one by one but he refused to tell them what they wanted to hear, so they hammered in more until 'his legges were crusht and beaten together as small as they might bee; and the bones and flesh so bruised that the bloud and marrow spouted forth in great abundance'. Naturally, he confessed all. That admission was retracted when it came to his execution, although he did confess to adultery with 32 women.

Among the charges of which Dr Fian was found guilty was one of being approached by the Devil while in a house in Tranent (the Devil, unaccountably, being dressed in white) and of being marked by him with a white wand, which sent him into ecstatic trances (some of which were witnessed by the King during questioning). He was also guilty of 'abusing his body' with a widow but, at Satan's command, refusing to marry her. He was found to have been transported from his bed in Prestonpans to North Berwick kirkyard, where he and others, including Agnes Sampson, paid homage to the Dark One. In addition, he was found to have moles' feet in his purse, which supposedly ensured he never lacked money.

Another man arrested, Robert Grierson, or Greyson, died 'it is thought by the extremyty of the tortours applied to him. He hath confessed litle, and yet it is said by the rest that he was pryvy to all their accions.'

It is clear from the fact that James VI went to the length of questioning Agnes Sampson and Dr Fian himself that the King took a great interest in the proceedings, during which the accused told some incredible stories. The reason for the King's fascination was simple: the brutal investigation had apparently uncovered a conspiracy to kill him and his new queen, Anne of Denmark. In October 1589, he had sailed from Leith to bring her back for the wedding but rough seas delayed the return trip – and when they did finally set sail, in May 1590, a storm blew up that threatened to swamp the ship. The royal couple survived but when he heard that it was the North Berwick witches who had summoned the tempest, at the behest of Satan, James was beside himself with rage.

In November 1590, the English ambassador sent a letter south to Lord Burghley saying, 'The King and Counsaill is occupied with the examinaciouns of sundry witches taken in this contrye, and confessing both great nombers and the names of their fellowes; and also strange and odiouse factes done by them.' Later, the same correspondent described the actions of the accused as 'filthy, lewde, and phantasticall'.

According to the wild tales told under torture, the Devil had appeared to the witches, 'his body hard lyk yrn; his faice was terrible; his nose lyk the bek of ane egle; gret handis and feit lyk the griffon, and spak with a low voice'. He took them out to sea in a ship 'lyke ane chimnay', which sounds like a demonic steamship, and there they threw a cat into the waves. This poor feline had already had its paws knitted to the private parts of a dead man, been drawn through a fire nine times, one for each life, and christened as the King. This apparently summoned the gale that was to kill the monarch and his wife (although, in the end, James's tremendous piety saved him from a watery grave). They then retired to the kirkyard at North Berwick, as they had done on other occasions, access gained by using the 'Hand of Glory' – cut from the corpse of a murderer, stuffed with herbs, pickled, dipped in wax and used as a candle. The hand could open any lock and protect the user from being observed. There they danced to the sound of pipes and the Jew's harp (dancing was seen by the Calvinists as the work of the Devil) and their Dark Master appeared to them again. They feasted on the flesh of the dead, they said, before Satan 'caussit them to kiss his erse'. Unsurprisingly, it was described as 'cauld lyk yce'.

The witches were able to give the King details of the pillow talk between the royal couple on their wedding night, which proved that some dark magics were being employed in the nation.

The conspiracy did not end there, for the witch-hunters uncovered yet another name, one that may well have struck fear directly into the King's heart, and that was Francis Stewart, Earl of Bothwell, nephew to Mary Stuart's third husband. The bold earl was, like his uncle, a free-booting Border lord, part rebel, part outlaw, fond of violence, although the nephew was prone to madness. He shared with his uncle a liking for action, once even storming the Tolbooth to free one of his men. He disliked the King and had little respect for him, once famously bursting in on the little monarch while he was on the toilet. Some of the witches claimed that the attempt on the lives of the King and Queen was made at his insistence. It was convenient for James that Bothwell had been implicated in the witch conspiracy, for it gave him the excuse he needed to have him arrested again. Agnes Sampson, for one, had been forced to claim Bothwell was in league with the Devil. One of the arrested men, Richard Graham, maintained that while he was in prison awaiting trial he had been sent money by the earl, with the instruction that he should stand fast to his denial that Bothwell had any part in the conspiracy.

Bothwell himself insisted that he be heard in answer to the charges against him. He denied them as 'incredible and unnatural accusations', demanding trial by combat. No one came forward to answer his challenge. He admitted he was acquainted with Graham and had received a ring from him 'of sundry colours', which reputedly had clairvoyant powers. According to rumour, Graham had healing skills that could be learned only through following the dark arts. Bothwell related that he knew of this and had sent Graham to tend the sick Earl of Angus – whose death had prompted the charge of murder by witchcraft against Barbara Napier. On another occasion, Bothwell said, he had met Graham and he had shown him 'a sticke with nickes in yt, all wrapped about with long heire eyther of a man or a woman, and [Graham] said yt was an enchanted stick; to which speech I gave small regard'.

The King dithered over bringing the swashbuckling Border lord to trial and eventually decided that he was merely to be outlawed. In June 1591, it was proclaimed that Bothwell

> for the bettir executioun of his wickit intentioun and tressonabill conspiracie aganis his Majesteis awin persoun, had consultatioun with nygromancris, witcheis, and utheris wickit and ungodlie pirsonis, bayth without and within this cuntre, for bereving of his Hienes lyff, confessit be sum of the same kynd alreddy exceute to the deid and sum utheris yit on lyve reddy to be execute for the same cryme.

The earl was to be banished from the realm, never to return unless by permission of the King. The reasoning behind this was that nowhere was secure enough to hold him – and he had too many powerful friends ready to come to his aid. In February 1592, Richard Graham, described as an 'arch-sorcerer of the day', was executed. Right up until he was throttled to death on the stake at the Cross, he continued his assertions that Bothwell had attempted to use magic to bring about the King's death.

Bothwell returned to Scotland without permission and in 1592 raided Falkland Palace in a bid to kidnap the King. In August 1593, he was finally brought to trial on the witchcraft charges and cleared. He proved to the lords judging him that Graham's evidence was false, pointing out that by executing the man, they showed they did not believe him. He called many 'diverse honest men of Edinboroughe' to testify that Graham had told them that 'he must eyther accuse the Erlse Bothwell falselye, or else endure such tormentes as no man was able to abyde'. Graham's brother said that Richard was forced to make the allegations out of 'feare of maymynge with the bootes and other tortures'.

Bothwell ended his days in Italy, penniless and reduced to performing conjuring tricks. The King could not further punish the earl but revenge could be wreaked on his brother, Hercules Stewart. Much to the chagrin of the mob, who believed Stewart was 'ane simple gentleman, and not ane enterpriser', he was arrested, tried and convicted for being concerned in the treasonous crimes of the exiled earl and on 18 February 1595 was hanged at the Cross. As his struggles ceased, he was cut down and carried to the Tolbooth to be dressed for his funeral, but after a short while he began to move. Word was sent to the King to request a reprieve but orders had already been given that the man was not to survive. In the Tolbooth, just as he had a second chance at life, Hercules Stewart was throttled to death by royal command.

The uproar died and the ashes of the dead cooled, yet the fear of witches continued. James unified his Scottish crown with that of England in 1603 when Elizabeth I died and he took his paranoia with him to London. In Scotland, other women were declared witches, tortured and executed until the Witchcraft Act was repealed in 1735. Until then, witch-hunters ran rampant, unscrupulous men who often used the superstition and religious frenzy of others to line their own pockets. The most notorious in England was the so-called Witchfinder General Matthew Hopkins. In Scotland, the most infamous was John Kincaid from Tranent. He was a 'pricker', a seeker of the Devil's mark. Prickers were paid according to the number of witches they exposed and some used a trick needle that retracted into itself when placed against the skin in order to create the appearance of an invulnerable spot. Others used sleight of hand to make it look as if the pin was being pushed in. A few, like Kincaid, had such knowledge of the human anatomy that they knew how and where to insert the needle without causing pain.

He and others of his ilk were much in demand but their activities brought disquiet to the more level-headed men in power. In 1662, Kincaid was imprisoned in the Tolbooth for 'unwarrantable pricking of persones suspect of witchcraft'. However, he was released by order of the Privy Council because he had become 'so infirme and diseased of bodie, being ane old man, that if he be not speedilie put to libertie it will be to the great hazard of his life'. Kincaid was duly ordered not to 'prick or torture ony persone suspect of witchcraft in tyme comeing without a warrant from the Lords of Counsell or his majesties Justice Deputtis, as he will be answerable to his utmost peril'. Other notorious prickers in Scotland were John Dick, John Balfour and, according to Dennis Wheatley, a person named Paterson from Inverness who was later revealed to be a woman in disguise.

Edinburgh, though, had not heard the last of demons and devils. Less than 100 years after the flames reduced the last of the North Berwick witches to ashes, the fire of the righteous was lit again. This time, though, the identity of the old devil was to shock the pious brethren to the very core – for he was one of their own.

Weir Tales

They were known as the Bowhead Saints, a group of tinsmiths who congregated in the old West Bow, an ancient thoroughfare that wound down from the Lawnmarket to the Grassmarket. It was along this route that sovereigns and state visitors would enter the city and receive the loyalty of their subjects as they ascended to the High Street and on to Castle or Palace. The name remains still but the West Bow that was does not, having long since been bulldozed in the name of civic improvements. The artisans who lived there in the sixteenth and seventeenth centuries were seen to be some of the godliest in the city, hence their nickname. Not all who took up lodgings among them worked the tin. One was Major Thomas Weir, a ferocious Presbyterian who had lately been captain of the Town Guard.

Born near Carluke in Lanarkshire, Weir had fought for the Puritans in Ireland in 1641, one of 10,000 Scottish troops sent to assist Oliver's army in the suppression of Roman Catholics. Weir then pledged his sword to the Scottish Covenanter forces when Montrose's conscience forced him to turn against them. In 1649, he came to Edinburgh with his sister Jean (in some accounts named as Grissel) and lodged in the house of a Cowgate widow woman. It was here that he met James Mitchell, a Covenanter preacher who would later achieve some renown for the attempted assassination of the hated Archbishop James Sharp. Later, Weir moved into one of the tall lands on the West Bow.

In 1650, when Weir was in command of the Town Guard, it fell to him to watch over the Marquis of Montrose during his sojourn in the Tolbooth. Ordered by his Presbyterian superiors to make the prisoner's life as uncomfortable as possible, the staunch soldier saw to it that the Marquis was tormented and verbally abused, personally calling him a 'dog, atheist, traitor, apostate, excommunicate wretch' as he was being led to the gallows. It was Weir who puffed vehemently on his pipe near to his charge, knowing well that the smell of tobacco turned his lordship's stomach.

Tall in stature and dark in aspect, Weir possessed, it was noted at the time (in an account quoted in Chambers' *Traditions of Edinburgh*), 'a grim countenance and a big nose'. It was also remarked upon that he was never seen without his staff – a habit that would prove damning in later years. It was a hefty instrument with 'a crooked head of thorn-wood' and carved with the faces of centaurs, an unusual adornment for such a sacred and sanctimonious man. He was a common sight on the streets, this towering, stern-faced soldier in a high black hat and flowing black cloak, the tap of his trusty rod echoing down the caverns of stone and wood that formed the Edinburgh streets. Weir was recognised as being a particularly devout man, even in those days when piety was commonplace. They said that he was so pious, that if four Presbyterians met together, it was certain he would be one. He had a prodigious memory for Scripture and could quote passages at will. He was no preacher but he could pray with such passion that people travelled 40 or 50 miles just to join in. 'Those who heard him pray,' the contemporary account went on, '[admired] his flood in prayer, his ready extemporary expression, his heavenly gesture; so that he was thought more angel than man, and was termed by some of the holy sisters ordinarily Angelical Thomas.' As he prayed, he always had his heavy, dark staff in his hands and as he listened to others sermonise, he rested his gaunt face on it. As is so often the case, that angelic exterior hid a black heart.

In 1670, during a prayer meeting, the sainted major stunned his 'congregation' with a confession of sins of which the Marquis de Sade would have been proud. What prompted this sudden outpouring of sexual adventures is not known – senility cannot be ruled out, for he was over 70 by this time – but the litany of lust was impressive. He had conducted an incestuous relationship with his sister for nigh on

40 years, he told them. He had been fornicating with his servant for more than 20 years. He had once been married and had abused his stepdaughter. There were other women with whom he had enjoyed sex, not to mention animals. There was more, he said, a lot more. 'Before God, I have not told you the hundred part of what I can say more, and am guilty of.'

The Saints were appalled by the nature and extent of their most revered member's crimes but conspired to cover the whole affair up. No doubt a few of them had some sins of their own, and undermining their piety by making public these crimes would do no one any good. They managed to keep a lid on the matter for some months, before one of them could not contain himself any longer and felt the need to unburden his soul. He took the information to Sir Andrew Ramsay, the Lord Provost of Edinburgh, who was equally amazed by the revelations but was compelled to take some sort of action. At first, and no doubt accurately, he felt the cause of the good major's spiritual stripping down was some medical complaint. A variety of doctors were sent to study Weir, for the provost believed that 'humane nature was uncapable of such horrid crimes' and so charged them to 'Physick him for his distempered brain'. The physicians, though, declared the patient to be 'free from Hyppocondriak Distempers' and that his 'intellectuals' were sound. So, with no diseases of mind or body being divined, it was decided that the major was suffering from an 'exulcerated conscience' that could be salved only by facing the wrath of Scottish justice, something the man himself desired with 'cryings and roarings'.

Charles II was at that time trying to bring the Presbyterians to heel – and revelations of the baser nature of one of their number would do nothing to hinder the King's cause. A desire to curry favour may well have played a part in the zeal with which the authorities moved against the clearly unhinged major and his sister. However, they could not have predicted the dark turn events would take.

The scandal was now the talk of the town and – with no exculpatory medical evidence to fall back on – they came under the cloak of night to arrest him. When they arrived, his sister counselled them to take possession of his black rod, for it had been given to him by the Devil – and if her brother got a hand to it, they would regret it. The good major was not only a fornicating sinner, he was also in league with Satan.

Major Weir found himself back in the Old Tolbooth, only this time on the other side of the cell door. His sister was also arrested and imprisoned. The major's staff was locked away but word spread through the streets that an arch-wizard was residing in the town jail. Ministers visited him to divine the nature of his crimes and his contact with the Dark One. Weir did not claim to have seen the griffin-clawed Devil of North Berwick but he did admit to having felt his presence in the night and that once he had appeared in the shape of a beautiful woman. In addition, he no longer recognised the difference between Presbyterianism and episcopalianism. 'Sir, you are now all alike to me,' he told the no doubt appalled clergymen.

Details of his past sins began to emerge. Years before, in Lanarkshire, a young woman had claimed to have witnessed him having sex with an animal in a field. At the time, she was not believed and was even whipped by the hangman for slandering 'such an eminent Holy Man'. A report of the major forcing his way into the bedchamber of another woman came to light, although nothing sexual had taken place. His sister revealed that the first time he had sexual knowledge of her was in Fife, between Kirkcaldy and Kinghorn, when she was 16. A visitor to the spot said that no grass had grown there since. The abuse continued until she was 50 years of age, when he lost interest in her ageing flesh. Thankfully, despite the 34 years of incestuous coupling, she had never become pregnant. According to the sister, this was achieved by 'means abominate'. Her interrogators wanted to know details but the ministers among them refused to allow any further questioning on that subject.

The clergy seemed more interested in the devilish side to the case. During his time in command of the Town Guard, it was recalled, the major had hesitated to cross running water (something that held great terror for those in league with Satan) and taken fright at the mention of the name 'Burns'. Whether Weir's fear was because 'burn' is the Scottish name for a stream or because he had a presentiment of his ultimate fate is unclear. In jail, he turned from the ministers sent to help him reject the Devil and all his works. 'Trouble me no more with your beseeching me to repent,' he reportedly told them, 'for I know my sentence of damnation is already sealed in heaven.' When they persisted, he cried out, 'I find nothing within me but blackness and darkness, brimstone and burning to the bottom of hell.' Still he refused to repent, saying that since he was to go to the Devil, he would not anger him. One minister refused to give up, saying, 'Sir, I will pray for you in spite of your teeth and the Devil your master, too.'

Jean Weir told them that her mother was a witch and bore the Devil's mark on her forehead – a little horseshoe that appeared when she frowned. She too carried the mark and was eventually allowed to show it. She said she had found a similar mark on her brother's back a few years before. She told her interrogators how they visited Dalkeith in a chariot of fire invisible to others and how a stranger gave her a root that enabled her to spin huge amounts of yarn in a very short space of time. Even when she was not in the house, the yarn would be spun, although no weaver could make anything of it.

The case against the Weirs was an easy one to make, for both admitted their crimes, although they were found guilty of the more physical transgressions rather than the metaphysical ones. The major was to be burned at the stake. The spot chosen for his death was on the Gallowlee, just off Leith Walk. Two days after his trial, on 11 April 1670, he was taken from the Tolbooth and placed on a sled to be transported to the execution site, being deemed too old and infirm to walk the distance. The hangman led the horse and the people lined the streets to watch the old devil pass by. At the Gallowlee, he was tied to the stake, a rope around his neck with which he would be wirreit. Even then, the ministers were concerned for his soul, for they pleaded with him to say 'Lord, be merciful to me'. But still Weir refused. 'Let me alone, I will not,' he snapped. 'I have lived as a beast and I must die as a beast.' The executioner either botched the strangulation or took Major Weir at his word, for the old man was burned alive. His staff, carried carefully from the Tolbooth, was thrown into the fire with him and it was said that it twisted and writhed in the flames with its owner.

Jean was told of her brother's death in her Tolbooth cell while she waited for her own date with the Devil. She asked of the fate of the staff and when told it had burned she 'in a furious rage fell on her knees, uttering words horrible to be remembered'. She was due to die the following day in the Grassmarket, a simple hanging for her, but she vowed that she would do so 'with all the shame that she could'. She was as good as her word, for on the gallows she tried to strip. A witness reported: 'On the scaffold she cast away hir mantell, hir gown tayle, and she was purposed to cast off all her cloaths before the multitude.' Naturally, the authorities could not countenance such an unseemly display of immodesty and Baillie Oliphant stepped forward to prevent her from removing anything further, telling the hangman to 'doe his office'. As the executioner tried to

> throw her ovir the leather [ladder], she smote [him] on the cheike; and her hands not being tyed when she was throwen ovir, she labored to recover herself, and put her head betwixt two of the steps of the leather, and keiped that powster for atyme, till she was put from itt.

And so died the diabolical Weirs of the West Bow. However, Edinburgh had not heard the last of them. For generations after their deaths, tales were told of the sound of Jean's satanic wheel spinning through the midnight hour and of the major himself galloping from his old home on a headless horse in a 'whirlwind of flame'. Brother and sister were also said to be seen on dark nights in a fiery coach pulled by six black horses and at the reins was the 'muckle Deil himsel'. They were borne off in this chariot of the damned amid the clatter of hooves and the snap of Satan's whip. And then there was the major's black rod, still heard tapping in the streets and taking on a life of its own in the popular imagination. There were other tales told and these stories were taken so seriously that the house on the West Bow was not occupied until long after the major and his sister were gone. However, the new tenants did not bide for any length of time, being forced out by bumps in the night and occult manifestations. It was used as a brazier's shop and a storehouse until, in 1878, it was demolished.

The tales of Major Weir were told to Sir Walter Scott, who said in 1798, 'If I were ever to become a writer of romances, I think I would choose Major Weir, if not for my hero, at least for an agent, and a leading one, in my production.' Scott, of course, did become a writer of romances but he never wrote about Weir. Robert Louis Stevenson's abiding obsession with the darker recesses of man's soul has been well documented and he was also fascinated by the tale. He learned the legends of Major Weir from his father, who had himself heard them as ghost stories in the nursery. Stevenson described Weir as 'the outcome and fine flower of dark and vehement religion' and went on to say that 'Old Edinburgh cannot clear itself of his unholy memory'. Eventually, the man who was Scotland's finest writer used the story as part of the inspiration for the double life of Dr Jekyll and Mr Hyde. There was another Edinburgh worthy who can also claim the credit for inspiring that famed tale and he too spent his final days in the Tolbooth.

But of Deacon William Brodie we shall hear later.

CHAPTER SIX

TWENTY-FOUR HOURS FROM TULZIE

Street Fighting

In 1640, a Major Somerville was hastening from the Castle, having had a meeting with his Covenanter superiors, when a grim-faced and cloaked man stepped before him with a determined look in his eye. The man was Captain Crawfurd and there was bitter animosity between the two soldiers. According to the *Memorie of the Somervilles*, a family history, the captain was determined that 'noe satisfaction acted in a private way could save his honour'. He resolved, therefore, to challenge the major in the High Street, and there they would settle the matter like men.

Near the Tolbooth, on the south side of the Lawnmarket, Crawfurd stepped into the major's path and shrugged off his cloak to reveal a long broadsword and a Highland dirk. He then pointed to Somerville and said, 'If you be a pretty man, draw your sword.' This seventeenth-century version of 'Come ahead if you think you're hard enough' was emphasised with the drawing of blade from scabbard and dagger from waist. Somerville, according to the family account, was 'at first somewhat startled at the impudence and boldnesse of the man that durst soe openly and avowedly assault him, being in publict charge, and even then on his duty'. However, Crawfurd was clearly bent on having some satisfaction and the major was not the man to disappoint him, even though all he had in his hand at the time was a 'great kaine staff'. He did have a 'half-rapper' sword on his person – a gift from a grateful general for a past service – but that was sheathed in a shoulder-belt far back from his hand 'as the fashion was then'. Crawfurd hacked two or three strokes and Somerville used his thick walking stick to parry the blows in order to gain sufficient time to draw his own weapon. He then stepped in close to his adversary, letting fly with thrusts of his own and forcing Crawfurd to back away a few steps. And so they continued, swords clanging in the morning sun, breathing becoming more laboured, as the people and tradesmen watched. At that time, there was a series of goldsmith shops in the luckenbooths, and it was here that Crawfurd realised that, with the stores being made of timber and he being in retreat, he was in danger of being 'nailled to the boords'. He feinted to Somerville's right, parrying an answering thrust with his dirk, then suddenly turned his hand 'and by a back-blow with his broadsword, he thought to have hamshekelled [hamstrung] him in one, if not both, of his legges'.

Somerville spotted the potentially debilitating stroke in time to leap back and used his cane, now in his left hand, to block the blade. Crawfurd put such force into the blow that his weapon sliced through the wood, the momentum swinging the captain round and temporarily leaving him open to attack. Now it was Somerville's turn to launch an offensive. He knocked Crawfurd's dagger out of his hand with what was left of his stick and battered the captain down with the handle of his sword. The major was at first 'mynded to have nailed his adversary to the ground' but thought better of it and offered the man mercy. His own soldiers, who had hurried from the Castle on hearing of the Lawnmarket duel, were 'soe incensed, that they wer ready to have cut the poor captaine all in pieces'. Somerville, though, held them back and saw to it that Crawfurd was safely ensconced in the town jail, 'where he was layd in irones, and continued in prisone in a most miserable and wretched condition somewhat more than a year'.

This morning duel was what was known as a 'tulzie' and the area around the Tolbooth was frequently the battleground for opposing factions to settle their differences with hackbutt and sword. Scottish politics is often seen as a centuries-long brawl between various noble families. The septs, or clans, forever bickered amongst themselves about which one should have power over the others. That bickering extended to full-scale feuds that made widows of women and orphans of children – who then continued the cycle of violence. The nobles argued in the council and parliament chambers of Edinburgh and when words did not make their point, then the point of a sword backed up their words. Such was the knife-edge state of Scottish power politics, not to mention the volatility of the city's various mobs, that it seems that at any given moment those streets were never much more than 24 hours from a tulzie. The mob often targeted the Tolbooth itself, storming its pitiful defences and freeing – or capturing – the object of their fury. For this reason, lawyer and criminologist William Roughead compared the building to the notorious Parisian jail famously breached by the revolutionary mob and dubbed it 'the Bastille of Auld Reekie'.

During the minority of James V, while the regent Albany was being held in France at the behest of Henry VIII, rivalry between Archibald Douglas, Earl of Angus, and James Hamilton, Earl of Arran, spilled into the streets. Angus had married the widow of James IV and so believed he should be regent. Arran could trace his bloodline back to the throne. Also, the former queen had tired of her new husband's womanising and was looking with favour on Arran. The feud erupted in a bloody skirmish that was later named 'Cleanse the Causeway'. Arran had been barred from Edinburgh by the citizens, who had taken exception to his attempts to force them into appointing a magistrate of his choice. The city fathers threw their collective hat in with Angus. In April 1520, Arran rode into Edinburgh at the head of a small army. Angus and 400 veteran soldiers were waiting for them in the High Street but they were outnumbered by Arran's force. Gavin Douglas, Bishop of Dunkeld and Angus's uncle, tried to prevent a slaughter by appealing to the Archbishop of Glasgow, James Beaton or Bethune, who had succeeded the executed Border noble Lord Home as Lord Chancellor. On the one hand, he had the power to order the two forces to stand down; on the other, he was related to Arran and therefore unlikely to go against him. As is so common in Scottish politics, the two hands might have come together in prayer but otherwise they were rarely on speaking terms. Beaton told Douglas, a poet of some renown, that 'on his conscience' there was nothing he could do, but when he hit his chest to emphasise a point, Douglas heard the unmistakable ring of armour beneath the archbishop's robes. 'How now, my lord,' he observed wryly, 'your conscience clatters.' Before taking to his own rooms to keep out of harm's way – for he was a writer, not a fighter – he told his nephew Angus to prepare for the worst.

The Douglas faction lined up in the streets, many of their long spears and other weapons passed to them by the citizenry through their windows. Barricades were quickly set up in the wynds and the men waited for the Arran army to surge up the Cowgate. The first casualty was Sir Patrick Hamilton, who was accused of cowardice. Incensed, he charged and was swiftly cut down. The fighting then raged up and down the High Street and around the Tolbooth, from where helpless city officials watched and hoped the warring factions would not break in. Finally, reinforcements for Douglas's outnumbered troops arrived in the shape of the Home family rough riders, who hounded the fleeing Arran army out of the city. Douglas's faction, as historian Pitscottie recorded, 'keiped both the gaitt [the street] and their honouris'. Arran and his son fled across the marshy Nor' Loch, ignominiously mounted upon a coal horse. Their kinsman Archbishop Beaton was found praying in Blackfriars Church and was saved from death by the pleas of Gavin Douglas. The victorious Home family took the opportunity to retrieve the heads of their executed lord and his brother from the Tolbooth spikes.

In November 1567, following a similarly bloody encounter between the followers of the lairds of Airth and Wemyss during which many were 'hurte on both sides by shote of pistoll', the council proclaimed 'the wearing of guns or pistolls, any sick-like fyerwork ingyne' forbidden 'under ye pain of death'. Only the King's guards and soldiers were excepted from the prohibition.

There is an impression now that the King's word was law and all his nobles followed it slavishly. This was not in fact the case, although the royal will was indeed a force to be reckoned with. Scots nobles were a proud, aggressive and arrogant body of men and they were not above taking their animosities onto the streets even when the King was present. On 7 January 1591, James VI was leaving the Tolbooth after overseeing the courts of justice when his companions the Duke of Lennox and Lord Home pursued a personal dispute with the Laird of Logie in the High Street. Blades were bared and while the two men attacked the laird, James, never the bravest of monarchs, fled into a close and took refuge in a skinner's booth.

Six days later, James's problems with Francis Stewart, Earl of Bothwell, flared up when the troublesome Border noble stormed into the Tolbooth while the King was sitting in judgment on a divorce case. Bothwell forcibly carried off an important witness and imprisoned him in Crichton Castle, where the man was threatened with the gallows if he spoke in evidence.

In July 1593, the legislation against the carrying of weapons was further strengthened when the Privy Council noted that 'vile murders have not only been committed within kirks and other places, but even within the burgh of Edinburgh and suburbs thereof [near] to his hieness' palace, to the great hazard of his awn person'. Accordingly, the Town Guard and members of the King's guard were ordered to search any person in the city or near Holyrood for 'all hagbuts and pistolets'. Anyone found carrying such a weapon was to be marched instantly to the jail. As an added incentive, the guards were allowed to keep any weapon they found. The moves were directly aimed at preventing anyone shedding blood in the presence of James VI. A new Act was written that made it treasonable to

> strike, hurt, or slay ony person within his hieness' parliament-house during the time of the halding of parliament; within the king's inner-chalmer [chamber], cabinet or chalmer of presence, the king's majesty for the time being within his palace; or within the Inner Tolbooth the time that the Lords of Session sit for administration of justice; or within the king's privy council-house the time of the council sitting there; or whaever sall happen to strike, hurt or slay ony person in the presence of his majesty, wherever his hieness sall happen to be for the time.

That same year, Sir James Sandilands was involved in a fight with John Graham, a Lord of the Session, at the foot of Leith Wynd. The two had been involved in a bitter court dispute over land rights and James VI had ordered Graham to leave the city for his safety. It was while he was doing so that he met up with Sir James and his supporters. Graham thought they had come to kill him, and his own party grew jittery. A shot was let loose by a nervous finger and this set the two sides to battle. Graham was wounded and carried into a nearby house but the servant of one of Sir James's friends followed him in and 'douped a whinger into him', thus killing him.

Sir James was a favourite of King James and so no action was taken at that time. However, in January the following year John Graham's kinsman, the powerful Earl of Montrose, decided that blood must be satisfied. Sir James Sandilands was warned of the impending attack and decided on the best form of defence. He and his party launched an offensive on the Montrose forces in the High Street. This time, matters did not go in Sir James's favour. He was 'dung down on his back, shot and hurt in divers parts of his body and head'. He would have been slain there on the street if a Captain Lockhart had not intervened to save him. The fighting grew so vicious that the Lord Chancellor, then with Montrose, 'retiret himself with glaydness to the College of Justice' in the Tolbooth. Eventually, the magistrates came seething out of the Tolbooth as an armed force and restored order. Sir James was seriously wounded 'bot convalescit agayne' and lived, no doubt to tulzie another day.

Despite being unreservedly Protestant, James VI seemed forever at odds with the leaders of the Kirk. He found that many of the strong-willed ministers continued to rail against him from their pulpits and in December 1596 he saw to it that one, David Black, was prosecuted for slandering him and his wife. Meanwhile, the King had further incurred the wrath of the Presbyterians by sanctioning the return of certain Catholic nobles from foreign exile.

On 17 December, while he was in session within the New Tolbooth, James was told, perhaps mischievously, that some of his ministers had convened in St Giles' Church and were planning an attack on his person. James ordered that the building's doors be locked against them. Word reached the ears of the common folk, and the mob split between those for Kirk and those for King. A blacksmith named John Watt, who was chief among the deacons, knew where his loyalties lay; he called the craftsmen to arms and positioned them around the Tolbooth. He demanded sight of the King or he and his men would 'ding up the yett [gate] with forehammers, sae that never ane within the Tolbooth sould come out with their life'. The King appeared and the army of tradesmen vowed to 'die and live with him'. James, emboldened by the martial authority of the guildsmen, left his sanctuary and was escorted to Holyrood.

Later, from the safety of Linlithgow Palace, James ordered that the courts be disbanded and wreaked revenge on the magistrates and baillies who had failed to protect him. A minister was imprisoned, others outlawed and one Sabbath day passed without any clergy available to lead services. James was furious that Edinburgh – the tradesmen apart – had failed to come to his aid. He filled the town with rambunctious Border forces of proven loyalty, thus prompting a worrying rumour that notorious freebooter Will Kinmont was coming under royal orders to plunder and despoil. The terrified merchants removed all their goods from the shops and booths to store them in the strongest house they could find. They armed themselves 'with hagbut, pistolet and other sic armour' and stood guard around their makeshift warehouse. Finally, after three months of haggling, James relaxed his position and the threat of attack eased on payment of 30,000 marks. The courts were allowed to sit in the Tolbooth again and the King shared a drink with the baillies and magistrates in the council house while bells were rung, drums beaten and trumpets blared to mark the occasion of Edinburgh returning to his favour.

John Watt, the Deacon of Deacons, had incurred the wrath of the clergy; he had during the high passions of the tumult actually offered to 'invade the person' of one notable minister and royal critic, Robert Bruce. In retaliation, the preacher had predicted that Watt would meet a violent end. In 1601, that prophecy was fulfilled when Watt was shot dead on the Burgh Muir. A man named Alexander Slummon was arrested and tried for the crime but cleared by the courts.

While lords settled private and public matters with blood-letting on the streets despite dire warnings from the Crown, the ordinary folk of the town often took to those same causeways to display their displeasure at events or to right what they saw as a wrong. These large-scale tulzies were known as 'tumults' and regularly centred on the Tolbooth. Afterwards, the ringleaders could be lodged in its cells, and often the target of the mob's displeasure cowered in the prison's dank rooms.

In 1565, the restless religious tapestry of the town was disturbed again when the Roman Catholic Easter Masses were set to take place at the same time as the more reserved Communion sacrament. The Catholic ceremonies were not just frowned upon but were actually illegal and priest Sir James Carvet was arrested by ministers of the reformed religion after he had conducted services. He was imprisoned in the Tolbooth along with other Roman Catholics. Later, he was dragged to the Mercat Cross where he was placed in the pillory, still clothed in his priestly garments and holding the chalice in his hand. They kept him there for around an hour, pelting him with stones and filth. John Knox gleefully stated that 'the boys served him with his Easter eggs'. The following day, Carvet was tried for celebrating Mass contrary to the law. Back he was taken to the pillory, where for three or four hours with 'the hangman standing by and keeping him . . . the boys and others were busy with eggs-casting'. Although the law of the day could have seen Sir James executed, the Catholic Queen Mary lodged a formal complaint and tried in vain to energise her supporters to take more direct action against the town and teach it some manners. The baillies and magistrates humbly apologised for the treatment meted out to the priest and promised to take stern measures to prevent such outrages happening again. They pledged to release the other prisoners still in the Tolbooth and Mary later demanded that the provost stand down.

In December 1561, Leith man William Balfour had led a tulzie in protest over the reformed religion. He and his gang arrived at St Giles', where minister John Cairns was taking Communion. It was the custom for the preacher to ask questions of the communicants and he inquired of one woman if she had 'ony hope of salvation by her awn good works?' Balfour, 'with thrawn countenance', responded for her: 'Thou demands of that woman the thing whilk thou nor nane of thy opinion allows or keeps.' The minister responded with a 'gentle admonition' and Balfour hit back: 'Thou are ane very knave, and thy doctrine is very false, as all your doctrine and teaching is.' At that point, weapons were drawn, blood was spilled and Balfour was eventually convicted of breaking the Queen's proclamation for the protection of the reformed religion.

The ugly face of religious intolerance reared its head again in 1680, when a group of English youths attending the College of Edinburgh were imprisoned in the Tolbooth. News had reached the council that Christmas Day was to be marked with an effigy of the Pope being marched through the town and burned. Any such display of force was viewed with alarm by the authorities and, in an unsuccessful attempt to prevent the procession, the boys were arrested as ringleaders. While soldiers concentrated on a band of marchers heading for the Castle, blocking the West Bow and the Grassmarket, the real procession was heading to the High Street via Blackfriars Wynd. There the effigy was pelted with debris and set aflame.

It was not just papist ways that beetled the brows of Kirk leaders. As we have seen, the older traditions were also something to be stamped out, and to that end the Scottish Parliament, under pressure from both the Catholic and the Calvinist sides, banned the ancient custom of springtime Robin Hood plays and festivals. It was the habit for the populace to nominate respected tradespeople to play the principal parts. If they felt capering and dancing in brightly coloured costumes was beneath their dignity, they were fined. The festivities took the form of a glittering armed procession and a fair at which the men playing the legendary outlaw and his companions robbed and fought and enjoyed archery contests.

However, the tale of Robin Hood we know today was originally much darker and also had strong connections with paganism. The name Robin was often given by witches as the name of the Devil, while Satan was known to appear hooded. According to some versions of the tale, the bandit had 12 men, his group therefore numbering 13, the same as a coven, and he was an enemy of the Church. The Catholics did not like the idea that the legends glorified the robbing of rich clergy, even if the spoils were being redistributed to the poor. The Calvinists mistrusted pagan ideas and besides didn't like the idea of anyone having any fun. So, in 1555 an Act was passed that made it unlawful to mark the coming of summer or to choose people to play 'Robin Hude, Litle John, Lord of Inobedience or Abbot of Unreason, or Queen of May'. Further, it was forbidden for 'onie weomen or others [to go] about summer trees singing, making perturbations to the Queen's lieges, the weomen perturbatoures sall be taken, handled, and put upon the cuck-stules of every burgh or toune'. Whether or not the women burst into song around the summer trees, the old festivals continued to hold a place in the hearts and minds of the people, despite the dire ramifications promised by those in power.

In 1561, while Edinburgh was getting over a riot during which the town's butchers had broken into the Tolbooth to free one of their number imprisoned for adultery, other tradesmen prepared to celebrate the coming of summer. A worthy named George Dune was named as Robin Hood and they massed on Castle Hill to begin the fun. The town's magistrates naturally heard of this and took a dim view. They relieved the people of weapons and a flag but the mob, never slow to make its voice heard, took over the city gates and forced the authorities to return the flag. The magistrates, piqued that their supremacy had been flouted, seized shoemaker's apprentice James Gillon, who was reputed to be one of the ringleaders. They trumped up charges regarding the theft of ten crowns and sentenced him to be hanged. A petition lodged by his brethren in the shoemakers' guild was refused. They even consulted that old bigot John Knox but he refused to be 'a patron of their impiety'.

The mob took matters into their own hands and tore down the gallows that had been erected to hang the unfortunate cobbler. They then chased the magistrates into a stall at the luckenbooths, where they could do nothing but watch as the rioters launched an offensive on the Tolbooth, which, the *Diurnal of Occurents* says, 'was then steekit [shut]'. When they could not obtain the keys, they took sledgehammers and proceeded to 'dang up' the doors. Gillon and other prisoners were freed and when the mob moved off to the Netherbow, which was also 'steekit', the magistrates left their hiding place and occupied the Tolbooth once again. The crowd surged back up the High Street and the furious magistrates took the opportunity to shoot at them from the windows of their jail fortress. After that, the *Diurnal* tells us, 'there was naething but tak and slay; that is, the ane part shooting forth and casting stanes, the other part shooting hagbuts in again'. The rioters laid siege to the city officials from three in the afternoon to eight that evening 'and never ane man of the town steirit [stirred] to defend their provost and baillies'. When asked for aid, the citizenry replied, 'They will be magistrates alone; let them rule the multitude alone.' Things might have turned even worse if reinforcements from the Castle had not arrived to bring order. Even so, the crowd did not disperse until about nine that night, when the Provost proclaimed publicly that no further action would be taken. Later, 13 men were fined for refusing to come to the aid of the besieged baillies.

More than 30 years later, another demonstration led to the murder of a leading citizen. In the courtyard of Riddell's Close, off the Lawnmarket, there was a square that held the house of Baillie John McMorran, or McMorrin. He was not a popular man with the common people but he was a very rich merchant, a magistrate and, despite having been a close ally of the executed regent the Earl of Morton, a favourite of James VI. In September 1595, he was called from his home to attend the High School of Edinburgh, situated at that time in the grounds of Blackfriars Monastery. The young students had staged a mutiny over extra holidays (they were only allowed five days a year) and had locked themselves into the school with provisions enough to weather any siege. This was a common enough occurrence; other similar protests ended with an attack by the authorities or the protesters giving up when their supplies gave out. This one would be different, for it would end with violent death. Baillie McMorran was unfortunate to lead the deputation formed to end the stand-off. The boys refused to budge and he ordered that the door be forced. The leader of the 'gentleman bairns' within was not willing to be defeated so easily and a warning rang down that anyone who tried to force their way in would be shot. The baillie ignored the caution and ordered his men to take a battering ram to the door. True to his word, the young student blasted away with a pistol and

McMorran fell, a ball in his brain. This galvanised the town forces and the school was stormed, the young mutineers being dragged to the Tolbooth. There were those who would have exacted summary justice but, for once, the excitable mob was controlled.

The youthful pistoleer was William Sinclair, son of the Chancellor of Caithness, and others of his rebellious friends were also sons of riches. King James, then at Falkland Palace, was informed of the death of his friend, and the boys lay in the foul arms of the Tolbooth for around a month. They subsequently petitioned to be brought to trial and the first day of December was set for the hearing. However, the powerful families of the young men brought pressure to bear and the King was persuaded to intercede on their behalf. He ruled that the boys were to be tried by a jury of gentlemen and not ordinary citizens of the town. Naturally, the boys were cleared, although the school's headmaster was sacked and his staff suffered a loss of salary. Someone, after all, had to pay. It would be a couple of generations before impartial justice would come to Scotland with Cromwell. The old High School was demolished in 1777 and until that time proud young scholars pointed out the window from which the fatal shot was fired as 'the Baillie's Window'.

More than 100 years after McMorran's death, baillies and privy counsellors found themselves besieged when the mob took to the streets over the disastrous Darien Scheme. In the latter part of the seventeenth century, trade legislation favoured England and prevented Scottish shipowners from foreign trade, giving their southern counterparts huge monopolies. In 1695, Scottish businessmen vowed to fight back by establishing a Company of Scotland and setting up trading routes to the Indies. The man behind the scheme was William Paterson, a London-based Scot who founded the Bank of England, and in 1698 he set sail from Leith with five ships loaded with trade goods destined to be parlayed into the riches of the Orient – spices, silk and precious metals. They also carried the hopes, dreams and financial security of their homeland. Their destination was Darien, a hellish spit of land on the isthmus of Panama in South America. Here a colony was to be established that would act as the doorway to the promised riches of the East, thus cutting out the long route round Africa.

At first, news was encouraging. The small fleet had landed, the colony of Caledonia was founded and an initial attack by the Spanish, jealously guarding their own trade interests, repulsed. In Edinburgh, the bells were rung in celebration and thanks were given in the churches. The ecstatic mob displayed their joy by setting fire to the Tolbooth door and setting free surgeon-apothecary Hugh Paterson and printer James Watson, who had produced a seditious pamphlet. Members of the Town Guard tried to stop them from their mission but were beaten back. During the scuffle, one turnkey was wounded and gudeman George Drummond, who would later be shamed following the escape of the aristocratic murderer Robert Balfour, was relieved of his hat, wig, cloak and ring and of the liquor and foods in the sutlery.

Some of the rioters were duly arrested and sentenced to be whipped, pilloried and banished, including one Charles Weir, found guilty of 'unlawful convocation and breaking open the prison of Edinburgh'. The mob reconvened and threw rose petals in the path of the convicted men as they made their way to the place of punishment. Feeling against the sentences was so high that the hangman was loath to fulfil his duty. The men were lined up on the platform for the public flogging and furious magistrates watched as the crowd brought them flowers and wine. To make matters worse, the hangman merely made a show of carrying out the sentence, wielding the whip but making sure that the lash never licked the men's backs. Arrested and tossed into a cell, he claimed that he had been threatened with death 'if he laid on but one sure stroke'.

The magistrates were determined that someone would pay with blood for the recent unrest and ordered that a second executioner be brought into the city to punish the first. The official from nearby

Haddington was given the duty but when it came to laying the lash against his Edinburgh colleague, he proved somewhat reluctant. Whether this was due to a sense of brotherhood or whether he was intimidated by the growls of the mob, it cannot be said. Whatever the case, he ran from the platform down one of the many wynds without laying on a single stroke. The magistrates, faced with finding a third hangman who would be willing to open the back of the first, decided to drop the whole matter. The mob's joy was short-lived, for news was yet to reach them that the Darien expedition had been abandoned.

Warnings over the unsuitability of the site chosen for the Caledonia colony had been ignored; the leaders – being Scots – quarrelled amongst themselves; disease struck with lethal intensity. When a small fleet arrived to bring aid, they found a graveyard of 400 people, among them Paterson's wife, who had succumbed within days of her arrival. A second expedition followed the first, news of the settlement's failure not yet having reached home, and it too fell prey to the elements, fever and Spanish forces. By April 1700, the disastrous venture was deserted. The empty huts eventually became part of the jungle again, while the dreams of the nation died in the damp vegetation and plague-infested waters. The trade routes were once again the sole province of the Spanish and English colonists, who had refused to give aid.

The scheme had all but bankrupted the tiny nation. Someone had to be blamed – and the English were a handy scapegoat. There had already been moves towards the establishment of a union of the two countries. However, although bound by one royal crown, Scotland and England were still separate nations and the peoples on either side of the border viewed those on the other with mistrust, if not loathing. The failure of the Darien venture was seen to be the result of yet another example of English treachery.

The ripples of the Central American disaster continued to wash over from far-off Panama. In 1704, the powerful East India Company seized a Company of Scotland ship, the *Annandale*, then being outfitted in the Thames for trade in India. Later that year, the exigencies of the North Sea weather forced the *Worcester*, a vessel belonging to the Two Million Company, to take shelter in the Firth of Forth. The Two Million Company was a rival to the East India but that did not matter – the ship was English and, by order of the Scottish Parliament, it was duly seized and the captain and crew taken into custody. The man behind the arrests was Roderick Mackenzie, the zealous Company of Scotland secretary whose hatred of the English and mistrust of moves towards union had already seen him spend time in the Tolbooth. In 1701, he had published a cartoon deemed libellous and was locked up. His release was bought by the directors of the company but he studied on revenge against the English. The *Worcester* scandal was to provide him with that. It is, though, one of the most iniquitous episodes in Scottish law. Although the accused were detained in the Castle dungeons, events subsequently raged around the Tolbooth and are worth repeating.

Apparently, it was the rum-soaked boasts of some of the crew that sparked things off. It was claimed that the men had talked of dark deeds off the Malabar Coast: an act of piracy during which the *Worcester* had attacked and sunk a Scottish ship, the *Speedy Return*, which had been dispatched to trade along the African coast in 1701 but had failed to live up to its name. In church pulpits, ministers thundered that God had sent the villains to Scotland for justice. The thirst for revenge over Darien and the *Annandale* seizure was still raw in the throats of many Scots. At Roderick Mackenzie's instigation, Captain Thomas Green, his first mate, John Madder, gunner James Simpson and 15 crew members were brought before the Court of Admiralty in Edinburgh and charged with piracy. There was no evidence that the *Speedy Return* had actually been attacked and no firm date given for such an act of piracy. In fact, it had been seized by buccaneer John Bowen to harry East-Indiamen and scuttled when he took a better prize. That mattered little, for the general feeling was one of vengeance, so the kangaroo court found the men guilty and they were condemned to be hanged 'twixt the high and low watermarks' on the sands of Leith. The sentence was further justified by confessions from crew members that apparently confirmed the attack on the Scottish ship and the subsequent murders of the captain and his men. Confessions, like eyewitness testimony, can make tricky evidence. In this case, there is every reason to suppose that the sailors told the authorities what they wanted to hear in a bid to save their own necks from being stretched.

In London, news of the impending executions was met with disbelief. Queen Anne became involved and in a bid to prevent the death of her subjects, expressed a desire that they be reprieved. The Privy Council took the plea seriously and postponed the execution for a week; they would have cancelled it altogether if the mob had not made its views known. Their lordships knew that if they submitted to the royal will and reprieved the men, trouble would follow. It has been said that if they had weakened, it would have been their necks on the line, while the condemned men would have been dragged from their cells and strung up on the streets of the town.

Execution day dawned and the city was already seething. Three men were to die that day: Captain Green, Madder and Simpson. Eyes watched the men of authority carefully for any sign of amnesty towards the condemned. One eyewitness to the event that day, Alexander Wodrow, wrote to his father that the privy counsellors

> came up to the Council-house about nine, against which time there was a strange gathering in the streets. The town continued in great confusion for two hours, while the Council was sitting, and a great rabble at the Netherbow port. All the guards in the Canongate were in readiness if any mob had arisen. About eleven, word came out of the Council that three were to be hanged ... This appeased the mob, and made many post away to Leith.

Thousands had gathered on the shore to witness the executions and a rumour began to surge through them that the whole scene was nothing but a sham, that the announcement had been a ruse in order to give the authorities time to spirit the three English sailors away. Word filtered back to the mob still waiting on the High Street and spleens were vented on the door of the Privy Council chamber. When the Lord Chancellor appeared in public to confirm the hangings were to proceed, he was at first cheered but then, as doubts began to fester, he was attacked. As a later government 'Account of the Mobbs of Edinburgh' related, his coach was 'broke to pieces, and my Lord run up the stairs of a house'.

Finally, the three men were led out of the Castle by the Town Guard and marched through the jeering mob past the Tolbooth, down the Canongate and through the Water Port to Leith, where a company of soldiers and cavalry was waiting to keep order. 'There was the greatest confluence of people there that I ever saw in my life,' Wodrow wrote, 'for they cared not how far they were oft; so be it they saw.' An estimate of the time said that around 80,000 people gathered in the streets of the town and on the waterside.

Captain Green died first, denying his guilt even as the rope was wrapped around his throat. His two crew members also protested their innocence. Their deaths brought the crowd to a sombre silence.

Within days, a pamphlet was on sale in the streets of Edinburgh carrying a ballad that purported to be the captain's 'Last farewell to the Ocean and all the World'. It is a surprisingly even-handed piece of work, given the prevalent feeling of the time, and suggests that perhaps there was more disquiet in Scotland over the incident than has been believed. It began:

> Adieu fair Ocean, on thee I long liv'd
> Plentifully, but now am sore griev'd,
> Thus shamefully to dye in thy bounds,
> Without a Drop of thee to wash my Wounds,

The ballad went on to repeat that the captain had nothing to do with the murder of the Scottish captain and his crew in far-off Malabar and fired a verbal broadside at the men who had betrayed him:

> . . . before God and the World I can,
> Truly protest I never knew the Man,
> Whose Murderer I was said to be,
> Nor ever saw him by Land or Sea:

As writer John Prebble observed, 'What was left of the company's honour and nobility died with those men on Leith sands.'

On 16 January 1707, the Act of Union was formally ratified in the Scottish Parliament by a majority of 43 votes. The bill passed unopposed through the English Parliament and finally the two nations were one. A total of £398,085 was to be paid to Scotland by England and the money – a mixture of cash and much-derided Exchequer bills – arrived in Edinburgh in 12 wagons, guarded by Scots Dragoons. The mob jeered the wagon train as it made its way to the Castle, pelting the horses and men with stones and filth.

A parcel of rogues may well have sold the Scots nation for English gold but the truth was that Scotland could not stand on its own. Political and financial manoeuvring by the South had set up the fall; the Darien debacle had helped topple the country over. Money changed hands, to be sure, but the Union was the only way for Scotland to prosper. And prosper it eventually did, as the old prohibitions regarding trade were swept aside, against the wishes of the English business classes. The investors in the Darien scheme recouped their losses, while the hated East India Company helped other Scots make their fortunes. But still, there was the final and absolute loss of independence and the tendency of the parliament in England to impose heavy tax burdens that were seen as favouring the southern shires.

Lynch Law

The Treaty of Union may have changed many things but it did not appease the hot blood of the Edinburgh mob, of which Daniel Defoe (in the city as an English spy and propagandist during the negotiations for union) commented, 'A Scots rabble is the worst of its kind.' The benefits of the union did not emerge for many a year and the citizenry was still prone to demonstrate its opposition. Stiff – and unfair – taxes imposed on the nation, including an export duty on linen, another on salt and a malt tax, proved crippling and hugely unpopular. When protest was made to the English Lord Treasurer, he observed, 'Have we not bought the Scots, and a right to tax them?' However, taxation was the indirect cause of a riot and subsequent slaughter that were seen as being tantamount to rebellion. The unrest left men and women dead and wounded in the streets and led to the Bastille of Auld Reekie being stormed once again, not to free prisoners but to bring to justice a man the people believed was guilty of murder.

One source of revenue to the Crown was the duty placed on imported goods. Brandy, rum, lace and other goods from the Continent were all subject to stiff taxation but were always in demand, so bands of smugglers sprang up who were willing to supply them. Revenue officers were charged with bringing these romantic desperadoes to justice and halt the flood of cash away from the official coffers. But the clerk would have his baccy and the parson his brandy, so the smugglers carried on their moonlight trade with the sanction and often assistance of all walks of life. Scotland's east coast was, naturally, a focal point for the traders in contraband. Andrew Wilson was an Edinburgh baker who supplemented his income by smuggling. By 1736, the swashbuckling Wilson had grown tired of the inroads excisemen had made into his illicit business and resolved to raid the Pittenweem customs house to recover goods seized by them. Among his band were George Robertson, William Hall and John Galloway. They managed to pull off the heist but were subsequently caught and sent to Edinburgh to face trial.

In the warding book of the Tolbooth for 12 January 1736, there is an entry recording that two of the band were subsequently liberated, while John Galloway was 'baled out of prison and examined as witness in the criminall tryall against Andrew Wilson . . . and did not return to prison'. With the evidence of their former co-accused against them, Wilson, Robertson and Hall were found guilty. Hall was to be transported to the penal colonies for his part in the robbery but Wilson and Robertson were due to hang. Wilson, though, was determined not to dance the hangman's jig and, according to legend, he and his accomplice, with the assistance of two horse thieves, cut through the iron bars of their window, singing psalms to cover the noise. According to the tale, one of the horse thieves squeezed through and slipped off into the night. Wilson was next but they had not made a hole wide enough for his bulky frame and he ended up trapped between the bars. The gudeman of the Tolbooth was alerted to the escape bid and Wilson and Robertson were placed in more secure lodgings within the prison.

What is certain is that on Sunday, 11 April, Wilson and Robertson attended services in the Tolbooth kirk, which was part of St Giles'. They were guarded by four of the Town Guard and just before the sermon began Wilson, according to a contemporary report, grabbed the younger Robertson 'by the head band of his breeks and threw him out of the seat'. With a cry of 'Run, Geordie, run!' Wilson intercepted three of the guards, reportedly seizing one in each hand and, incredibly, a third in his teeth. Robertson saw his chance and punched the fourth guard to the ground before sprinting for the door of the church. No one got in his way and he disappeared into Parliament Close. He managed to escape through the city gates before they were sealed. Friends were waiting with tools with which to strike off his chains and a swift horse to take him to Dunbar, from where, it was said, he took a fast boat to Holland. For many years, it was rumoured, he kept a bar in a village near Rotterdam. The entry in the Tolbooth records states in its customary spare style that 'the aforementioned George Robertson made his escape out of the tolbooth kirk a little before sermon and was not apprehended again'.

Wilson may have made up for ruining the earlier bid for freedom but he had sealed his own fate. Security around him was strengthened while he lay in the Tolbooth awaiting his execution. Sympathy for him among the mob grew. As a smuggler and known as such for thumbing his nose at the hated authorities, he was already well liked but his selfless act in holding down the guards while his young friend got free made him into a hero. He was due to hang on 14 April but word reached the magistrates that the mob might be tempted to help him break free. A detachment of Royal Welch Fusiliers was drafted in to beef up the Guard on the appointed day.

The captain of the Town Guard at that time was John Porteous. According to the *Newgate Calendar*, a true-crime compendium from the latter part of the eighteenth century, he was a former tailor who caught the eye of a high-ranking official, said to be the Lord Provost of the time. This gentleman had a wish to offload his mistress and he suggested that Porteous, well regarded by Edinburgh society but as poor as a church mouse, take her off his hands. To make the match more attractive to the lady in question, who wrinkled her nose at the thought of marrying a tradesman and a penniless one at that, a one-off payment of £500 was offered and accepted. Porteous duly married the woman and set out to rise in his profession. However, the young man was 'much addicted to company' and neglected his business, losing many customers in the process. His wife, fearful of being left destitute, used her influence with the provost, who offered Porteous the captaincy of the Town Guard, with a salary of £80 a year.

The truth is that Porteous was more likely to have come to the Town Guard through military service, first as drill-master following the 1715 Jacobite uprising. Within ten years, he had been promoted to captain. A keen golfer, he famously lost to Alexander Elphinstone in

1724 before a large crowd in a match that was the very first reported by a newspaper. Where the accounts agree is that his personality tended towards the arrogant and the truculent. He was officious, self-important and often brutal. He soon developed a reputation for overly enthusiastic use of violence in quelling disturbances. The *Newgate Calendar* states that 'he would exceed the bounds of his commission and treat the delinquents with the utmost cruelty by knocking them down with his musket and frequently breaking arms and legs'. He was no less brutal when dispatched to investigate reports of tumults in 'a house of ill fame':

> Notwithstanding he was a most abandoned debauchee himself, he would take pleasure in exposing the characters of all he found there, thus destroying the peace of many families. He would treat the unhappy prostitutes with the greatest inhumanity and even drag them to a prison, though many of them had been seduced by himself.

This was the man who was in charge of the Town Guard when Andrew Wilson was sentenced to hang. His mood was already foul over Robertson's escape and he may also have resented the fact that the magistrates felt it necessary to bring in the Fusiliers to strengthen the execution detail. (The *Calendar*, incidentally, says that it was Porteous himself who requested that the soldiers be present.) On 14 April, Porteous led the Guard as Wilson was taken from the Tolbooth to the Grassmarket, where the 'hanging tree' awaited. The soldiers lined the route and the crowd watched the procession go by, but there was no suggestion of trouble, even when Porteous forced the manacles on Wilson's wrist so tightly that he was in obvious agony. The condemned man was led to the gibbet, where the customary psalms were sung, prayers were said and still there was no sign of unrest. Wilson was turned off the ladder 'with all decency and quietnes', as one spectator wrote, and still there was no disruption. It was as the body was being cut down that it began.

It started with some boys throwing stones at hangman Jock Dalgliesh, a common enough occurrence, for the post of 'hangie' was fraught with danger, but it was enough for Porteous to wade into the crowd himself, followed by his men. The mob first pulled back then surged forward. One man leaped to the gibbet and cut the body of the dead smuggler down, while Porteous and his Guard were assailed from all sides by missiles. Either the magistrates, fearful for their own safety, gave Porteous an order or he made the decision himself, but whatever the case it was the biggest mistake of his life – he told his men to fire. The first volley was aimed over the heads of the rioters but the Guard hit spectators who were leaning from the tenement windows. Far from cowing the mob, the gunfire merely served to push it further into a frenzy and the captain ordered the Town Guard to shoot directly into the throng, before beating a retreat up the West Bow, the men forming a thin line of red snaking through the press of bodies. Striking out at all sides and being hit by stones and filth from around and above, Porteous once again told his men to fire, ordering them to 'level their pieces and be damned'. He snatched a musket from the nearest man and fired himself, killing one man. Another volley rattled out and more people slumped to the ground, blood seeping from wounds, before the Guard were able to reach the comparative safety of their headquarters and the Fusiliers helped bring some semblance of order to the streets.

The number of dead varies from six to nine people depending on what version you read. Porteous was called to account before the town council, 'where there was an abundance of witnesses to fix the guilt upon him', as a witness wrote. He continued:

> The uproar of the mob encreased with the loudest din that ever was heard and would have torn him, the Council and Guard all in pices, if the Magistrates had not sent him to the Tolbooth by a strong party and told them he should be tried for his life.

On 5 July, Captain John Porteous faced the High Court of Justiciary. Against him was the evidence of those in the crowd who claimed that he had personally fired into the mob and had ordered his men to do the same. His position was that his men had fired of their own volition and that he had not pulled a trigger. He also argued that the magistrates issuing him and his Guard with ball ammunition amounted to an order to fire if it became necessary. Sixteen witnesses testified that they had not seen the captain fire on the people. However, the strength of public opinion was formidable and Porteous's own reputation and the number of dead and wounded counted against him. He was found guilty and sentenced to die in the Grassmarket, where it all began, on 8 September.

News of the case reached Queen Caroline in London, then acting as regent while her husband, George II, was on the Continent. She was disposed to pardon the captain and issued orders that a six-week reprieve be granted. Naturally, her compassion did not sit well with the Edinburgh mob, who saw it as yet another example of an English government supporting the slaughter of innocent Scots. Captain Porteous was not to be allowed to avoid paying the ultimate penalty for his actions.

They came for him on the night of 7 September. At first there were but few of them, men and women, but as they walked from the suburb of Portsburgh towards the West Port, the grave beat of a drum in the dark alerting like-minded folk, their numbers swelled. They took control of the West Port gate, nailing it shut and barricading it. Into the Cowgate then, bodies joining them from every side, and finally onto the High Street. A band of strongly armed and determined men seized the Netherbow Port in order to cut off any possibility of aid from the Welch Fusiliers then stationed in the Canongate. The headquarters of the Town Guard was stormed and taken, the officers and men disarmed and isolated. The Guard's muskets, cutlasses and Lochaber axes were plundered and distributed among the multitude.

And now they turned their attention to the Tolbooth. They surged around the ancient building, flaming torches sending tall shadows dancing against its walls, the sound of their voices reaching the soldiers in the Castle, where the commander of the troops stationed there refused to mobilise his forces. Whatever his reasons for not interfering – procedural or personal – he took the wisest course. The mob was not to be diverted from its course that night and military interference would only have led to further bloodshed.

The door to the Tolbooth had been barred against them but that would not stop them. Sledgehammers were wielded against the wood and, when they made little more than a dent, axes were swung to hack a way through. Finally, tar and brushwood were brought and the door set alight. When the flames weakened the thick wood, the crowd pushed it open and blazed through the portal, snatching the keys from the terrified turnkey. Into the stairway and up the stairs then, doors being thrown open and rooms searched, but their quarry was nowhere to be seen. The hapless gudeman was forced to divulge in which room Porteous was being held but it was, it seemed, empty. It appeared the mob's efforts had been in vain until someone thought to peer up the chimney. The terrified captain had crawled into the space as soon as he heard the din outside but an iron grate placed there to prevent prisoners from escaping had halted his upward progress. The desperate man screamed for mercy as he clung to the ironwork while the resolute band below hauled at his legs. But there was no mercy in that room that night. Some could recall the groans of the dead and wounded that day in April, some had perhaps suffered at Porteous's hands on other occasions. There was no mercy, only a grim determination that their dark work would be carried through to its inescapable conclusion.

Finally, Porteous was dragged from the chimney. He would have known what fate was in store but did not know exactly where he was to meet it. There were men there, he knew, who would have done for him on the spot but their leaders had other notions. Perhaps hope rose in the breast then. Perhaps he thought the longer they kept from fulfilling their dread purpose, the better were his chances of rescue by the authorities. Perhaps that slim hope sustained him through his final minutes.

The captain was manhandled out of the Tolbooth and the procession turned towards the West Bow and the Grassmarket. The streets were clogged with people and many more watched from the tenement windows above, the whole scene lit by the fierce glow of countless torches. The flambeaux illuminated grim faces and the guttering flames glinted from the metal of blade and axe. Porteous could be heard praying as he descended the winding street. When he stumbled, he was caught and propelled onwards. At one point, a shoe came off a foot and he was halted in order for it to be retrieved and replaced. A shop in the West Bow was forced open and its owner, a Mrs Jeffrey, was asked for a rope. When told it was to be used to hang Porteous, she said they were welcome to all she had. The people took what length they needed and left a guinea as payment.

They reached the Grassmarket but the gibbet had been taken away. The mob were not to be discouraged from their intent, however, and one end of the rope was thrown over a dyer's pole on the south-east corner of the square and the other wrapped around the neck of their proposed victim. They allowed him to pray. They permitted him to hand over what money he had on his person to a wealthy man nearby on the promise it would be delivered to his brother. (Some accounts say he gave his money to a debtor in the Tolbooth.) Then he was hauled up by the neck. As he struggled on the rope, the executioners realised that they had not covered his face, so he was lowered again to the ground and his shirt pulled over his head to conceal the hideous grimace of death from the crowd. Then the men strained at the hemp and dragged him upwards once more. Again he was let down as his freed hands feverishly fluttered at the rope biting into his neck. Some men came forward at this, tiring of the time the killing was taking, and struck at him, some trying to saw off his ears with the long Lochaber axes taken from the guardhouse. But they were pushed back and Porteous was a third time hoisted aloft, his body jerking as the life was throttled from his body. His legs flailed wildly, spasmodically, then slowed and finally stilled. His body swung from the pole, the breath finally drained from it.

The cheer that greeted the expunging of life from the hated captain reverberated round the Grassmarket, carried up the West Bow and reached the Castle. And then, with surprising swiftness, the borrowed weapons were thrown to the ground and the mob dispersed, melting into the night like wraiths. Only the discarded axes and muskets and above all the body still gently swaying from the makeshift dule tree, the rope creaking softly in the now silent night, showed that they had ever been there.

The city's populace had not only killed Porteous, they had also shown a violent disregard for the royal prerogative. It was known that Queen Caroline had had a mind to pardon the captain and the events of 7 September 1736 proved that the mob had scant respect for her wishes. Sir Robert Walpole's government took steps to punish someone – anyone – for the flagrant scorn the people had shown for their authority. The question was, who could they bring to justice? It was felt that this mob had a quality that others lacked and so it was believed that many men in high office had taken part in the events, some even dressed in women's clothes. The guinea left for payment in the corder's store was cited as proof that men of wealth were present, for the ordinary Edinburgh mob would not have had that kind of cash to leave. One nobleman rumoured to have taken part was the Earl of Haddington, dressed like a cook-maid. Rewards were offered in a bid to track down the ringleaders and it was ordered that a proclamation be read from every pulpit, although many ministers refused to do so. Arrests were made but the leaders were never found, reinforcing the claims that the conspiracy reached high into the upper echelons of society. Other theories laid the blame at the feet of Covenanters, criminal friends of Andrew Wilson and even Jacobite sympathisers who wished to overthrow the Government.

One man arrested was William Maclauchlane, a footman to the Countess of Wemyss. He had been sent earlier that day on an errand for his mistress. Having delivered his message, Maclauchlane retired to John Lamb's alehouse in Parliament Close, where he enjoyed a few drinks. Then, so much the worse for drink that he did not know where he was or what he was doing, he joined the throng in the Grassmarket. He was implicated when witnesses identified his 'showy livery'. His liking for drink saw him very narrowly miss being made a scapegoat for the shocking events that night.

However, according to Sir Daniel Wilson in his *Memorials of Edinburgh in the Olden Time*, the real mastermind behind the lynching was a baker's apprentice named Alexander Richmond. He describes him as 'a wild and daring lad, who took a prominent share in all the riotings of the period'. His father was said to have deprived him of his clothes and locked him in his room on the night of the riot but the young man managed to escape, dressed in his sister's clothes. He was in the vanguard of the attack on the Tolbooth and among the leaders as Porteous dangled on the dyer's pole in the Grassmarket. When his name was mentioned in connection with the hellish events, he ran off to sea and did not return for many years. When he was a successful merchant captain, he told a few of his closest friends his secret, one of whom passed it on to Sir Daniel many years later. Another mooted as being one of the leaders was journeyman carpenter James Maxwell.

Although no one was directly punished for being part of the mob, the government's ire did descend on the Lord Provost, Andrew Wilson. He was arrested and jailed for three weeks before being freed on bail. Further moves against him – including preventing him from holding office anywhere in the country and imprisoning him for a year – were blocked by Scottish MPs in the House of Commons. They also managed to prevent the Government from demolishing the Netherbow Port and disbanding the Town Guard. Someone had to be punished, of course, and the city was ordered to pay £2,000 to Mrs Porteous. In the end, the widow accepted £1,500.

Two days after his death, Captain John Porteous was laid to rest in Greyfriars kirkyard, for over two centuries marked by a small stone with the letter 'P' and the year 1736. In 1973, a headstone was placed there stating: 'John Porteous, a captain of the Edinburgh City Guard, murdered 7 September 1736. All Passion Spent.'

CHAPTER SEVEN

THE GREAT ESCAPES

Taking Liberty

It is often said that the Tolbooth was notoriously insecure, especially when it came to holding prisoners of high rank. Although this is a generalisation, the walls were, like those of many other prisons, breached from the inside on a number of occasions. The keeper was liable for stiff penalties if anyone fled while under his care. As the jailer, he was, of course, responsible for the security of the prisoners. While it would have been easy for some of them to hatch escape plots with outsiders – the jail was open every day from 9 a.m. until 3 p.m. and then again from 4.30 p.m. to 9 p.m. – he was expected to check each and every apartment during lockdown periods. If bars had been weakened or walls damaged, it was his duty to find out. If someone did escape while in his charge, he had to bring them in again or he might suffer the financial consequences. Of course, the men he hired to act as wardens or turnkeys were perhaps not so fearful of repercussions and would gladly turn a blind eye or even actively assist in escapes in return for coin of the realm.

How often punishments were actually levied on the gudeman after an escape is open to question. However, the threat of reprisals was certainly there, as is exemplified by the case of the Master of Burleigh. An account of the crime for which he was sent to the

Tolbooth – one of jealousy and murder – is contained in the *Newgate Calendar*, compiled by London lawyers Andrew Knapp and William Baldwin in 1824. Some of their 'facts' are suspect, so I have drawn also on another version, told in Robert Chambers' *Domestic Annals of Scotland*.

Robert Balfour, the eldest son of Lord Burleigh, was born in 1687 at the family seat in Kinross. It was his lordship's intention that the young man should pursue a career in the military and distinguish himself on the field of battle in Flanders under the Duke of Marlborough. The family was related to the Duke of Argyll as well as the Earl of Stair, both generals in Marlborough's force, and so it would have been no great chore to have the young man granted a commission and perhaps even a plum posting. Matters of the heart, though, were to prevent this plan from being fulfilled.

Before military glory could be won, young Burleigh had first to receive an education, so he was sent off to university at St Andrews. It was on a visit home during vacation that Robert Balfour met Miss Anne Robertson, tutor to his sisters. The *Calendar* tells us that 'this young lady was possessed of considerable talents, improved by a superior education' and the young man promptly fell under her spell. Talented she may have been, educated she most certainly was, but Lord Burleigh took a dim view of the liaison and had her fired from her position. Accounts say that the young master made improper advances, which might mean that sexual overtures were made that may not have stopped short of rape, and the girl was sent away to avoid a scandal. The lovesick swain was then packed off for the rest of the vacation on a tour of France and Italy. He was still obsessed with the girl, though, and before he left he wrote a letter warning that if she married before his next trip home, he would kill her husband.

Time passed and, of course, Miss Robertson clearly did not take the threat seriously, for she met and married a Mr Henry Stenhouse, a schoolteacher in Inverkeithing. Balfour, however, had been in deadly earnest, for when he next returned home one of his first tasks was to track down his former love. On being told she was married, he went to Inverkeithing to carry out his threat. The *Calendar* claims that, his passions already high, he was pushed over the brink of madness by the sight of the woman he loved sitting in the window of her new home, nursing a newborn child. She saw the young man watching her from the street and knew instantly by the look in his eye that his earlier threat of murder was no idle fancy. She cried out to her husband in the schoolroom 'to consult his safety'. The schoolteacher, not knowing what the fuss was about, remained where he was and looked up as the rival in love he did not even know existed walked in, a pistol in his hand. The *Domestic Annals* records that while Stenhouse's pupils watched, the following conversation took place. 'I am the Master of Burleigh,' said the young man. 'You have spoken to my disadvantage, and I am come to fight you.'

'I never saw you before and I am sure I never said anything against you.'

Balfour was spoiling for a fight, however: 'I must nevertheless fight with you, and if you won't, I will at once shoot you.'

'It would be hard to force a man who never injured you into a fight. I have neither horse nor arms, and it is against my principles to fight duels.'

But the young, no doubt insane, peer was insistent. 'You must nevertheless fight or be shot instantly.'

Stenhouse continued to try reason but the time for talking had passed. With the words 'take that to be doing with', Balfour put a ball into the schoolteacher's shoulder. Stenhouse died of his wound within days. In the confusion, Balfour escaped but he was spotted a few days later at an inn four miles from Edinburgh and arrested. Brought to trial for murder, he was duly convicted and sentenced to die on the Maiden, it being thought more fitting to his station in life to be decapitated than to dangle on the rope.

Although some sources – notably James Grant in *Old and New Edinburgh* – report the following part of the tale as being true, Robert Chambers admits it was told to him by Sir Walter Scott but does not insist it was young Balfour who took the central part. Eager to avoid death, the prisoner, or members of his influential family, bribed jailors to turn a blind eye as he was smuggled out of the Tolbooth in a trunk. An unwitting porter was tasked to carry the trunk to Leith, where it was to be loaded onto a boat destined for the Continent. The porter, not knowing what was inside, lifted the trunk the wrong way round, so that the young nobleman was hanging upside down. He was bumped and battered as the porter swung his burden from side to side while manhandling it towards the docks. The young man, however, knew that he could not cry out, for if he did so, he would be returned to the Tolbooth and ultimately delivered up to the kiss of the Maiden. So he kept silent, even though his cramped and inverted position in the trunk must have been agonising.

At the Netherbow Port, the porter met a friend, who asked him where he was going. When he heard he had been paid to carry the trunk to Leith, the man's friend asked him if he had been well enough rewarded to afford a glass or two. The porter, having decided that he had both time and money enough to wet his throat, dropped the heavy load. The thud with which it landed brought forth a scream of pain from inside and, once they got over their shock, the porter and his friend opened the lid. They found the young Master of Burleigh inside, doubled over and unconscious. The Town Guard was summoned and the prisoner was returned to his apartment in the Tolbooth. He did not remain there for long.

The Maiden had been erected in preparation for his execution but Robert Balfour would never grace its platform. The day before his due date, he was visited in the Tolbooth by one of his sisters, who was by all accounts 'very much like him in face and stature'. The two changed clothes and he walked out of the prison without challenge and made his way to one of the city gates, where friends had a change of clothes and a horse waiting for him.

Balfour's escape brought the keeper of the Tolbooth problems. A letter dated 3 January 1710 from Mungo Graham of Gorthie requested his kinsman, James, first Duke of Montrose, to bring his influence to bear in order to help the beleaguered gudeman. Mungo Graham had been asked to elicit the duke's aid by David Drummond, treasurer of the Bank of Scotland, on behalf of the keeper, George Drummond (who may well have been a relative), 'so that he might not suffer' over Burleigh's escape. Montrose was asked to 'do Mr Drummond all the favours you can', especially as there appeared to be some conspiracy over the break-out. The letter implies that the escape was 'winked at', the inference being that people in high places had been aware of the plot, an idea that Graham thought was 'not altogether groundless'. In the keeper's defence over the escape itself, the master and his sister were so alike that 'it was impossible almost to distinguish' between them. A pardon was requested for Mr Drummond, although what action was subsequently taken is not recorded. The keeper, however, remained in office for some years afterwards: his name crops up again in a note in the warding books when, on 25 September 1714, he recorded that 'Euphan Deans made her escape furth of the prison and retired to the abbey cliffs'.

David Dalrymple, the Lord Advocate, took the escape of Robert Balfour seriously. He issued letters to sheriffs, judges and magistrates of neighbouring shires urging them to employ the 'utmost diligence for searching for and apprehending the person of the said Robert, Master of Burley'. The sheriff of Berwick received such a communiqué, dated 2 January 1710 and marked 'Haste haste post haste'. It stated that 'Robert Balfour, eldest son of the Lord Burley, under sentence of death for a barbarous murder . . . made his escape this night out of the tolbooth of Edinburgh.' The letter ordered that if the sheriff or his deputies managed to capture the fugitive, they were to hold him 'until a sufficient guard may be had to transport him . . . to the prison of Edinburgh'. They were authorised to make 'strict' inquiries and to undertake what searches and examinations of witnesses they thought fit in order to capture the escaped prisoner and any accomplices he might have had. The Government pledged to cover 'whatsoever charges is laid out'.

A description of the wanted man was appended, although not of his clothes, he 'having made his escape in women's apparel'. The Lord Advocate provided this pen portrait:

> He is a young man of about one or two and twenty, of a fine complexion, sharp nose and a countenance rather long than round, speaks thick and after the dialect of Fyfe, strong, well made and of a middle stature, he wears a fair piriwig but at his tryall appeared twice in a black piriwig, his eyebrows are fair. I believe the colour of his hair will [not] attend a mean of discovery because he prefers to shave his head but his hair is yellowish inclining to red.

However, according to the *Newgate Calendar*, the shaven-headed killer had fled the country. He waited abroad until Lord Burleigh had engineered a pardon from Queen Anne. He inherited the title and estates on the death of his father and died himself in 1752 'a sincere penitent for the murder he had committed'. The far more reliable *Domestic Annals* paints a different end to his life.

> He was not again heard of till May 1714, when he appeared amongst a number of Jacobite gentlemen at the Cross of Lochmaben, to drink the health of James VIII. The family title had by this time devolved on him by the death of his father; but his property had all been escheat by sentence of the Court of Justiciary. His appearance in the rebellion of 1715 completed by attainder the ruin of his family, and he died unmarried and in obscurity in 1757.

Cross-dressing seems to have been a common means of gaining unlawful liberty from the Tolbooth. On 24 February 1610, Margaret Maxwell, Lady Amisfield, was interviewed by the Privy Council over the 'forme and manner of the eschaiping of Thomas Kirkpatrick . . . hir son-in-law, furthe of his warde within the Tolbuith of Edinburgh'. It seems the prisoner and his mother-in-law had been given permission for a private interview and took the opportunity to swap clothes. He escaped and she was jailed in the Tolbooth but later transferred to more suitable lodgings in the Castle. Andrew Whyte, an assistant keeper, was implicated in the escape and was ordered to be 'layed in irnes'. The sentence did not appear to affect his upward mobility, for he was later recorded as keeper of the jail.

In 1681, Covenanter Alexander Smith was arrested for his part in the Battle of Bothwell Bridge and sent to the Tolbooth to await what was certain execution. He escaped dressed as a woman. He was subsequently caught near Glasgow and lodged in the Tolbooth there. The authorities planned to have him returned to Edinburgh but fellow Covenanters had other ideas. In a bid to avoid any attack, Smith was to be taken to the capital by a slightly circuitous route but his friends had been tipped off and at Inchbelly Bridge near Kirkintilloch they struck. A soldier died in the gunfire and Smith was set free. Two men unconnected with the attack, who were in the wrong place at the wrong time, were arrested and cruelly executed as a reprisal for the death of the soldier.

Charles Capells, or Caples, staged a different type of escape. This Causewayside grocer was jailed on 8 July 1792 accused of 'stabbing and wounding in the belly with a large knife or other such weapon Robert Weir, silk weaver'. One week later, Capells was found hanged in his cell. An inquiry was launched but the result is not recorded. Naturally, Capells was not the only prisoner to see suicide as a way out of the hell in which he had found himself; other men tried to cheat the hangman by taking their own lives. In 1754, Hugh Lundie was due to be executed for stealing the grand total of one pound, fifteen shillings and ten pence in five highway robberies. On the night before he was due to die, he tried to hang himself in his cell with his own coat and shirt. A surgeon was called and the unconscious man was bled to bring him round. The following day he died in the Grassmarket.

The story of Ayrshire man Mungo Campbell is well known, for even after his suicide he still suffered the wrath of the mob, although by that time he was, of course, beyond feeling or caring. Campbell was part of a family of 24 from Saltcoats in Ayrshire. He was ostensibly a God-fearing and law-abiding individual, for as an exciseman he was one of the scourges of smugglers bringing in contraband to the beaches and coves between Troon and Ardrossan. Although he pursued his duties diligently, he was seen as a fair man and was well respected. He had one vice, however, and that was poaching. Whether it was through a desire to take what was not his or a need to put food on the table, he was known to tread softly through the woods and heather of lands belonging to great men and take their game. His habits were well known but accepted, for poaching was a common practice.

One of the estates on which he plied his soft-footed trade belonged to Alexander Montgomerie, the 10th Earl of Eglinton, a landlord not terribly popular with some of his tenants thanks to his mania for improving the land. Farmers were forced to cultivate ryegrass against their wishes and even compelled to swap lands with one another. He meant well but his tenants did not take kindly to his interference. However liberal-minded and forward-thinking he might have been, he guarded his own property jealously. He liked to do a spot of shooting and parts of his estate were reserved for him and his guests to blast away at anything that moved. The earl took a dim view of Mungo Campbell's poaching but stopped short of taking recourse to the law. The wayward exciseman had already been caught red-handed on the earl's preferred shooting lands and had, according to legend at least, sworn an oath never to return.

Naturally, return he did and in October 1770 he was again found trespassing by his lordship. The earl demanded that Campbell hand over his gun but the poacher refused. The gun was his property and he was not going to give it up. The earl insisted and stepped closer. Campbell again refused and stepped back, with a warning that the earl might get more of the gun than he bargained for if he came any closer. The earl paused and brandished his own weapon. Campbell stepped away again – and tripped backwards over a stone, much to the merriment of the nobleman. Some accounts say the gun went off accidentally, others that Campbell, embarrassed by his clumsiness and outraged at the earl's laughter, sat up and purposely fired. Whatever the case, the outcome was the same: the Earl of Eglinton took the blast in the chest. He stumbled away, blood bursting through his clothes, and staggered towards his servants before slumping to the ground. He died in Eglinton Castle, insisting that he had meant only to frighten the man with his gun, which was unloaded.

Whether it was accident or murder, Mungo Campbell was arrested and taken to Edinburgh for trial. Sympathy was with him in his homeland but justice in the east was sure to be more unforgiving. Death awaited him but he cheated the hangman of the pleasure by hanging himself in his cell in the Tolbooth. Word got out that the murderer of the Earl of Eglinton had avoided justice and the mob, never a group to miss the opportunity for a tumult, discovered that the body was to be given over to the anatomists, as was the custom for condemned men and suicides. It is said that friends of the dead man managed to get the authorities to release the body to them and it was quietly buried. The mob, though, dug it up and the corpse was unceremoniously hauled down the High Street to what was then the King's Park at Holyrood and manhandled up to the top of Salisbury Crags. It was then tossed down the chasm known as the Cat's Nick. Later, his friends retrieved what was left of the body and buried it at sea.

The dead man was a Campbell, though, and soon there were rumours that the powerful Argyll family had intervened to save him. It was not his body that had been found hanging in his cell but that of a dead soldier from the Castle. Money had changed hands and Campbell had been placed in the soldier's coffin to be spirited from the city. Tradition tells of gravediggers being frightened half to death as the coffin lid was forced open from the inside and the 'dead man' leaped out to run off into the night.

A graveyard played its part in one of the most celebrated escapes from the Tolbooth, that of James Hay, son of a Grassmarket glazier. He had been imprisoned in the Tolbooth on 15 October 1783 with two others, John Paterson, stocking maker, and James Andrews, a former soldier with the Scots Fencibles. They were charged with attacking a journeyman printer, John Stirling, 'in the meadow on the south side of Edinburgh'. They beat him to the ground and relieved him of two shillings and a pair of spectacles. Another victim, brewer's servant David Dukes, was attacked on the east side of the Meadows. He too was knocked down and robbed of what money he had in his pockets, as well as his watch. This attack was so brutal that 'by the blows they gave him the said David Dukes was so wounded that his life was in danger'.

The three were found guilty and sentenced to death but Hay's family had no intention of allowing him to die on the scaffold. Notwithstanding the rule that the keeper had to check the cells and chains every day, somehow Hay and his father managed to file through the iron bonds. Then, on 24 November 1783, some time before the hour when the prison was to be cleared of visitors, Hay senior invited the turnkey into the room for a glass or two of something strong. A few such potations later, the man was drunk enough to agree to anything – especially if it involved further ingestion of alcohol. A coin was produced and a suggestion made that the turnkey go off and buy some more. He agreed and weaved away, forgetting to lock the door behind him. Young James Hay, who had not touched a drop, followed close behind him. He watched as the man was allowed out of the main door and waited until his father stuck his head out of an upper window and cried, 'Turn your hand!' The doorkeeper, used to hearing the order as visitors began to file out, automatically opened the portal and James Hay shot out of the shadows and into the street. He made off down Beth's Wynd, opposite the jail, and gave any pursuers the slip by climbing over the wall of Greyfriars kirkyard. Everything had been arranged beforehand, even down to a large stone being laid against the tall wall to help him get over.

Shortly after the escape, the *Edinburgh Advertiser* carried the following announcement:

> Escaped from the Tolbooth of Edinburgh
>
> James Hay, indicted for highway robbery, aged about 18 years, by trade a glazier, 5 feet 10 inches high, slender made, pale complexion, long visage, brown hair cut short, pitted a little in the face with the small-pox, speaks slow with a haar in his tone, and has a mole on one of his cheeks. The magistrates offer a reward of twenty guineas to any person who will apprehend and secure the said James Hay, to be paid by the City Chamberlain, on the said James Hay being re-committed to the Tolbooth of this city.

Twenty guineas was a lot of money and there must have been many in the city who would have turned in their own mother for such a sum. Hay was obviously well liked, for none of his confederates betrayed his location.

Greyfriars kirkyard is where the National Covenant of 1638 was signed and it is ironic that it is also the last resting place of one of the Covenanters' greatest enemies, the prosecutor Sir George Mackenzie. 'Bluidy' Mackenzie had been interred in a circular mausoleum that held particular terrors for the superstitious townsfolk. The Kirk had successfully demonised him and it was said that the ghost of this ferocious Lord Advocate haunted the graveyard. Young Hay, though, seemed undaunted by the terrifying prospect of meeting the spectre of the great persecutor, for it was in this mausoleum that he hid while waiting for the hue and cry to die down. He was a 'Herioter', which meant he had been educated in George Heriot's Hospital, a charitable school that adjoined the kirkyard. As children, he and his friends had often played among the tombstones and he used his boyhood bond with other former pupils to help him through the days and nights of his voluntary incarceration among the dead. They smuggled him food and water and even kept him company in dead of night when the ghosts were said to walk abroad. He hid in the graveyard for six weeks until it was felt it was safe for him to emerge. He is believed to have escaped to the Continent.

His co-accused suffered mixed fates. On 1 January 1784, John Paterson, 'being in a bad state of health, was liberated under warrant by the sheriff'. The third man, former soldier James Andrews, was not so fortunate, for on 4 February he was executed in the Grassmarket.

Another escape attempt – even more audacious, perhaps, but less successful – saw Robert Auchmutie using aquafortis (nitric acid) to burn through the bars of his window. The barber-surgeon had been arrested for killing a man, James Wauchope, in a duel on St Leonard's Hill in April 1600. While in jail, he claimed to be ill and in need of darkness, and he covered the window with a cloak. This concealed the work of the acid as it gnawed through the bars of the window. When the time came, his apprentice boy was instructed to watch in the street for the Town Guard to move away and then wave his hand, at which point Auchmutie planned to descend down a rope to freedom. However, one of the guards spotted the accomplice waving and the scheme was uncovered. Auchmutie lost his head to the Maiden at the Cross a few days later.

Ayr merchant William Harris did manage to get away from the Tolbooth, if only for a short period. He had been convicted of forging £10,129 in 20-shilling notes – a sizeable fortune in those days. Naturally, the authorities took a dim view of this kind of free enterprise. On 7 November 1769, he was transferred from the Ayr jail to the Tolbooth in Edinburgh to await trial. There, he resolved to circumvent the judicial process by sawing through the bars. A reward of 50 guineas for his recapture ensured he remained at liberty for only a short time. Even then, he thought he had a trick or two up his sleeve. At his trial in April 1770 he behaved in so outrageous a manner that insanity was suspected. However, doctors examined him and found him to be sane, so he was duly convicted and breathed his last in the Grassmarket.

Leith bucklemaker William Purcell was luckier. He had been arrested for stealing ten of the King's weights from the port of Leith. According to the note in the warding book for 23 September 1765, these weights 'had been fixed to the scales with an iron chain'. One of the stolen items was found opposite his shop and he was duly arrested and sent to the Tolbooth of Leith. However, as he was to be tried in the Edinburgh courts, he was transferred to the Heart of Midlothian so that he would be 'at hand at the examination'. It was also noted that 'there might be some hazard of the prisoner making his escape'. How right they were, for on 10 December 1765, William Purcell 'escaped from the prison the night twixed the ninth and tenth having cutt the window of the West Gallery and fastened a rope to the barrs by which he gott clear off'.

Some men tried not to get free of their cells but rather to avoid going to the gallows. On 19 December 1750, Sergeant Major John Young of the 4th Regiment of Foot barricaded himself into his cell in the Tolbooth. He was due to hang for forging bank notes and witnesses against him included the young soldiers he had used to engrave the plates. His notion was that if he could hold the besieging magistrates at bay until after 4 p.m., the hour the judge had decreed he was to die, his sentence would be nullified. The magistrates pulled up the floorboard of the room above Young's cell and six volunteers from the Town Guard dropped down. One was knocked down but the remaining five managed to subdue the former soldier. Young died in the Grassmarket at 6 p.m.

The Kate Escape

Easily the most famous of all escapes from the Tolbooth came in 1766. The escapee was a young woman, beautiful but notorious, and she gained her freedom almost certainly with the connivance of her rich and powerful family. She had been found guilty of murder but the fatal hour had been postponed because of her pregnancy. Her confinement gave her family the chance to devise a daring escape plan. Her supposed lover, who was condemned along with her, received no such favours. He died on the scaffold while his pregnant co-accused reclined in her cell.

In the Tolbooth records for 24 June 1765, there is an entry regarding the warding of Katharine Nairn and Patrick Ogilvy, who had until then been in custody 'in Forfar prison and council rooms which were not sufficient'. They were to be brought to Edinburgh under 'sure guard' and placed in the jail 'therein to remain until they are liberated in due course of law'. Appended to the order was a warning that the jailers were 'to take the utmost care that [they] be kept separate and have no communication with one another'.

The pair had been charged with murder and incest. Katharine Nairn came from a good family. Her father was Sir Thomas Nairn, Baronet of Dunsinane, and in 1765 she was married off to Thomas Ogilvy, Laird of Eastmiln in Glenisla, Fife. She was a beautiful 19-year-old girl, wilful, high-spirited and able to captivate any man she met. He was the 40-year-old third son of a family already steeped in tragedy. His Jacobite father had marched with Bonnie Prince Charlie but died during an attempt to escape from Edinburgh Castle. His depressed eldest brother had committed suicide by hanging himself in a sheepcote. (It was said that, having made the drop too short, he had dug a pit at his feet in order to finish off the job, an act that William Roughead, in his account of the tale, declared 'showed considerable force of character'.) Another brother was crushed to death while serving on a man-of-war. Yet another, although not dead, had brought disgrace to the family by marrying beneath him when he took to wife a porter's daughter.

Young Katharine's arrival at the house should have been the beginning of a brighter future for the Ogilvy family. Instead, it brought more death and scandal. Thomas was not a well man, or rather he appeared to enjoy ill health, but his young and vibrant wife managed, for a time, to bring him out of his hypochondria. He began to dress well, certainly in a manner more fitting to his station in life, and, finally, happiness came to live in Eastmiln.

Naturally, it did not last. Thomas had another brother, Patrick, a lieutenant in the 89th Regiment of Foot, who came home from the East Indies. He was younger and more dashing than his brother and, according to the case against them, it was not long before he and Katharine were sharing a more than familial affection. Eastmiln was not a large house – the family and servants lived in four rooms – and if such an intrigue was taking place it would not be long before Thomas heard about it. Anne Clark, a cousin of suspect motive and dubious virtue, had come to stay and she seems to have been the prime mover in the telling of tales. There was a falling out between the brothers after which Patrick left the family home and within weeks Thomas was dead. Suspicion fell on his young wife and there were stories of poisons being bought by Patrick Ogilvy and delivered to Eastmiln. Matters were further darkened by the arrival of Alexander Ogilvy, the family black sheep who had married poorly. This failed medical student demanded that the funeral be halted because he had a suspicion his brother had been poisoned. Alexander had led a far from blameless life and in the past had been partnered, professionally and personally, by Anne Clark. It is possible that she planted in his mind the poisonous seeds of the idea that Thomas had been done to death by Katharine and her lover. Given Alexander's own dissolute habits and lifestyle, it is also not unreasonable to suggest that the murder – if murder there was – had been carried out by Anne herself on his direction in order that he might inherit the estate. He insisted that doctors open the corpse to determine if poison had been used. However, although three different medical men scrutinised the body, not one of them conducted a post-mortem; they based their comments on an exterior examination only. They decided that poison could have been administered but conceded that the symptoms they found could also have their roots in natural causes.

Nonetheless, Katharine and Patrick Ogilvy were arrested, largely on the testimony of Anne Clark and at the insistence of Alexander. They were accused not only of murder but also of incest, for although they were not blood kin, they were related by marriage and the strict laws prohibited any sexual shenanigans among members of the extended family. They were, as we have seen, locked up in Forfar Tolbooth before being transported to its more secure Edinburgh counterpart. Meanwhile, Alexander looted the estate six ways from Sunday, even though he was not yet legally entitled to it.

News of the coming of the young murderess and her soldier lover reached Edinburgh and a vast crowd gathered at Leith to await their arrival. The person who stepped ashore from the ferry was not the demure, penitent lady they expected, even demanded. Instead, she was a beautiful young woman who laughed with her captors and showed no sign of remorse for her deeds. The crowd grew restive and a black mood settled: perhaps they should teach this arrogant wench a lesson in manners. The authorities had to force their way through the ugly mob to lodge the couple in the Tolbooth.

The trial was a farce. The jury was empanelled at 7 a.m. on 12 August and, as was the custom then, evidence was heard non-stop until 2 a.m. on 14 August. The jury wandered about the courtroom, discussing the case – and no doubt much else – with witnesses and counsel. As the trial proceeded without a breather, food and drink were necessarily brought in. Three judges sat on the bench on the first day but that was whittled down to one as the other two went off to join the melee in the various parts of the courtroom. A total of thirty-three hours was spent listening to the prosecution case but only three hearing the defence; the judges and jury were simply not interested in hearing what the lawyers for the accused had to say. The suspects themselves were prohibited by law from testifying, their words heard only through pre-trial statements.

Much of the damning evidence came from Anne Clark, who had shown great willingness to tell all and sundry that the young couple were guilty but was less than forthcoming when it came to repeating her allegations in court. She had to be taken into custody and kept under lock and key in Edinburgh Castle to ensure her appearance. Unfortunately, she was placed in the same room as servants from Eastmiln who were also due to testify against their erstwhile mistress. There can be little doubt that stories were compared and changed during those hours of captivity. At the close of the trial, the judge, Lord Kames, broke with tradition and summed up for the jury – the first time this had been done in a High Court matter. How fair he was in his summary is open to question given the prevalent mood in the court. It must come as no surprise that both Katharine Nairn and Patrick Ogilvy were sentenced to death.

Later, the attitude of the court was criticised in print by an English lawyer, who also lampooned the way Nairn and Ogilvy were charged with two crimes on the one indictment. Basically, his point was that each of the two charges – one of murder and one of incest – had been used to corroborate the other: 'The intrigue was supposed to be certain, because the husband was supposed to have been poisoned; and, on the other hand, the man was believed to have been poisoned, because there was supposed proof of intrigue.' The criticism excited the proud emotions of the Scottish justiciary, and the various Scottish publications that had reprinted the article were accused of contempt (even though the proceedings were done and dusted by that time). The publishers were sharply rebuked but not fined.

The lieutenant spent his time in the Tolbooth perfecting his mastery of the violin. The sad notes he made wafted down the corridors of the Heart of Midlothian and reached the ears of his alleged lover, who had managed a temporary reprieve due to the fact that she was pregnant – by whom is unknown. Ogilvy's execution was delayed three times as friends tried to have the verdict overturned, but to no avail. On 13 November, Patrick Ogilvy was told to lay his fiddle aside for the last time and escorted to the Grassmarket. If he had hoped for a rescue by any of his former messmates, he was to be disappointed, for they had been penned up in Edinburgh Castle as a precaution against any such folly. Standing on the gallows, he continued to proclaim his innocence of the crimes for which he was about to die. As he was turned from the ladder, the rope snapped and he tumbled to the ground. The hangman and a chimney sweep grabbed him and propelled him back up the ladder. A new noose was rigged; this time the drop held and Patrick Ogilvy died. The Society of Tron-Men, the guild of Edinburgh chimney sweeps, were so incensed at the involvement of one of their members in this shocking incident that he was drummed out of their ranks and banished to Leith for five years.

Katharine Nairn remained in her Tolbooth confinement, enjoying ale, white wine, rum and tea twice a day, until her child, a daughter, was born on 27 January 1766. She was visited regularly by members of her family and a well-known midwife named Mrs Shiells, or Shields. When the child was little more than one month old, the authorities debated whether her mother was strong enough yet to be put to death. A decision was delayed for seven days. Katharine and her family knew that if something was to be done, it would have to be done soon.

On 15 March, Katharine Nairn vanished, leaving her infant daughter behind. The official line at the time was that she had simply walked out of her unlocked cell. Some say she followed the Tolbooth tradition of cross-dressing to make good her escape, wrapping her slim body in a man's greatcoat. The most likely method of egress was a deception achieved with the connivance of Mrs Shiells, who had continued to visit the new mother. The midwife had feigned a toothache for some time and a large scarf had become something of a fixture over her face. All Katharine had to do was swap clothes with the other woman, swathe her face with the cloth and hobble out of the jail, receiving, apparently, a slap on the behind from a turnkey and being dismissed as 'a howling old Jezebel'. What happened to the midwife when the escape was discovered the following day is not recorded. It is known she continued in her professional duties, bringing many respected Edinburgh men into the world and occasionally hinting that there was more to the escape of Katharine Nairn than was generally known. This suggestion that the break-out was 'winked at' is underlined by the manner in which the fugitive avoided capture.

As has already been stated, she came from a good if not overly wealthy family – hence the need for her marriage to the comfortable but not terribly well-placed Thomas Ogilvy. Her uncle was William Nairn, a respected lawyer who was at that time commissary clerk of Edinburgh and was later promoted to judge when he adopted the title Lord Dunsinane. Clearly, he was a man not without influence in the Scottish judicial establishment and strings were probably pulled to ease his niece's departure. On leaving the Tolbooth, so the story goes, she knocked on the door of a house in James's Court, which she thought was that of her father's lawyer but which was in fact the home of Lord Alva, a judge. The servant who opened the door had supposedly attended the trial (even though it was held in private) and recognised her immediately. He raised the alarm and Katharine, still in her midwife's garb, scuttled off to the home of her uncle. He hid her in a cellar until the furore had passed and it was felt safe enough to smuggle her out of the city in the company of his clerk. A more likely story, however, is that a coach and horses was waiting for her at the foot of Horse Wynd when she left the Tolbooth. As it sped from the city, she changed into the clothes of an officer, complete with cocked hat, but still caused her companion, her uncle's clerk James Bremner, some disquiet due to her frivolous manner. Chambers, in his *Traditions*, claims that the coachman was ordered to drive the carriage into the sea and allow the fugitive to drown herself – preferable, it seems, to a public execution – if any pursuers managed to catch up with them.

After that, nothing definite is known of Katharine Nairn, but rumours there are aplenty. She went to the Continent, they say, and married a French nobleman. She moved to America and died, old and happy, surrounded by her grandchildren. She came through the French Revolution and ended her days in England. She entered a convent in France, or England, and died in regret for her past sins. Her end is as much a mystery as the alleged crime itself, for it cannot be stated with any certainty that Thomas Ogilvy was murdered – although Patrick did buy arsenic in Brechin and sent it, or at least some substance, to Katharine at Eastmiln. There is no firm evidence linking them either to murder or incest, as most of the damning testimony came from Anne Clark, a woman who, by all accounts, had little more than a nodding acquaintance with the truth.

The baby daughter born in the Tolbooth died there two months later. They say she was 'overlaid', that is smothered, but no one knows by whom. Mrs Shiells continued to practise her arts until 1805. Anne Clark vanished from history but her proclivities were unlikely to have kept her out of trouble. Alexander Ogilvy, the rascally brother who may or may not have conspired with her in murder or at least in manoeuvring events to his own ends, failed to profit from his brother's death. Although he sold off parts of the estate before Patrick was executed, he was prevented from doing further harm by a court order raised by Katharine Nairn on behalf of her unborn child. On 11 March 1766, he found himself in the Tolbooth at the same time as his sister-in-law; his crime was bigamy. He was legally married to the porter's daughter, Ann Rattray, but had 'taken up with one Margaret Don [or Dow], late a milliner's apprentice and has procured himself to be married to [her] on the twenty-fourth day of February last'. He pled guilty to the charge and was banished from Scotland for seven years. He was given two months to put his affairs in order and it was during that time that he leaned too far out of a window in one of Edinburgh's tall tenements and plunged to his death. It is tempting to imagine the shadow of Anne Clark behind him in the room, assisting him in his flight.

CHAPTER EIGHT

HELL'S BELLES

Pregnant Pauses

Katharine Nairn's execution was delayed due to her pregnancy, a common enough occurrence in those days of capital punishment. After all, the child in the womb was innocent of the crimes for which the mother had been found guilty and, of course, to kill the woman would also mean the death of the unborn. The practice of having a death sentence postponed in this way became known as 'pleading the belly' and there was many a felon who attempted to deprive the hangman of his fee by claiming she was pregnant, even if it was not the case.

In 1751, two women were lodged in the Tolbooth for the murder of a child. One tried to escape the noose by pleading her belly. The case was also one of the earliest documented killings committed for a cash payment, prefiguring a more sensational series of such murders by almost 80 years.

In the eighteenth century, medical science was trying very hard to slice its way out of the Middle Ages but superstition and religious scruples often got in the way of progress. The Kirk was still enormously powerful and the notion of dissecting corpses was anathema to it, as the flesh of the godly had to be whole come Judgement Day; an anatomist who cut up a corpse faced excommunication. Surgeons were allowed the cadavers of executed criminals, of which there were many but not enough to satisfy the doctors' need for experimentation. Eventually it was decided that the bodies of foundlings who had died before they were put to a trade were also to be given over, as were those of infants who had died at birth.

Still it was not enough, so students took their own steps to obtain the raw materials for their studies – and the body-snatching trade was born. They raided fresh graves, usually in dead of night, and corpses were hauled out and carted off. The grave-clothes were left behind: taking the corrupting flesh of the recently deceased was done in the name of science and humanity; taking the garments would be theft. The entrepreneurs who spotted a means of making profit from the trade – the 'resurrectionists' or 'sack-'em-up boys' – had no such scruples, for a shilling or two could be earned from a dead man's clothes as well as from his body.

Not all suppliers gleaned their stock-in-trade during moonlight raids on the kirkyard, as the first known case of a murder intended to produce a specimen for dissection proves. In the Tolbooth warding book for 1751, there is the following entry:

March 18

Helen Torrence and Jean Waldie were executed this day, for stealing a child, eight or nine years of age, and selling its body to the surgeons for dissection. Alive on Tuesday when carried off, and dead on Friday, with an incision in the belly, but sewn up again.

The boy was John Dallas and he was what could be termed a sickly child. He suffered from scrofula, a condition once known as 'the King's Evil', which attacked the lymphatic glands and bones. In his case, the disease had left him deaf, unable to speak and so weak he was housebound. He had contracted the illness four years before but he was showing signs of improvement. That mattered little to needlewoman Helen Torrence. In need of cash, she knew that the surgeons of the town would pay well for a cadaver. She had already approached one physician's assistant with the offer of a body for his master's use but had been turned down, as she was not a known supplier. However, the young student, knowing that specimens were relatively hard to come by, regretted his hasty decision, so some time later he approached Torrence and offered to treat some sores on her leg if she could rustle him up a body or two. The woman, in desperate need of medical attention, agreed. The only problem was that she did not have a corpse to hand. That was when she realised that the young Dallas boy was not long for this world.

The child's father was a sedan-chair carrier and was often away from home making his living. His mother was a hopeless drunk, who could easily be distracted with a dram or two. Given the boy's condition, Torrence probably thought at first that he was at death's door but when he steadfastly refused to breathe his last, she grew desperate. The medical student was also becoming insistent that she uphold her end of the bargain. He had provided her with treatment and had even parted with some coin, now he wanted his pounds of flesh. Torrence recruited the aid of her friend Jean Waldie and they hatched a plan to kidnap the boy from his home and bring him to their lodgings in Fairlie's Close. Their notion was that the trip in the cold night air would probably do for him. The boy's mother was lured away with the promise of grog and Jean Waldie snatched the young lad from his bed. As expected, he expired before he reached Fairlie's Close, although the hand of woman may have played more of a part in that little death than the hand of God.

A further fee for delivery had already been negotiated, the little corpse was duly handed over to the anatomists, and Torrence and Waldie toasted their good fortune. Meanwhile, the mother sobered up and found her boy gone. Inquiries were launched and it was not long before the finger of suspicion was pointed at the two women. The rumours of foul murder permeated through to the anatomist's chamber, where the boy was lying on a slab. Students had already sliced open his abdomen but when they realised they had been party to homicide it was swiftly stitched up again and the corpse dumped in Libberton's Wynd.

Torrence and Waldie lingered only briefly in the Tolbooth. During their time there, each blamed the other, while Torrence attempted to escape execution by claiming she was pregnant. Midwives were summoned to her cell and she was minutely examined for any sign of child-bearing but they announced there was none. A few days later, she and her accomplice died in the Grassmarket. On the scaffold, Waldie admitted she was responsible for the boy's death but claimed he had been smothered accidentally as she carried him through the streets. She also pointed the finger of guilt at Torrence, probably correctly, saying that she had talked her into the plan while she was drunk. Torrence, however, appeared to have come to terms with her fate and merely warned the crowd against the perils of 'drunkenness, bad company and uncleanliness'.

The two had murdered and traded their victim for profit to the anatomists. It was the first such crime recorded in Scotland but it would not be the last. William Burke and William Hare later turned their crime into a near science and kept the respectable Dr Robert Knox in corpses. But that was in another century and the Tolbooth had been gone for 12 years when that case shocked the city.

In 1806, Kirkcaldy woman Margaret Cunningham, or Masson, succeeded in delaying her execution due to her pregnancy. She had been found guilty of poisoning her husband, John Masson, with arsenic. Her accomplice, lover John Skinner, had managed to evade arrest, so the full weight of the law fell on the woman. At the High Court of Justiciary, a panel of midwives confirmed that she was indeed pregnant but five months later she appeared in court again, her newborn child in her arms, to hear sentence of death being passed. On 7 January 1807, she was taken from her cell in the Tolbooth and led to the platform at the west end of the building, where she died.

While the law protected the unborn babies of murderesses, it, like the Kirk, took a dim view of pregnancy out of wedlock. If there was one thing that got the ministers in a sweaty frenzy, then it was immorality, and a variety of punishments were devised for men and women who were discovered to be enjoying sexual relations without benefit of clergy. Fornication and adultery were proscribed acts and heaven help anyone who was caught indulging – unless they were high born or wealthy. Fines could be levied, of course, but these were sins of the flesh and for those the flesh must pay. Whipping, scourging and piercing were all inflicted on those convicted. The ministers could have the guilty party placed in the stocks or 'jougs' (a heavy iron manacle that bolted around the neck, which can still be seen outside some churches), where they would be subject to ridicule and physical abuse. Sitting on the 'cutty stool' to do penance in front of the congregation was less painful but no less shameful. If the accused showed little remorse for the crime, then he or she could be excommunicated, which was worse than it might sound, for it meant a person could not work, marry, baptise children or even expect a decent burial at life's end. Of course, there was also that perennial favourite – hanging by the neck till dead. And all for a bit of pleasure.

Men could be punished but women had a rougher time. If a woman was unfortunate enough to fall pregnant while unmarried, she alone was considered responsible and suffered the consequences. This forced many to attempt to hide their condition but if the deception was discovered, it carried dire repercussions. Even if undiscovered, the concealment of a pregnancy involved great threat to the lives of the mother and the child. Deaths in childbirth with a midwife present were common but without expert help the danger increased. Even if the mother and her baby survived, the temptation for her to simply kill the newborn to avoid scandal, ruin or judicial punishment was often too great to resist. In 1690, an Act was passed against concealment of pregnancy, stating:

> If any woman shall conceal her being with child during the whole
> space, and shall not call or make help of assistance in the birth, the
> child being found dead or missing, the woman shall be [deemed]
> the murderer of her own child, although there be no appearance
> of bruise or wound upon the body of the child.

In the same year, Kirk ministers rejoiced as three women were hanged
for child murder. One, Christian Adams, had hidden her pregnancy
to protect her married lover. For the same reason, she had smothered
the child shortly after giving birth and had buried it in a field. The
year before the new legislation was passed, Highlander Margaret
Craig was sent to the Tolbooth to await trial for murdering her child.
She had carried the bairn from her home in northern Scotland to
Peebles to confront the man who had seduced her. Unable to obtain
satisfaction, she drowned the child in a stream. She lay in the Tolbooth
for three years before she was finally tried and hanged.

The annals of crime throughout Scotland are littered with the
names of women punished or judicially murdered for concealing
a pregnancy and/or killing their newborn child. One of the most
famous is that of Maggie Dickson, from Musselburgh; the events
following her execution in 1728 have given her some sort of
immortality among drinkers in the modern-day Grassmarket.

The *Newgate Calendar* tells us that she was born to poor folk in
Musselburgh, who 'brought up their child in the practice of religious
duties and also instructed her in such household duties as was likely
to suit her future station in life'. The town then being 'almost entirely
inhabited by gardeners, fishermen and persons employed in making
salt', Maggie was married to a fisherman and bore him a number of
children. However, as was not uncommon at that time, her husband
fell prey to a press gang and was carted off to serve in His Majesty's
Navy. While he was fighting for King and country, Maggie 'had
an illicit connection with a man at Musselburgh, in consequence
of which she became pregnant'. She denied her condition but
neighbours insisted it was so. Finally, the child was born but, the

Calendar tells us, 'it is uncertain whether it was born alive or not'. As a consequence, Maggie Dickson was carted off to Edinburgh and the Tolbooth.

At her trial, witnesses came forward to say that 'she had been frequently pregnant' and that a newborn child had been found near her home. A doctor had put the lungs of the child in water and 'they were found to swim, which was deemed proof that the child had been alive. For it was a received opinion that, if no air be ever drawn into the lungs, they will not swim.' This belief, even then, was open to some doubt but the jury was happy to conclude that murder had been done and condemned Maggie to death.

In the Tolbooth, awaiting the appointed day, the woman 'behaved in the most penitent manner'. She confessed that she had been guilty of a number of past sins, including having 'departed from the line of duty to her husband', but continued to deny that she had murdered a child. In fact, she had no clear idea exactly what had happened. She admitted concealing her pregnancy for fear of being exposed to ridicule at church. She had been 'suddenly seized with the pangs of childbirth' and, being unable to call on assistance from neighbours, 'a state of insensibility ensued, so that it was impossible she should know what became of the infant'.

Her execution was to take place in the Grassmarket. Everything seemed to go according to plan. She addressed the crowd, insisting she did not kill the child but admitting her other sins, before her face was covered to protect the delicate sensibilities of the spectators and she was turned off the ladder. Here accounts of the case diverge. Normally, the bodies of convicted felons were given to the anatomists but, according to one version, permission had been given for friends and family to take possession of the corpse so that it could be returned to Musselburgh. Another version says that a scuffle broke out among medical students, who had a legal right to take possession, and relatives of the deceased, who felt they had a moral right to take her away for burial. In the end, the latter faction won the day and Maggie's body was placed in a coffin and the coffin in a cart and the cart driven from Edinburgh towards home. According to the *Calendar*, the party stopped for a drink at a village called Pepper Mill, about two miles from the city. The account goes on: 'While they were refreshing themselves, one of them perceived the lid of the coffin move and, uncovering it, the woman immediately sat up.' It is no surprise that 'most of the spectators ran off with every sign of trepidation'. Another customer at the inn may well have been a physician, or at least a barber-surgeon, for Maggie was bled a little and put to bed. The following day, she was so much recovered that she was able to walk home. From that day on, she became known as 'Half-Hangit Maggie Dickson'. The *Newgate Calendar* continues the story:

> By Scottish law, which is in part founded on that of the Romans, a person against whom the judgement of the court has been executed can suffer no more, but is thenceforward totally exculpated. It is likewise held that a marriage is dissolved by the execution of the convicted party, which indeed is consistent with the ideas that common sense would form on such an occasion.

In the eyes of the law, due process had been carried out. She had been accused, tried and hanged. Death had no doubt been pronounced. The fact that she had somehow survived mattered little. The legal writ did hit the fan, but the argument was between the Lord Advocate and the sheriff for not ensuring that she had actually been hanged by the neck till dead. Maggie, though, went on with her life. She even remarried her husband, who seems to have been a forgiving soul, and she was said to be alive as late as 1753.

Although much of this account follows that given in the *Newgate Calendar*, there are other versions of the story. One, featured in *Ghostly Tales and Sinister Stories of Old Edinburgh*, says that Maggie was a fish hawker and well known in Edinburgh. When her husband deserted her, she moved to Kelso, where she took up employment in an inn. The landlady had a son. Love, or at the very least lust, blossomed and she became pregnant. She hid her condition and when the baby was born, placed it among some reeds along the River Tweed. The baby drowned, the tiny body was discovered and it was traced to Maggie. She was transported to Edinburgh and executed, only to survive. In this version, the events took place in 1742.

It was a case of concealment of pregnancy that provided some of the inspiration for Sir Walter Scott's *The Heart of Midlothian*, which gave the Tolbooth its most popular nickname. The novel, the seventh of the Waverley books, was first published in four volumes in 1818 under the pen-name Jedediah Cleishbotham, 'Schoolmaster and Parish-clerk of Gandercleugh'. One strand of the story features the Porteous Riot while another focuses on one of Scott's most memorable heroines, Jeanie Deans, a young Presbyterian woman who tries to save the life of a sister accused of child murder. Her epic trek to London was based on actual events, of which Scott said he had first learned in an unsigned letter. The real-life Jeanie was Helen Walker, from Kirkpatrick Irongray in present-day Dumfries and Galloway. The dramatic events that set her apart from her neighbours might not have involved Edinburgh's Tolbooth but, thanks to Sir Walter Scott's pen, the story has become so inextricably linked to the Heart of Midlothian that it is worth retelling here.

In 1736, Helen and her sister Isobel, known as Tibbie, were scratching a meagre living by spinning and knitting wool. When Tibbie became sexually involved with a man named Waugh and the inevitable happened, she hid the fact from her friends and neighbours. When the child was born, she drowned it in the Cluden Water. The body was discovered and a handkerchief around its neck identified as Isobel's. The dead child was placed in her arms to see how she would react and when she threw a fit they decided that they had the culprit and arrested her. The case against her grew when the authorities questioned Helen. A devout Christian, she could not lie when asked with her hand on a

Bible if she had known Isobel was pregnant. 'It is impossible for me to swear to a falsehood,' she was reported many years later to have said, 'and, whatever may be the consequence, I will give my oath according to my conscience.' It was deemed that concealment had been proved and as the condemned woman was led from the court she turned to her sister and said, 'Oh, Nellie, ye've been the cause of my death.'

Whether the words stung her conscience or whether her stubborn nature would not let the matter lie, Helen Walker vowed to do everything in her power to save her sister from the gallows. She could not damn her own soul by lying under oath but she could throw herself on the mercy of those in power. While her sister was consigned to jail to await execution, she prepared herself for a heroic journey to London, where she would lodge an appeal with the King. Armed with a correctly worded plea, she set out on foot to cover the 300 miles between her home and the great city. There were few roads and she had not enough money for the coach fare all the way but this short, sturdy woman set out all the same, her feet bare, her body wrapped in a woollen skirt and a tartan shawl. Over her shoulder was a bag filled with supplies for her trip as well as shoes and stockings to wear when she arrived to converse with the great and the good. It took her 14 days to reach London and by then her feet were 'sorely blistered'. She would have been amazed and a bit confused by the metropolis, which was certainly much smaller than it is today but would still have appeared huge and bustling to a country woman more used to the comparative peace of Dumfries. Once there, she found her way to the home of the Duke of Argyll. She did not bang on the door, it seems, but waited in the street for him, for she knew that unless she could personally face his lordship and make her plea, it would fall on deaf ears. So she stood outside and waited, according to one account, for two days and two nights until she finally caught sight of the duke leaving the house. She approached him in the street and told her tale, handing the bemused man the document containing her written plea. He agreed to do all he could and within days she had a royal pardon for her sister, provided Tibbie left Scotland. Helen Walker made her way back home the way she had come and secured her sister's release.

Isobel Walker married the man whose child she had borne and moved to Whitehaven in Cumberland. Every year, she sent a cake or a cheese back to Scotland as a remembrance. Helen Walker remained in their small cottage in Kirkpatrick Irongray. She never married and seldom spoke about her trek to London. As one local observed, she was 'a wily body, for whene'er ony o' the neebors asked onything aboot the journey to London, she aye turned the conversation'. She died in 1791 and was buried in the village kirkyard.

In an introduction to the 1830 edition of his novel, Sir Walter Scott named the 'anonymous correspondent' who had told him the tale as Helen Goldie, wife of Thomas Goldie of Craigmuie, Commissary of Dumfries. She first met Helen Walker when she spent a summer in a rented cottage near the Abbey of Lincluden. She went to buy chickens from

> a little, rather stout-looking woman, who seemed to be between seventy and eighty years of age; she was almost covered with a tartan plaid, and her cap had over it a black silk hood, tied under the chin, a piece of dress still much in use among elderly woman of that rank of life in Scotland; her eyes were dark, and remarkably intelligent.

Mrs Goldie fell into conversation with the woman and learned that she earned a crust during winter footing stockings,

> that is, knit feet to country-people's stockings, which bears about the same relation to stocking-knitting that cobbling does to shoe-making, and is of course both less profitable and less dignified; she likewise taught a few children to read, and in summer she whiles reared a few chickens.

Later in the conversation the woman announced she was Helen Walker and added, 'but your husband kens weel about me'. Thomas Goldie told his wife the tale and she resolved to speak more to Helen Walker when she returned to the area the following spring. Unfortunately, before she could 'prosecute [her] acquaintance' with the woman, Helen died. Mrs Goldie tried to find out all she could about the mission of mercy to London but found that she had seldom spoken of it. 'Helen was a lofty body,' one distant relative told her, 'and used a high style o' language.' A relation of Mrs Goldie, however, did by chance visit an inn in the north of England where he met a serving woman who introduced herself as 'Nelly Walker's sister'. As Mrs Goldie's daughter put it in her correspondence with Sir Walter, by introducing herself thus, Tibbie showed that she 'considered her sister as better known by her high conduct than even herself by a different kind of celebrity'.

It was Mrs Goldie's daughter who suggested that a memorial be placed over Helen Walker's grave – a fervent wish of her mother. She stated that 'a little subscription could easily be raised in the neighbourhood'. Sir Walter saw to it that the request was 'most willingly complied with, and without the necessity of any tax on the public'. He paid for the tombstone and wrote the inscription, which praises Helen's virtues.

Like that of Half-Hangit Maggie Dickson, Jeanie Deans' name lives on in the memory of Edinburgh's drinkers. Maggie has a pub in the Grassmarket named after her while Jeanie Deans Tryste is a bar in St Leonard's Hill. In 2004, the bar, its fictional inspiration and Helen Walker were back in the news when it was announced that an insurance firm had sent the fictional Ms Deans a circular telling her she could win £30,000 if she signed up for disability insurance. The company explained the gaffe by claiming that the name and address must have been picked up from an online source.

In 1803, the threat of execution for concealing pregnancy was removed and replaced with a sentence of transportation. Given the conditions women faced on the convict ships and then in the colonies, it is a matter of opinion which punishment was more humane.

Of course, women were not imprisoned only for murdering children. Like men, they could be jailed and even executed for the pettiest of crimes. There is an astonishing entry in the Tolbooth records from 1653. On 11 February, Margaret Rennie, who is described as being 'both man and woman', was hanged for 'irregularities of conduct'. As was the custom, the cadaver was given over to anatomists, who found her to be 'two in every way, having two hearts, two livers, two every inward thing'.

A Maiden's Kiss

While the low-born would hang for a capital crime, those higher up in the nation's pecking order were generally executed in a manner thought to be more fitting to their status. Slowly throttling on the end of a rope was not a death to be wished for and the rich and infamous would not expect to be executed in this way. The losing of the head with one sure blow of a blade was a much swifter way to go. Of course, there was all that blood to be contended with but the mob liked a bit of gore with their entertainment. What the accused might not have factored in when wishing for this speedy death was the competence of the headsman, who was generally the common hangman and who might already have been paid his fee in ale. Headings were easily botched and what should have been a quick and relatively painless exercise might become a bloodbath, with a number of strokes from the weapon needed before the head left the neck. When Mary, Queen of Scots was executed at Fotheringhay, it took three blows of the axe to finish the job.

In Scotland, a more efficient method was found. The beheading machine known as the Maiden was, as we have already heard, supposedly introduced into Scotland by the Earl of Morton, who would himself feel its kiss of death. He may or may not have brought back plans following a visit to northern England, where such a device had been in operation for some years. It was based on a notorious device long in use in Halifax, where there were such strict laws against vagrancy that beggars used to intone, 'From Hull, hell and Halifax the good Lord deliver us.' An example of the Scottish machine can be seen in the National Museum of Scotland in Edinburgh. Although it is not the original device, this replica gives an idea of just how efficient the Maiden was. The ten-foot-high and five-foot-wide structure sports a blade ten inches long, topped with lead weights to strengthen the downward trajectory and ease the passage through flesh and bone. It was cunning in its simplicity and easy to use – pull the pin and watch the blade fall in its regularly greased grooves.

Mystery surrounds the reason why the machine was called the Maiden but one theory suggests it was a slang reference to Mary, Queen of Scots, for the first man to die under its blade was the Under-Sheriff of Perth, Thomas Scott; he and Henry Yair were both found guilty of involvement in the murder of David Rizzio, the Queen's secretary, in 1566. However, in the official expense sheet for those executions, the machine was already called the 'Madin'.

More than a century later, the Maiden claimed a notable female victim. Christian Hamilton murdered her lover, James Baillie, 2nd Lord Forrester. She was the wife of city merchant Andrew Nimmo and she had been conducting an affair with the older nobleman, who also happened to be her uncle. He was a notorious philanderer and at the same time as he was 'living and cohabiting in one house' with Christian, he was also fooling around with local woman Bessie Ritchie. This open fornication was too much for the Corstorphine kirk session, who, mindful of his rank and position, referred the matter to the Presbytery. However, fate – and the fiery Christian Hamilton – took a hand. On 26 August 1679, her uncle/lover was enjoying a convivial drink in the Black Bull Inn on Corstorphine's High Street when he received a message from her asking for a tryst. She wanted to meet him in the grounds of Corstorphine Castle, his own home, at the huge sycamore tree beside the dovecot. Thinking perhaps that he was on a promise, Sir James hurried to the appointed place at the appointed hour. However, his niece did not want to have at it but to have it out over his other extramarital affairs. She had already borne him a child, a girl, and he had promised to marry her. A furious row developed, during which, she said, Sir James, drunk as a lord, 'called hir whoor'. When intoxicated, he was prone to anger and she claimed that he attacked her with his sword bared. She protected herself and he somehow contrived to fall on the blade himself, no doubt thanks to the debilitating effects of the alcohol he'd consumed.

Self-defence it might have been but the woman knew her life would be forfeit if she was arrested. She hid in an attic room in the castle but was detected, tradition states, when one of her shoes fell through a floorboard. Her new lodgings in the Tolbooth were infinitely less comfortable than her attic hidey-hole but she was less concerned with that than she was with keeping her head attached to her body. She tried to avoid execution by pleading her belly but physicians found no evidence to support the claim. She tried to flee the prison altogether, following the traditional route of dressing in men's clothing, but was rearrested and returned to her cell. On 12 November 1679, she went to her death on the Maiden at the Mercat Cross, wearing a 'white taffetie hood'. In later years, the ghost of a woman in a white hood was seen around the sycamore tree where the fatal row took place.

The last person to die under the blade was gentleman John Hamilton, in 1716. He could have been a lawyer but lacked the application. He might have become a soldier but lacked the discipline. Instead, he became a wastrel and a drunkard, for which occupations he lacked no skill. He killed a tavern owner during a drunken brawl but fled the country and remained at liberty for two years. When he was finally caught, having returned on the death of the parents he had let down so badly, Hamilton tried to convince the courts that his being drunk at the time was reason for clemency. The jury saw it another way and he lost his head.

One of the best-known and perhaps the saddest of tales related to the Maiden and its dealings with the fair sex is that of Lady Jean Livingston. It is celebrated in ballad and by the pens of Scottish criminologists, including William Roughead. It is a tale of passion, murder and, according to a Scots clergyman, of redemption finally found within the dank walls of the Edinburgh Tolbooth.

On 1 July 1600, John Kincaid of Warriston was, according to the diary of Edinburgh councillor Robert Birrel, 'murderit be hes awin wyff and servant man'. Kincaid was the laird of an estate that lay to the east of the city (and which would later be the home of Sir Archibald Johnston, the Presbyterian lawyer who helped draw up the National Covenant, backed the torment of Montrose and died himself on the gallows). The Kincaids had money and they had power. John's wife, Jean Livingston, had a good name and even better looks, if the ballads are to be believed. They had married young or he was considerably older than she, depending on which account you read. What is known is that she bore him a son who was only a few months old when the following events unfolded. The old songsmiths would also have us believe that Kincaid was an abusive man, although this is something we may have to take on faith. A later indictment does seem to bear this out, stating that she had conceived 'ane deadly rancour, hatred and malice' against him for 'the alleged biting her on the arm and striking her divers times'. How he came to bite her on the arm can only be guessed at but the fact of the matter is that she grew to hate the man she married. She confided this loathing to her nurse, Janet Murdo, who soothed her little lamb with dark thoughts of homicide.

Lady Jean was receptive to the notion and Janet told her she had an idea who she could call on to do the deed. Jean's father, Sir John Livingston, was at that moment attending King James VI at Holyrood. In his company was one Robert Weir, a horse-boy with whom her ladyship was well acquainted. There is little detail in the scant official records of this case, so it is tempting to imagine a personal bond between the young woman and the groom. Given subsequent events, there must have been some strong link between the two, or else why would he so readily agree to become a killer? Janet Murdo believed he was just the man for the job but, according to Lady Jean's later confession, the nurse vowed, 'I shall go seek him and if I get him not, I shall seek another; and if I get none, I shall do it myself!'

The groom was indeed willing to commit murder for his ladyship but she seems to have suffered an attack of cold feet. Twice he was sent for and twice she refused even to speak to him. But the third time, on 1 July, the plot was hatched. Here we do have an official record of what supposedly happened, in the indictment, or 'dittay', of Robert Weir. That night, he was concealed in a cellar. Meanwhile, Lady Jean made sure her husband imbibed more than his usual amount of drink – all the better to make him sleep soundly – and then, around midnight, she fetched Weir from his hiding place and conveyed him up the stairs to the master chamber. But either Kincaid had not drunk enough or they made too much noise, for he woke up as they entered and Robert 'came then running to him, and most cruelly, with clenched fists, gave him a deadly and cruel stroke on the vane-organ'. Having thus delivered a debilitating blow to the jugular, Weir then threw his victim to the floor and kicked him in the stomach. Kincaid cried out and the groom fell on him, sitting on his chest and wrapping his powerful hands around his throat. According to the indictment, Lady Jean stood in the room while the murder took place. However, the confession she made in the Tolbooth states that she fled soon after the struggle began, although she could still hear the muffled cries and groans as her husband vainly fought for life.

Afterwards, while Jean's husband lay dead on the bedchamber floor, Robert Weir came to her and told her he would flee the country. 'I desired him, I say, to take me away with him, for I feared tryall,' she said in her confession, 'albeit flesh and blood made me think my father's moen [influence] at Court would have saved me.' Weir, though, felt this was the wrong course of action. 'You shall tarry still,' he told her, 'and if this matter come not to light, you shall say he died in the gallery, and I shall return to my master's service. But if it be known, I shall fly and take the crime on me, and none dare pursue you.' In other words, if the authorities did not buy the claim that Kincaid died of natural causes, then Weir would do a runner and draw any blame towards him.

However, the authorities suspected foul play – why, we do not know – and Lady Jean, nurse Murdo and two other servants were duly arrested. Weir was true to his word: he fled and remained free for four years. His disappearance did not have the desired effect, though, for the women were imprisoned in the Tolbooth and brought before the magistrates of Edinburgh. Under the law of the time, because they had been caught 'red-hand', they were to be tried by the Burgh Court and not by the High Court of Justiciary. The term 'red-hand' here seems to have been interpreted broadly, as they were not discovered over the body with a smoking gun, figuratively speaking. They were, however, caught in the house with a murdered man lying on a bedroom floor and that must have been enough.

Lady Jean might have thought her family would intercede on her behalf but she thought wrong. Perhaps her disappointment that no strings were pulled to save her partly explains her wild attitude prior to being found guilty. On the day of her trial, two days after the murder, Kirk minister James Balfour visited her cell. He found her

> raging in a senseless fury, disdainfully taunting every word of grace that was spoken to her, impatiently tearing her hair, sometimes running up and down the house [cell] like one possessed, sometimes throwing herself on the bed and sprawling, refusing all comfort by word, and when the book of God was brought to her, flinging it upon the walls twice or thrice most unreverently.

She heaped scorn on his words and dismissed them as 'trittle trattle'. Her behaviour was such that it is not surprising those present believed Satan had caused her to commit the murder. The thought of being consigned to hell did not worry her. 'I will die but once,' she told them. 'I care not what be done with me.'

The minister and his companions predicted that her demeanour would change when she was found guilty, which verdict appeared to be a foregone conclusion. Then, they said, 'you will be better tamed and the pride of your heart will be broke in another manner.' Lady Jean did not answer but called for a drink, which she drained before tossing the cup on the floor and turning her back on her visitors.

She may yet have harboured hope of paternal interference in due process but again that hope was to be dashed. No record of the trial exists, so no one can say what evidence was given against her, but it is known that one of the servants charged with her was freed. We already know how prodigiously the prosecutors were prepared to wield methods of torture in order to make their case, so perhaps the other woman had been coerced into testifying against her mistress. The charge was found proven and Lady Jean stoically took the news that she was to be first wirreit at the stake and then burned.

Back in her cell, she asked that Mr Balfour return and it was this and subsequent interviews that formed the basis of his *Memorial*, or to give its full title:

A Worthy and Notable Memorial of the great Work of Mercy which God wrought in the Conversion of Jean Livingston, Lady Warriston, who was Apprehended for the vile and horrible Murder of her own husband, John Kincaid, committed on Tuesday, July 1, 1600, for which she was Execute on Saturday following. Containing an Account of her obstinacy, earnest repentance, and her turning to God; of the odd Speeches she used during her Imprisonment; of her great and marvellous Constancy, and of her Behaviour and manner of her Death, observed by one who was both a seer and hearer of what was spoken.

How much of what he wrote was honest repentance on her part and how much he added to satisfy the Kirk's need for such repentance is unknown. She still defied them over her prior lack of religious fervour and when asked why she had not regularly attended church, replied that those who attended services not in the proper spirit would 'weary more sitting in the Kirk one hour than in ten days spent in vice'. The poor young woman had been arrested on Wednesday, tried and convicted on Thursday and was due to die on Friday. In between, with only a few hours sleep, she was pestered and preached at by Mr Balfour and other good men of the Kirk with an earnest desire to save her soul. It would not be surprising if she did break under their ministrations and agree to everything they said. On the other hand, perhaps the account is more or less verbatim and the contrition contained therein was sincere. However, it is the only record we have and we have to consider it, even if we do not take it as Gospel.

'Such an odd mercy, such deep feeling, and such high measure of grace saw I never in any creature as I saw in her, considering the ignorance and profanity of her whole life before,' wrote the enraptured Mr Balfour. She told him she had found 'a spark of grace beginning in her' and during the following 37 hours that spark grew 'to a great height'. He said she repeated one prayer many times: 'Lord, for mercy and grace at Thy hand for Thy dear son, Jesus Christ His sake, to the glory of Thy mercy and the safety of my silly soul.' Mr Balfour wrote: 'This prayer had she afterwards ever in her mouth as a common proverb, that I may say she uttered five hundred times before her death.'

Together they prayed hour after hour. He remained with her till eight that night before he had to retire for an hour to rest. When he returned, he found her 'very joyfull at her supper, mixing her bodily feeding with words of spiritual comfort, to the great joy and contentment of very many who heard her'. Back they went to praying until midnight, when it was decided some of her few remaining hours must be spent sleeping. The minister promised to return the following morning and in the meantime he thought to visit the nurse, who was also condemned to die. She, though, was a hardier creature than her mistress and he could not break through her 'evil' to find salvation. Giving her up as a lost cause, he returned to Lady Jean. He took with him Robert Bruce, a minister who only a few short weeks later would defy his king over the authorised version of the Gowrie affair (James VI claimed that two brothers had tried to assassinate him, although doubt raged over the truth of the matter). Lady Jean begged leave to see her infant son one more time. The ministers were unwilling to allow this as they thought the sight of the boy would make that 'spark of grace' leave her and she would rebel once more against the laws of man and the wish of God for her death. However, they relented and she kissed the child's head before asking that Robert Bruce look after him and bring him up 'in the fear of God'. Then the infant was taken away and she returned to her prayers.

It was while Mr Balfour was seeing Mr Bruce out of the Tolbooth that he learned that Lady Jean's method of execution was to be amended. She had hoped her family would use their influence and save her; all they did was see to it that she was not wirreit and burned but beheaded on the Maiden. The exact time she was to die was still not known. Traditionally, condemned persons went to the platform at around four in the afternoon, but the family wished that changed to nine at night. The crowd, knowing that a grisly spectacle awaited them, began to gather in the High Street and the young woman could hear their voices growing louder through the prayers and exhortations of the assembled preachers. There was also a crowd of onlookers crammed into the Tolbooth stairs and hallways to witness her miraculous conversion and defiance of the Devil. The people mobbed the High Street and climbed up the tall lands to secure vantage points in rooms overlooking the jail, keen to catch a glimpse of the notorious murderess. Lady Jean ceased her devotions to stand at a window and let them see her. As William Roughead slyly observed, this 'in a less saintly person, might savour of the "grievous sin" of vanity'.

Still she did not know when the deathly hour would come. Rumour after rumour reached her but she only said, 'You give me many frights, but the Lord will not suffer me to be affrighted.' Finally, she gave an account of what had happened on the night of the murder. 'I think I shall hear presently the pitiful and fearful cries which he gave when he was strangled,' she told Balfour,

> and that vile sin which I committed in murdering my own husband is yet before me. When that horrible and fearful sin was done, I desired the unhappy man who did it – for my own part, the Lord knoweth I laid never my hands upon him to do him evil – but as soon as that man gripped him and began his evil turn, so soon my husband cried fearfully, I leapt out over my bed and went to the Hall, where I sat all the time, till that unhappy man came to me and reported that mine husband was dead.

She asked God to forgive Janet Murdo, 'for she helped me too well in mine evil purpose'. The other two servants arrested with her were 'both innocent, and knew nothing of this deed before it was done, and the mean time of doing it; and that they knew they durst not tell, for fear; for I compelled them to dissemble'. She went on,

> As for mine own part, I thank my God a thousand times that I am so touched with the sense of that sin now: for I confess this also to you, that when that horrible murder was committed first, that I might seem to be innocent, I laboured to counterfeit weeping; but, do what I could, I could not find a tear.

Jean also 'purged herself very sincerely from many scandalouse things she had been bruitted with, that she might clear herself from those false reports that her house was charged with'. Some commentators take this to mean she denied rumours of an affair with Robert

Weir. Finally, at 3 a.m. on Saturday, 5 July, the magistrates arrived to accompany her to the Maiden. Under pressure from her family, they wanted her done away with as discreetly as possible, at an hour when there would be few witnesses. Lady Jean pleaded with them to allow her one last sunrise but they were determined that the deed be done in the dark of night. Mr Balfour, who had remained with her, also tried to stop the execution going ahead at this hour, not through any feeling of mercy for the accused but because he wanted the citizenry to witness it:

> Will you deprive God's people of that comfort which they might have in this poor woman's death? Will you obstruct the honour of it by putting her away before the people rise out of their beds? You do wrong in so doing; for the more public the death be, the more profitable it shall be to many; and the more glorious, in the sight of all who shall see it.

But the decision had been taken and the condemned woman was led away. Before she left her cell, her brother-in-law kissed her and forgave her.

At the Girth Cross on the Royal Mile she gazed up at the Maiden's blade as it reflected the light of the torches around them and shuddered. Mr Balfour tried to comfort her. 'This is a dead enimy,' he counselled, 'a piece of wood and iron; there is no death here but a parting, and entering into a better life.'

Despite the hour, a crowd had gathered and Jean Livingston addressed it from the four corners of the platform. Mr Balfour continued to attend her and noted that 'there appeared such majesty on her countenance and visage, and such a heavenly courage in her gesture, that many said, "That woman is ravished by a higher spirit than a man or woman's"'. However, when it came time for the blade to fall, he could not bring himself to stay and left his recent charge to her fate.

A friend or relative brought her a 'clean cloath' to tie over her face and she handed this person a pin to help fasten it at the back of her head. She knelt at the foot of the Maiden and gently laid her neck on the groove. Her head was fastened in place and the executioner pulled out her feet to lengthen the neck ready for the stroke. A man sat before her, holding her hands, and reported that she twice tried to pull her knees up to a kneeling position to offer up more prayers – but the time for that was past. Even as the blade fell, she continued to mouth pleas to God. 'Lord Jesus receive my spirit,' she intoned, 'O Lamb of God, that taketh away the sins of the world, have mercy upon me. Into thy hand, Lord . . .' Then the words were stilled as the blade hit its mark and the friend who held her hands watched as her head was struck from her shoulders.

The family had done everything they could to prevent the death of the young woman from becoming entertainment to the eyes of the crude and vulgar. They had even seen to it that her nurse Janet Murdo and the serving woman were executed at the same time on Castle Hill, in the hope that what spectators there were would find a double burning more of a draw. The ruse failed, for the greater crowd was at the Cross to see Lady Jean's beheading than attended the conflagration on the Hill.

It was four years before Robert Weir was taken prisoner. It is not recorded how he was finally caught but he did face Scottish justice on 26 June 1604. He confessed to the murder and he would pay a terrible price for his crime. Weir was a mere servant and he had raised his hand against a man seen to be his better. The method of death was particularly brutal, even for its day. Weir was to be 'tane to ane skaffold to be fixt beside the Croce of Edinburgh, and there to be broken upon the Row'.

The row was a wheel and this brutal means of dispatch was employed only twice in recorded cases in Scotland, the first occasion being in 1591, when John Dickson was convicted of murdering his father. Weir was spreadeagled and bound to a cartwheel. Then every bone in his body was systematically broken by the executioner, wielding 'ane coulter of ane pleuch' – the iron blade of a plough. The beating continued until Weir was dead. His broken and bloody body was then strung up between Warriston and Leith as a lesson to others not only to refrain from committing murder but also to remember their place.

CHAPTER NINE

FALLS FROM GRACE

The Divine Touch

There is no class distinction when it comes to crime. Lords and ladies of the realm, even men of God, are as capable of committing a felony as are the poorest beggars in the street. History is peppered with outwardly respectable people who have turned to homicide to solve a problem. Lady Jean Livingston, Katharine Nairn and Patrick Ogilvy we have already heard about. Linlithgow-born John Kello was another who spent his last few hours in the Tolbooth on a charge of murder. In his case, the crime was made even more horrendous by the fact that he was a Kirk minister and it was committed to further the cause not of his faith but of his own ambition.

In 1567, Kello became the minister of Spott, a small East Lothian town about four miles from Dunbar. He was married to a woman named Margaret Thomson and they had three children, Bartilmo, or Bartholomew, Barbara and Bessie. He was a well-respected preacher, with a reputation for delivering an eloquent and barnstorming sermon in the fire and brimstone mode of the early Presbyterians. He believed in heaven and he believed in hell but as he preached from his pulpit he could not have known it was for the latter he was destined. It was ambition that was his downfall. Passionate he may have been, pious very probably, but he was also of the opinion that he was meant for better things. He received a very basic stipend and his wife was loyal and steadfast but from poor stock. He wanted more out of life, so he speculated a little in property. His initial investment reaped a small profit and, as he confessed later, 'This manner of dealing kindled in me a desire of avarice which the Apostle Paul, not without cause, termed "the root of all evil".'

However, as in many a similar case, Kello sowed more than he reaped. Inspired by the success of his first foray into real estate, he bought more property but this time the venture failed and he found himself in debt. Stress levels began to rise and he searched feverishly for a way out. He butted heads with the Presbytery over his income but they were unmoving. With creditors clamouring, his mind turned towards much darker thoughts. Matters would be simpler, he reasoned, if he were single. For one thing, he could make his income stretch further; for another, he might marry again, perhaps someone with a more substantial financial foothold. His eye had fallen on the daughter of a local laird, for instance. Now, she would make a fine wife – and her father's connections would not go amiss.

So the Reverend John Kello began to circulate rumours about his wife's state of mind. She was showing signs of madness, he whispered, and he feared she would take her own life. All the while, he was tipping doses of poison into her stew but the woman refused to shuffle off this mortal coil. Whether Kello ingested some of the toxin himself or whether his conscience was proving a burden, he fell sick and was plagued by dreams, the nightmarish content of which he confided to a Dunbar colleague. In the dreams, a grim-faced man took him before a stern judge; to escape sentence, he threw himself into a swift-flowing river but sword-wielding angels pursued him.

Finally, on 24 September 1570, Kello tired of his wife's determination to remain hale and hearty and decided a more hands-on approach to her demise was necessary. On that Sunday morning, he crept up on her as she prayed in their bedroom and strangled her with a towel. Later, he insisted that even as she breathed her last she imparted to him that she was glad 'to depart if her death could do me an advantage or pleasure'. This highly unlikely claim no doubt served to salve his conscience slightly but it did nothing to prevent his own death. With poor Margaret finally gone, Kello set about putting the rest of his plan into action. He had already laid the fictional groundwork about her propensity to self-harm and now he made it look as if she had at last committed suicide. He wrapped a rope around her neck and hauled her up to the ceiling so that it would appear that she had hanged herself. Locking the front door from the inside, he then left the house through a seldom-used rear entrance and, amazingly, considering what he had just done, went to church. During that morning's sermon, he was more vehement than usual in railing against sin. Either his conscience was putting words into his mouth or his blood was on fire after his morning exertions. Following the service, he invited some prominent members of his congregation back to the house, for it was vital to his plan that there be witnesses present when he found his wife. He threw himself into a frenzy of grief when they came upon the body hanging in the bedroom.

However, not everyone was taken in by his seeming devotion. The Dunbar minister to whom he had confided his dream returned and said that he had analysed its content and had deduced that Kello had, in fact, murdered his wife. The judge in the dream represented God, the angels were not those of the Lord but agents of justice, while the river into which Kello fell represented his own hypocrisy. Only by confessing, Kello was told, could his spirit be saved. His words had the desired effect: the murdering minister realised what a terrible wrong he had done and took himself off to Edinburgh to confess.

He did not tarry long in the Tolbooth, for within a day he was sentenced to be hanged and his body burned. From the scaffold, he exhorted the multitude not to use his transgression as a stick with which to beat the faith or to excuse the sins of Queen Mary, who was then the subject of gossip over her possible complicity in the death of her husband, Lord Darnley. It was common in those days to explain acts of murder with reference to witchcraft or at least the influence of Satan but Kello himself was quick to point out that no supernatural beings had forced him to his crime.

'The Confessione of Mr Johnne Kello, Minister of Spott; together with his earnest repentance maid upon the scaffold befoir his suffering, the fourt day of Octiber 1570' was published in Edinburgh soon after his death. Some of it (including Kello's dream and the minister's interpretation of it) may have been subjected to the attentions of early spin doctors of the Kirk, for the murder had indeed given its critics – described as 'the poisonous sect of the anti-Christ' – an opportunity to undermine the faith. But, as we know, the 'new religion' survived both this and the more widespread and bloody tribulations to come.

The hand of God may or may not have forced John Kello to confess his crime but there were other cases in which it was believed that the divine touch could play a vital part in exposing the wrongdoer. These investigations used the ancient rite of *Bahr-recht*, a word that to modern ears sounds vaguely Klingon but which means 'law of the bier' and is better known as 'ordeal by touch'. King James VI, in his *Daemonologie*, summarised this now somewhat unbelievable approach to detection: 'In a secret Murther, if the dead carkasse be at any time thereafter handled by the Murtherer, it will gush out of blood; as if the blood were crying to Heaven for revenge of the Murtherer.'

The *Bahr-recht* rite came into play in one particular famous case – if only in popular retellings of the tale. However, it was not 'God's revenge on murderers' that led two Ayrshire noblemen to a brutal death in Edinburgh but the possibly perjured testimony of an alleged accomplice. The roots of this case lie in a long-standing feud in that county between rival factions of one family. The intricacies and sheer power of the tale have attracted the attentions of Sir Walter Scott and the lesser-known Scots novelist S.R. Crockett.

The Kennedys had long been known as the Kings of Carrick and a battle for supremacy over the family raged for generations between the rival branches of Cassilis and Bargany. On 11 December 1601, John Kennedy, 5th Earl of Cassilis, heard that his kinsman and rival Gilbert, Laird of Bargany, was due to pass near Cassilis' Maybole stronghold on his way from Ayr to his own lands at Girvan. The earl, as the local lord and master, learned that some members of Gilbert's party were wanted men and he decided to use his baronial powers of *fossa et furca* to bring them to justice. At Pennyglen, just outside the town, John Kennedy, with a large posse of men behind him, confronted the much smaller Bargany force and demanded the delivery of the hunted felons. The arrest turned into a tulzie in the teeth of a ferocious blizzard, during which the 25-year-old Gilbert of Bargany was mortally wounded. He succumbed to those wounds in Ayr less than a day later.

The death sent the young laird's followers into a fury. Among them were John Mure of Auchendrane and his son James, who apparently plotted revenge. John Kennedy was too powerful and too well guarded to attack but there were other members of his branch of the family who were not so secure. Sir Thomas Kennedy of Culzean, known as 'the Tutor', had approved the ambush, so they resolved to have their vengeance on him. Despite his nickname, Sir Thomas was no bookish academic. He was a Kennedy, red in blood and claw, and his past was littered with violent deeds. His daughter had married James Mure in a bid to calm an earlier outbreak of violence but there appears to have been little in the way of familial devotion. In May 1602, Sir Thomas sent his servant William Dalrymple to Auchendrane with a letter to his son-in-law, urging him to meet with him at Duppil Burn, on the shore near Ayr. On 12 May, a rendezvous was kept but it was with Gilbert Kennedy's brother, Thomas Kennedy of Drummurchie. There was a brief skirmish and Sir Thomas was left dead in the fine sands. It is not clear if John and James Mure were present at the murder but it was alleged that they had steered the information about Culzean's whereabouts to the vengeance-seeking Drummurchie. According to the evidence given against them later, young Dalrymple, the only proof that the Mures knew of the dead man's plans, vanished soon after the killing. He was kept for a time in Auchendrane House, outside Maybole, and then carried off to Arran. Finally, he was sent abroad to fight in Holland.

Rumours, of course, circulated that the Mures were complicit in the murder. Knowing that there was nothing to link them with the crime, John Mure went to Edinburgh and more or less dared the courts to charge him. He even challenged anyone who accused him to hand-to-hand combat. With no evidence, the courts dismissed him.

Some years later, Dalrymple returned from fighting in those foreign fields. The Mures were uneasy at the news. This young man could conceivably doom them with a word, so they resolved to shut him up forever. The young soldier was lodging in the home of his uncle James Bannatyne, an Auchendrane tenant, using the name William Montgomery. On a lonely stretch of beach between Girvan and Turnberry, the Mures are said to have murdered the hapless Dalrymple, who had been lured there by his uncle. They first attempted to bury the body in the sands but the tide waits for no man and proved too impatient for their gravedigging. They resolved, therefore, to dump the corpse at sea. Troublesome as Dalrymple was in life, he proved even more so in death, for the body drifted back to shore and was within days discovered.

Suspicion fell on the Mures and they quickly realised that now another man had the power to hang them – James Bannatyne. The farmer knew just how dangerous these men were but was also canny enough to realise the gravity of his own situation, so he made himself scarce. Meanwhile, legend tells us, the Mures were brought to the young man's body to undergo ordeal by touch. In his book *The Grey Man*, Crockett vividly describes the scene:

But James Mure seemed to flame out suddenly distract, like a madman being taken to Bethlem. He cried out, 'No, no, I will not touch. I declare that I will not go near him!'

And when John Mure strove to persuade him to it, he struck at him with his open hand, leaving the stead of his fingers dead white upon his father's cheek. And when they took his arm and would have forced him to it, he threw himself down headlong in the sand, foaming and crying, 'I will not touch for blood! I will not touch for blood!'

But in spite of his struggling they carried him to where the body lay. And, all the men standing back, they thrust his bare hand sharply upon the neck where the rope had been.

And, it is true as Scripture, I that write declare (though I cannot explain it), out from the open mouth of the lad there sprang a gout of black and oozy blood.

God himself, it seemed, had pointed the finger of judgement at the culprit. There is another version of the story of the ordeal. In this, Lady Culzean viewed the body with her granddaughter, the daughter of James Mure. As soon as the child neared the corpse, the blood began to flow. As it was clear that a child of her tender years could not be the culprit, suspicion fell on her father.

Supernatural evidence aside, the King was convinced of the men's guilt and had Mure the elder brought to the Tolbooth for further examination. His son – who, some accounts claim, arranged for Bannatyne to disappear in Ireland – remained at liberty but gave himself up to face trial. The King, no doubt influenced by the powerful Cassilis faction, ordered that he be tortured. Despite his legs being crushed in the boot, he refused to confess. Nevertheless, the King ordered that he and his father be held in prison.

Four years after the murder on Girvan shore, Bannatyne was discovered in Ireland and prevailed upon to come forward. Under pressure from the King and knowing that the Mures had been arranging from their prison cells to have him murdered in Ireland, he confessed all. John and James Mure were tried 'for the tressonable murthour of Sir Thomas Kennedie of Culzean' and the killing of William Dalrymple. The fact that the only evidence was that of an accomplice mattered little to his accusers, for both men were executed on the Maiden. They died clinging to their innocence and claiming that James Bannatyne, who was pardoned in return for turning King's evidence, had perjured himself.

Whether the Mures were guilty of either murder must be open to some doubt, for as was proved in the witchcraft trials of the period, torture can make even the most innocent person admit anything and implicate anyone. It was a brave man or woman who could withstand the agonies of flesh being pierced and bones being crushed to insist on their innocence. The fact that James Mure managed this must, to a modern mind, tell us that there may have been something in his protestations of innocence. However, the Mure name has for centuries been linked to the violent events of 1601–2 and, thanks to Crockett's adventure novel, also with the legend of Sawney Beane, the Ayrshire cannibal said to have lived in a deep cave at Bennane Head, north of Girvan. Crockett's blood-and-thunder narrative details the epic struggle between the warring Kennedy septs, with John Mure being the Grey Man of the title, a sinister villain in league with the Devil and using the hideous Beane family as hired killers.

Their story first appeared in a broadside around 1700. It is a matter of debate whether they ever existed at all, but the story goes that they were arrested when their cave was penetrated by a hunting party and found to be lined with the corpses of their victims strung up like sides of beef in a butcher's shop. The entire pack – Sawney and his wife, their eight sons, six daughters, eighteen grandsons and fourteen granddaughters – were transported en masse to Edinburgh and may have bided a while in the Tolbooth. Legend, if not documentary evidence, tells us that their end was no less brutal than the fates of their victims. The men were taken to Leith, where their hands and feet were lopped off. They were then castrated and impaled on stakes to bleed slowly to death. Their corpses were then incinerated in a huge pyre. The womenfolk were forced to watch this grisly spectacle before they too were burned, strapped to three stakes. According to the *Newgate Calendar*, the family spat and snarled at their executioners and the mob all the while, 'venting the most dreadful imprecations' until 'the very last gasp of life'.

The work of Samuel Rutherford Crockett (1860–1914), although dated now, is long overdue for a reappraisal; *The Grey Man* and his other books should take their place if not alongside the works of Scott and Stevenson then certainly just a little way behind them. Scott, it should be pointed out, also used the Kennedy feud in his work, as the basis for his play *Auchendrane; or, The Ayrshire Tragedy*.

Another true-life case to attract the interest of both Crockett and Scott was that of Philip Stanfield. It too involves ordeal by touch, and Scott (who, though he may have been an old romantic, was still a lawyer at heart) was rightly dubious about the legitimacy of the case, resting as it did on supernatural evidence. In a notebook dated 15 March 1797, he writes:

> Read Stanfield's trial, and the conviction appears very doubtful indeed. Surely no-one could seriously believe, in 1688, that the body of the murdered bleeds at the touch of the murderer, and I see little else that directly touches Philip Stanfield. It was believed at the time that Lady Stanfield had a hand in the assassination or was at least privy to her son's plans; but I see nothing inconsistent with the old gentleman's having committed suicide.

William Roughead, on the other hand, was certain that murder had been committed: 'We may rest assured that Sir James Stanfield died by some hand other than his own, and that Philip ... was, in [Scottish judge] Braxfield's classic phrase, "nane the waur o' a hangin"'.' But that game old crime commentator did admit that

> [The tale] is a tragedy of old years of blood and superstition;
> grim, indeed, but with here and there quaint glimpses of the
> ghostly marvellous, wherein we perceive malice domestic incite
> to midnight murder, and in the end the guilty designated by the
> manifest finger of God.

The victim in this story of murder and, it would seem, madness was the aforementioned Sir James Stanfield, a Yorkshireman by birth, a Roundhead by choice and a businessman by design. Having first come north with Cromwell's forces and participated in the 'miraculous' victory at Dunbar, he settled in Scotland, buying a site at New Mills, near Haddington in East Lothian, on which he erected a cloth factory. His devotion to the Protector did not seem to get in the way of his rise in riches come the Restoration, for he was knighted by Charles II and involved with the Duke of York (later James VII and II) in a scheme to build Scotland's textile industry. He also owned other land, including a house in Edinburgh, which stood close to the city wall, on the spot where the famed World's End pub now sits.

He had two sons, the elder, Philip, being a wastrel described by Roughead as 'a prince of prodigals'. At university in St Andrews, he was noted for having thrown a missile at John Welsh, the great-grandson of John Knox, during a sermon. The minister showed the Presbyterian gift for prescience when he stated that 'there would be more present at [Stanfield's] death than were hearing him preach that day'. The younger son, John, was not much better. Lady Stanfield doted on the boys, particularly Philip (it was suggested later that the love between them was more than that of a mother for her son), and her husband was forever called upon to bail him out of some trouble or other. James told friends that Philip was 'very wicked' and that it was 'sad that a man should be destroyed by his own bowels'.

The young man continued to prove troublesome to his father. He joined the army but continually found himself in prison for some outrage or another, usually as a result of his temper or his tendency to get into debt. On one occasion, he was sentenced to death but he managed to escape from the foreign jail before his day of reckoning. When he returned home, he continued to be something of a millstone around his father's neck and on two occasions tried to kill the older man. Philip's behaviour, coupled with the less outrageous but equally costly habits of his young brother, dragged the family fortunes down and Sir James was put in the position of having to sell some of his holdings. When he resolved to disinherit his elder and more troublesome son, events began to hurtle towards sudden death.

In November 1687, Sir James was found face down in an icy pool of water that formed part of the River Tyne near Haddington. A man passing by stated that he had seen Philip Stanfield standing on the banks looking down at the body. A guest at the Stanfields' house told of strange noises he had heard during the night, which, being a minister of the Gospel, he had put down to 'evil spirits about the house that night'. He said that he was roused from sleep by a cry and 'heard for a time a great dinn and confused noise of several voices, and persons sometimes walking, which affrighted me (supposing them to be evil wicked spirits)'. The voices were sometimes outside his bedroom door, sometimes in the passageway or on the stairs. However, instead of getting up to investigate, the good reverend merely got up to 'bolt the chamber-door further, and to recommend myself by prayer, for protection and preservation, to the majestie of God'. The voices then moved outside the house but he could see nothing from his window. He later heard footfalls on the stairs and in the corridor on the floor above.

The following morning, Philip Stanfield asked the guest if he had seen Sir James, telling him that he had been out looking for him along the riverbank. He mentioned nothing about seeing a body in the river. As the minister left the house, a servant ran up to him and told him that the master's body had been found. 'If the majestie of God did ever permit the Devil and his instruments to do an honest man wrong, then Sir James Stanfield has received wrong this last night, which the Lord will discover in his good time.' Having thus consigned the matter of his friend's death to God's judgement, the minister left without further investigation. After all, he had a sermon to preach.

Philip told everyone that he believed his father had killed himself. He would not allow the body to enter the house 'for he had not died like a man but like a beast'. The dead man was taken to an outhouse, while Philip went through the house and took possession of everything of value, including the dead man's silver buckles. When the minister returned that night, he told Philip that he believed this was not a case of suicide 'but a violent murder committed by wicked spirits'. Philip had told the authorities in Edinburgh of his father's death and was expecting a visit from them that night to view the body.

However, tongues were wagging and Sir James's mill manager, Umphray Spurway, suspected foul play. Within hours of the discovery, he managed to convince the Lord Advocate, Sir John Dalrymple (who two years later would plan the massacre at Glencoe), that all was not well. A letter was sent ordering Spurway and two or three 'discreet persons' to examine the body but Philip managed to intercept the message before it reached the manager's hands. That night, torches glowed in the frost-filled air as Sir James's corpse was moved secretly from the outhouse to the kirkyard in Morham, three miles away, and there buried under orders of Philip Stanfield.

But Sir John Dalrymple was not to be deterred. The next night he sent two surgeons with three other witnesses to have the body exhumed from its hasty grave and properly examined. Umphray Spurway and Philip Stanfield were both present when the corpse was carried into the church. The doctors found, according to their report, 'a large and conspicuous swelling' on the neck. This livid three-inch bruise ran 'from one side of the larynx round backwards to the other side thereof'. The neck was dislocated while the lungs were dry. It was deduced that strangulation, not drowning, was the cause of death.

But what happened when Philip Stanfield helped heft the dissected corpse back into its coffin excited more interest. As he gripped the head, the witnesses were startled to 'see it darting out blood through the linen from the left side of the neck which the pannel [accused person] touched'. The blood spurted over Philip's hands and he dropped the body. He rushed from the church, wiping the blood away and saying, 'Lord have mercy on me!' To the men who watched, this was God playing a part in unmasking a murderer – and it was this, more than anything else, that brought Philip Stanfield to a horrible death on the scaffold.

In the Tolbooth warding book for 14 February 1688 – the same day as Covenanter James Renwick was imprisoned – a 'Philip Stampfield' is listed as being 'wardit'. His trial had taken place the week before and he had been found guilty not only of parricide but also of high treason, for it was alleged that he had 'drunk confusion to the King', and of cursing of his parents. His defence, although no witnesses were called to support it, was that his father had committed suicide while in a 'frainzie or melancholy fit'. In support of this depressed state of mind, there was cited an occasion when he had tried to throw himself from a window of his house at the Netherbow Port. There was also a claim that he had tried to ride from Scotland to England, never to return, 'but his horse stopped and would not go forward, which he looked upon as the finger of God, and returned home again'.

God was never far from these proceedings – Sir George Mackenzie saw to that. The prosecutor was as capable of calling down fire and brimstone as the Covenanters he pursued with such vigour. 'You will discern the finger of God in all the steps of this probation as evidently as Philip's guilt,' he intoned, 'and this extraordinary discovery has been made as well to convince this wicked age that the world is governed by Divine Providence, as that he is guilty of this murder.'

Philip had denounced the King and had certainly cursed his

father on more than one occasion. As we have seen, his father had even taken steps to disinherit him and it was claimed that Philip had made renewed threats to kill him. The father had latterly lived in fear of the son – not surprising since the young man had indeed tried to kill him twice. Also, Philip had been heard to boast before the murder that he would be 'laird of all before Christmas'. What's more his mother, in bad health, had said to him, 'You will shortly want your mother, which will be a gentle visitation to Sir James,' to which Philip replied darkly, 'By my soul, mother, my father shall be dead before you!'

It was alleged that he murdered his father with the aid of his mistress, a married woman named Janet Johnston, and two others, George Thomson and his wife Helen Dickson. Significantly, all three were tortured with the 'thumbkins', the thumbscrews, but revealed nothing and so were not charged with him. There was some testimony from the son of Thomson and Dickson, who overheard his father say that 'he never thought a man would have died so soon' and that 'they had carried him out towards the waterside and tyed a stone about his neck'. As to the suggestion of suicide, Bluidy Mackenzie pointed out that for this to be so, it would be necessary to suppose that 'after he had strangled himself and broke his own neck, he drown'd himself'.

But it was the ordeal by touch that proved the most damning – and Sir George made the most of it. 'The divine Mejesty, who loves to see just things done in a legal way, furnished a full probation in an extraordinary manner,' he proclaimed. Thanks to God, things were indeed 'done in a legal way', for Philip Stanfield was found guilty of his crimes and sentenced to die on the scaffold – just as that minister in St Andrews had prophesied. The date was set for 15 February but the sentence was stayed for a further eight days while Stanfield made legal moves to have his alleged co-conspirators questioned again. These efforts failed and on 24 February he was led from the Tolbooth to the Mercat Cross and strung up on the gibbet.

However, the knot on the noose was insecure and he slumped down so that his feet and knees rested on the platform. The hangman then had to manually tighten the rope and strangle him. His tongue was cut out and burned before the crowd. His right hand was hacked from the arm and nailed to the East Port at Haddington. His body hung in chains on the Gallowlee for all to see. After a few days, the body vanished and was found lying in a water-filled ditch. The parallels with his father's death were obvious: the murderer had first been strangled on the scaffold and now he lay face down in water. The body was again hung in chains but soon disappeared again, to be seen no more. The removal of corpses from gibbets was not unknown even in later years. On 23 April 1755, Nicol Brown was executed for burning his wife to death. His body hung on the gibbet at the Gallowlee but vanished within weeks. It was found in a nearby quarry and hung back up again only to disappear again two weeks later, never to be found.

Of Philip Stanfield's reputation as a reprobate there can be no doubt. That he had little or no respect for his father there is also no doubt. But did he murder him? The evidence is far from conclusive and the revelation of the ordeal by touch can be disregarded. The body had been opened during the post-mortem, and an incision had been made into the suspicious bruise on the neck. It is entirely likely that the wound ruptured again as the cadaver was lifted. Certainly Sir George Mackenzie tried to defuse any possible probing of the incident. The wound had been stitched closed, he insisted, and the body had been some time dead 'which naturally occasions the blood to congeal'. As Sir Walter Scott noted, it is hard to believe that level-headed men even then could take such evidence seriously. The statement of the child is certainly compelling but it implicated Stanfield only by hearsay. The surgeons were not even questioned regarding their medical findings, only about what they had witnessed when the body was lifted. Lady Stanfield was also on the suspect list, for, a contemporary chronicler said, she 'had the dead-clothes all ready' before her husband was even defunct. And then there were the dark murmurings about her relationship with her elder boy. Could she have murdered her husband because he planned to disinherit Philip?

William Roughead may have been certain of Philip Stanfield's guilt but Robert Chambers, in his *Domestic Annals*, like Sir Walter Scott, entertained doubts over the safety of the verdict:

> It will be acknowledged that in the circumstances related there is not a particle of valid evidence against the young man. The surgeons' opinion as to the fact of strangulation is not entitled to much regard; but, granting its solidity, it does not prove the guilt of the accused. The horror of the young man on seeing his father's blood might be referred to painful recollections of that profligate conduct which he knew had distressed his parent, and brought his grey hairs with sorrow to the grave – especially when we reflect that Stanfield would himself be impressed with the superstitious feelings of the age, and might accept the haemorrhage as an accusation by heaven on account of the concern his conduct had in shortening the life of his father. The whole case seems to be a lively illustration of the effect of superstitious feelings in blinding justice.

The Crime of Miscreant Brodie

From the warding book, 17 July 1788:

> William Brodie, wright in Edinburgh, was this day incarcerated in the Tolbooth thereof in virtue of a warrant of the Sheriff of Edinburgh untill liberate in due course of law . . . that on the night betwixt the sixteenth and seventeenth day of August last the shop of John Carnegie Grocer in Leith was broke into and a quantity of tea, about 45 pounds in weight, was stole and carried off therefrom. That also in the night betwixt the fifteenth and sixteenth days of March last the Excise office in the Canongate of Edinburgh was broken into and 17 pound stolen therefrom. That

> from information received and circumstances since discovered
> there is the greatest reason to suspect that the said thefts were
> committed by William Brodie, wright in Edinburgh, or at least
> that he was aiding and assisting thereof. In order therefore that he
> might be apprehendit and examined and if guilty punished, his
> Lordship's warrant was raised as above.

If Mure of Auchendrane and Philip Stanfield are forever associated
with Scott and Crockett, then William Brodie remains always the
domain of Robert Louis Stevenson. So fascinated with the story
was he that, along with W.E. Henley, he wrote a play entitled
Deacon Brodie, or The Double Life. And, of course, it was that notion
of a double life – on the one hand respectable and God-fearing,
on the other dark and sinister – that led to the creation of what
Stevenson called 'a fine bogey tale', *The Strange Case of Dr Jekyll
and Mr Hyde*. The good deacon was one of two inspirations for
that influential work of psychological horror. The other seemingly
respectable worthy leading a dark and secret life was, of course,
Major Thomas Weir. Unlike Weir's, though, Brodie's secret life
was not one of lust involving hints of Satanism. Not that there
was no debauchery in the outwardly solid master carpenter's life,
for Edinburgh in his day was not lacking in places in which to
pleasure the flesh. Brodie's sins, though, were principally of larceny
and greed, and he paid the ultimate price, reputedly spending his
final hours playing a makeshift game of draughts on the flagstones
of the Tolbooth floor.

William Brodie was, like his father before him, a deacon in the
Incorporation of Wrights, or cabinetmakers. The family was solid,
successful and wealthy enough to have a close named after them in
the Lawnmarket. William inherited the business, the family fortune
of some £10,000 and valuable property when his father died in
1782. At that time, he was 41 years of age and a dab hand with saw
and plane. Business was good. Being on the town council, Brodie
could ensure that he had his share of the tastiest municipal contracts.

His reputation was as fine as his workmanship and he knew all the best people.

The good deacon, however, was not what he seemed. There was another side to him, a darker side. His Mr Hyde appeared at night, when the Town Rats beat the drum through the streets to signal the dying of the day. As darkness fell, Edinburgh's businesspeople gave up the pursuit of profit to chase their pleasures – and the night people made the cobbled streets their marketplace. Old Edinburgh was littered with taverns both high and low, and within them could be found every pleasure of the flesh imaginable. In these dingy back-street establishments were prostitutes to satisfy physical needs and gambling to cater to a craving for thrills. Cockfighting was popular and Brodie was a devotee. Perhaps he saw something of himself in these swaggering, game creatures, for he too was slight of stature but sure of himself. Such was his addiction that he began to breed fighting birds in Brodie's Close. The daytime deacon knew all the right people and was welcome in polite society. The night-time Brodie knew all the fleshpots and alehouses of the old town and was well kent by them in turn. Not only was he a gambler but he was also a womaniser – he had two mistresses, Jean Watt of Libberton's Wynd and Ann Grant of Cant's Close, both themselves married with children. It takes cash to keep a legitimate family plus two extramarital relationships going, and Brodie's gambling addiction also made its dent in his fortune. With his debts rising, he looked around for other ways to make a shilling.

It was in Michael Henderson's tavern in the Grassmarket that he met Englishman George Smith. Another gambler, albeit one who preferred to bolster his luck with loaded dice, Smith had left his own country under a cloud and travelled north. Although a locksmith to trade, he set himself up in Edinburgh as a grocer and soon sniffed out the nightlife – and his future partner-in-crime, Deacon William Brodie. Together they embarked on a crime spree, Brodie using his local knowledge to identify targets and his social connections to gain access in order to 'case the joint'. The series of burglaries shocked Edinburgh and was no doubt discussed at the town council, Brodie himself shaking his head as if in disbelief that such calamities could befall his neighbours.

If his cabinetmaking business was good, his lock-breaking activities were even better. He and Smith decided to take on extra hands, John Brown and Andrew Ainslie. The latter was a weak link in the crime chain and was used merely as a lookout but Brown was something else. Like his countryman Smith, he was a professional who was wanted in his homeland for theft and escaping from the long arm (but weak grasp) of the law. If he were caught again, he would pay for that cheek at the end of a rope. The gang proved energetic. Homes were robbed, goods went missing from shops and most, but not all, of the profits were duly lost at the gaming tables. The canny Brodie sent some of the more valuable hot goods to Newcastle, to be stored for a rainy day.

Then, on 5 March 1788, everything changed. Up until then, the furtive four had led charmed lives but now they were about to take a crooked step too far. It had been Brodie's plan for some time to make his big score by breaking into the excise office in Chessel's Court in the Canongate. The place had been cased and Brodie had managed by sleight of hand to make a duplicate key to the door. The fact that it hung in the passageway when the office was open made it a matter of some ease for the honest, upright and respectable deacon to palm it long enough to make an impression. Between eight and ten o'clock at night, the office was devoid of either doorman or nightwatchman, so the robbers identified that two-hour period as their window of opportunity. While Brown made sure the last employee was safely home, Brodie and Smith used their duplicate key to breach the front door. Ainslie stood outside to keep watch, an ivory whistle in his hand. By the time Smith had used the coulter of a plough and wedges to force his way into the cashier's office, Brown had rejoined them. They were, of course, looking for cash but all they found was £15 16s. 3d (although in the Tolbooth records the sum appears to have increased to £17). What they did not know was that £600 lay in a drawer unnoticed by them. Perhaps they would have found it, given time, but time was the one thing of which they were desperately short, for fate, or at least what Brodie later with a shrug called *fortune de la guerre*, was about to take a hand.

Too late, Ainslie spotted someone dashing into the excise office but failed to blow his whistle. The newcomer was an office worker looking for some papers and he proved to be a very lucky man indeed. All three robbers were armed with a brace of pistols each but the only one he encountered was Brodie, who panicked and rushed out of the building. Had the man met up with Smith or Brown, the situation might well have been very different. Ainslie, hiding behind his wall, saw Brodie leave but did not recognise him. More importantly, he still did not raise the alarm. The clerk obtained his papers, and thinking that the man he had bumped into was a fellow worker staying late, took his leave. It was only when Ainslie saw his shadowy figure emerge from the building that he blew his three warning notes on the whistle. Smith and Brown heard the shrill triple shriek and, thinking the jig was up, made good their escape.

The robbery was the talk of the town and a reward of £200 was offered for the capture of the guilty parties. John Brown saw a way of getting himself out of this scrape – and wiping his slate clean. If he turned King's evidence, he could see to it that he was pardoned for his English crimes while obtaining a Get Out of Jail Free card for the excise office job. Scottish justice has always been willing to overlook serious crimes if it brings someone – anyone – to justice. In addition, Brown reasoned, he would be £200 richer. So he did what any self-respecting thief would do: he 'peached' on his mates. But even then, the wily Brown had an eye to the future, for he named only Smith and Ainslie. Brodie's name he kept to himself, tucking it away in his mind as a means of accruing blackmail income. Later, under pressure, he caved and ratted Brodie out too.

Naturally, news of the arrests had Brodie worried. He was no fool; he knew even before Brown's betrayal that there was no honour among thieves. It was only a matter of time before Smith or Ainslie, or both, gave him up in order to avoid the gallows. Ever daring, Brodie decided to visit his old companions in crime in the Tolbooth to try to ensure their silence but was not allowed in. He lost his nerve and decided that discretion was the better part of valour. He took the *Flying Mercury* coach south, tapping into his emergency fund at Newcastle on the way. He reached London to learn that Smith had finally given him up.

Brodie went to ground in London before taking ship for Holland. There, as John Dixon, he planned to set sail for New York and lose himself in the wide open spaces of the colonies. However, he had made a mistake that proved fatal. He had written letters to friends and placed them in the keeping of a man called Geddes, who was returning to Scotland. Geddes recognised him and gave the letters to the authorities. Brodie was subsequently arrested in Amsterdam, where he hid himself in a cupboard in an attempt to avoid capture. Following an unsuccessful attempt to beat extradition, he was dragged back to Edinburgh.

Tossed into the Tolbooth, Brodie learned that his erstwhile companion in crime – and his accuser – John Brown was awaiting trial on a charge of culpable homicide, having been party to the death of a man during a brawl. The authorities needed Brown untainted by a sentence, so while his co-accused was found guilty their star witness in the Brodie case got off. Meanwhile, Ainslie had also turned informer in order to evade becoming gallows bait. Only Brodie and Smith were to face the music and their trial began, after some legal delays, on 27 August 1788. The court sat continuously from 9 a.m. until it was adjourned at 6 a.m. the following morning. Brodie had more or less confessed to the robbery in the letters passed on by Geddes, while his flight from justice also went against him. In addition, certain items were found at the scene of the crime and later, under direction by Smith, the duplicate key to the office was recovered. Other items, tools of a burglar's trade, had been found in Brodie's home. But it was the evidence of Brown and Ainslie that sealed the deacon's fate. His defence tried to undermine their statements by pointing out that they were accomplices who had only turned informer to save their own necks. Brodie tried to save himself with an alibi, backed by his brother-in-law and Jean Watt, but that was easily dismissed by the prosecutors. The jury, many of them former friends or acquaintances of Brodie, had little difficulty in finding the two men guilty.

Back in the Tolbooth, Brodie seemed to accept his fate with some stoicism, singing verses from *The Beggar's Opera* to himself while he played draughts on the floor with anyone who cared to take him on. If no one challenged him, then he played against himself. There was a gap of over 30 days between the verdict and the fulfilment of the sentence. On 1 October 1788, they led Brodie and Smith from their cell. As they made their way towards the gallows, built atop the platform on the west end of the Tolbooth, the pair passed James Falconer and Peter Bruce, who had robbed a Dundee bank of £422. Also sentenced to death, they had received a respite of six weeks. Smith commented that six weeks was too short a time but Brodie, ever the pragmatist, disagreed: 'George, what would you and I give for six weeks longer? Six weeks would be an age to us.'

Finally they reached the dread platform where public executions had been held since 1785. Clad in black, with a freshly powdered wig, Brodie showed a professional interest in the new device that was to speed the passing of felons from this world to the next. There was no undignified turning off from a ladder for William Brodie. He himself had been involved in the decision to adopt the new trapdoor system but he was not, as legend states, the first in Edinburgh to die on it – nor did he have a hand in its design or construction. The device did not work the first time the bolt was sprung. As the hangman and labourers worked to address the problem and Smith waited patiently to die, Brodie calmly chatted to friends in the crowd. To all intents and purposes, he appeared ready to make his leap in the dark. Again the noose was placed around his neck and again the proceedings were delayed by technical problems. 'What would you have?' Brodie called to the crowd. 'It is *fortune de la guerre.*' He was led to the noose a third time and this time everything went smoothly. The life of Deacon Brodie, cabinetmaker and gentleman thief, was over – but the legend had begun.

It was his demeanour during his last days – and moments – that spawned that legend. Brodie's slender body, as that of a convicted felon, should have been handed over to the anatomists for dissection but a special dispensation had been obtained that allowed it to be given to friends almost immediately after the hanging. A French doctor was waiting nearby who, it was believed, had the skills to reanimate him through bleeding. Brodie would have heard of Half-Hangit Maggie Dickson and of Hugh Lundie, who was revived in his Tolbooth cell following his suicide attempt. If they could be revived after hanging, then so could he. Naturally, the attempted reanimation failed.

But the storytellers of the town would not let him die. Brodie knew his life was not to be snuffed out on the scaffold, they said, which explained his buoyant mood at the end. His powerful friends had planned to rescue him but heavy security had prevented it. However, he had been given a silver tube that was to be swallowed, thus preventing the rope from strangling him, while a harness of wires beneath his clothes protected his neck from snapping when the trapdoor opened and he plunged into the darkness below. According to these urban myths, Brodie's grave was empty and he had been seen alive and well in Paris.

Brodie did live on, if only in the imagination of Robert Louis Stevenson. Modern-day tourists are also aware of him, thanks to Deacon Brodie's Tavern on the corner opposite the site of the Tolbooth and to the Deacon's House café in Brodie's Close.

CHAPTER TEN

GUNPOWDER, TREASON AND PLOT

Royal Blood

If a 1566 miniature purporting to depict James Hepburn, 4th Earl of Bothwell, is accurate, then the Border noble would not have looked out of place wielding a razor in a Glasgow street fight. Although it is impossible to be sure from the tiny portrait, there is no feeling of great height about the man, while his close-cropped dark hair and a nose that bears evidence of having been broken at least once lend weight to the comparison with a street thug. There are no scars visible but they would have been there, for the earl was a brawler. His sideways gaze is challenging, as if daring the viewer to take him on, while even the effeminate ruff, the style of the time, fails to soften his air of menace. Here was a Border terrier of a man, no worse than some of his contemporaries but infinitely superior to many. He had his own honour, this small firebrand, and he never betrayed it. John Prebble called him 'a rogue but a bold rogue and a brave one, more likeable, or at least more forgivable than many noble Scotsmen who died secure in the titles and estates which they had bought with treason, treachery and murder'.

On Saturday, 12 April 1567, Bothwell faced his fellow lords gathered in the Tolbooth and defied them to bring charges against him for murder. That Bothwell had killed men, and had ordered men killed, there is no doubt, but that was the way of the world in those days. This particular murder was especially heinous, as the victim was of the blood royal and the word on the street held Bothwell responsible. On this day, in the Tolbooth, he faced the nobles, his hand on his sword, and challenged them to find him guilty of a crime that is one of Scotland's most enduring mysteries.

Mary Stuart, Queen of Scots, met Henry Stuart, Lord Darnley, in February 1564 during one of her many royal progresses through her kingdom. There had been much discussion of marriage revolving around the young queen, a widow these past three years, and a great deal of political engineering on both sides of the border to create a match. Despite her changing the spelling of her name, Mary was a Stewart and she had all the ambition of her line. Scotland was merely a stepping stone on the route to the ultimate prize, the throne of England, which she believed was hers by right. Elizabeth, then on the throne, was the daughter of Anne Boleyn, whom Henry had married without permission from the Pope, a move that led the fat king to break away from the Roman Catholic Church. The rich rents, tithes and lands that had thus fallen into those fleshy royal hands were a bonus. In the eyes of the Mother Church, Elizabeth was illegitimate and Mary, descended from Margaret Tudor, Henry's sister, was the rightful heir. To strengthen her position, Mary must marry and marry well. A son or two would not go amiss to ensure the future stability of the Stuart dynasty. Mary saw the 18-year-old Darnley, declared him to be the 'lustiest and best proportionit lang man' she had ever clapped eyes upon and decided they would be wed.

Darnley was certainly handsome, if effeminate, but, despite Mary's glowing review, he was also a petulant brat who had ambitions of his own. He was of royal blood and he had his eye on the throne. This man who would be king was also Roman Catholic, like Mary, and the idea of such a union did not fill the leaders of the Reformed Church with enthusiasm, even if Darnley did have sympathy with the Protestant cause. Nevertheless, the two were married amid great pomp and circumstance on 29 July 1565. John Knox condemned the match from the pulpit of St Giles' and attacked the Lords of the Congregation for their seeming inability to prevent it: 'I see before me your beleaguered camp. I hear the tramp of the horsemen as they charged you in the streets of Edinburgh; and most of all is that dark and dolorous night now present to my eyes, in which all of you, my Lords, in shame and fear, left this town.'

Wedded bliss did not last long. Mary fell pregnant within months and many affairs of state were left in the hands of her Italian secretary David Rizzio, or Riccio. This did not please either her noble lords or her husband and on a stormy night in March 1566, Rizzio was murdered in Holyrood Palace. The killing party was led by Darnley, who held his heavily pregnant wife back while the little secretary was carried away by the armed men and stabbed 56 times. It was a horrific scene and it was a wonder that Mary did not suffer a miscarriage because of it. Bothwell was not part of the murder crew, for he had remained loyal to his queen. He and another loyal noble, John Gordon, the Roman Catholic Earl of Huntly, had been decoyed elsewhere in the palace that night; they too were on the hit list but they managed to escape.

Mary knew that she must play to Darnley's vanity if she and her unborn child were to survive, so despite his involvement in the murder, she used all her charms, all her wiles, to convince him that she did not blame him for the violent act. He had been used, she told him, by ambitious men. More or less imprisoned in Holyrood Palace, she convinced Darnley that they must escape. They galloped headlong for Dunbar, where Bothwell and Huntly were waiting with a small army. Darnley's apparent change of heart, and news that a force of 8,000 men was heading for Edinburgh, sent his co-conspirators in the murder into a panic. They fled south. In the end, only two men – Under-Sheriff of Perth Thomas Scott and his servant Henry Yair – were caught, tried and beheaded on the Maiden for their part in Rizzio's assassination.

Bothwell's hour had come and he was ready for it. With Rizzio gone, Mary soon came to believe that this wiry Border lord was one of the few men she could trust, especially as her due date came close. For his part, Bothwell remained loyal. Perhaps it was through ambition or perhaps he had fallen under her spell, but the swashbuckling nobleman never let her down. Darnley realised he had been too hasty in abandoning his former accomplices and knew that the Border lord would not be as easy to dispose of as Rizzio. Despised by both sides, the Queen's husband fell into a sulk and soothed his hurt feelings by whoring and wenching his way through Edinburgh and Stirling.

On 19 June 1566, the Queen of Scots was, as Elizabeth put it, 'lighter of a fair son and I am of barren stock'. Darnley pouted, believing the child was not his but Rizzio's. Mary assured him that the boy James – set to become the sixth Scottish king of that name and the first of England – had been 'begotten by none but you'. Darnley went off on a bout of drinking and fornicating and in doing so may have contracted a dose of syphilis, although some believe it was smallpox with which he became infected. Whatever kind of pox he had, it marked his face and for a while he hid himself in Glasgow. Mary convinced him to return to Edinburgh and he took up residence in the Old Provost's lodging at Kirk o' Field, just inside the city wall, where Drummond Street stands today. It was here, on 9 February 1567, that he died.

Mary was in Holyrood Palace, three-quarters of a mile away, when she was awakened by the sound of a huge explosion. Someone had stored gunpowder in the room she used as a bedroom during her regular visits to her sick husband and had set light to a fuse. The house at Kirk o' Field had been completely destroyed and the bodies of Darnley and his valet were found in the garden. According to reports, they had been killed not by the blast but by strangulation. It was presumed that Darnley had got wind of the threat and tried to escape, only to meet a conspirator lurking in the garden. The mob had no doubt as to who was responsible – neither did the Earl of Lennox, Darnley's father. The finger of guilt was pointed firmly in the direction of Bothwell and soon notices calling for his arrest were hammered under cover of night on the Tolbooth door. These notices also brought into question the Queen's honour in the matter. These 'seditious libells' proliferated to such a degree that an Act was passed to repress 'ane licentious abuse enterit laitlie and cum in practize within this realme'. The Act prohibited the printing and placing of 'placardes, billies and tiquetties of defamation ... under silence of nyt in divers publicit places ... to the slander, reproche and infamye of the quenies Majestie'. These defamers of the Queen, if caught, would be subject to 'the pane of deid without favour'.

Bothwell, though, showed no fear, although he did threaten to wash his hands in the blood of the men who published the 'libells'. He denied the rumours, while the Queen, although offering a reward of £2,000 for information, chose not to have him brought to court. The defiant Border lord remained in Edinburgh but surrounded himself with 50 of his best men, just in case. However, the clamour proved too much and Mary eventually agreed that Bothwell must be called to answer the accusations. He filled Edinburgh with his men and strutted into the Tolbooth court confident that he would be walking out a free man. Although the jury included men who were no great fans of his, they were forced to acquit him of the charge of being 'art and part of the cruel, odious, treasonable and abominable slaughter' of Henry Stuart. No witnesses were called, no evidence was lodged and even the dead man's father was absent from the court, having been forcibly detained by some of Bothwell's Border troops. Bothwell backed up his plea of innocence by challenging anyone who wished to continue the rumours to hand-to-hand combat. No one was unwise enough to take him up on the offer.

It was James Hepburn's crowning moment. From then on, it was all downhill. Following the news that he and Mary were to marry, critical placards again decorated the Tolbooth door. There had been a delay while his divorce was finalised and then Mary herself had hesitated to cleave to another husband. Finally, Bothwell could wait no longer. He apparently abducted her and carried her – perhaps willingly – to his fortress at Dunbar. What actually took place there – if it was rape or consensual sex – no one can say for certain but afterwards Mary announced she was to marry the rough-hewn Border lord. The wedding marked the beginning of the end of Mary's rule: the nobles mistrusted Bothwell, the public still believed him responsible for Darnley's death, the Kirk thought she was the Whore of Babylon anyway. The couple were forced to flee when a thousand-strong force came to arrest the Queen's new husband. At Carberry Hill, there was a ludicrous non-battle as the Confederate Lords faced Mary's troops and demanded that the earl be handed over to them. She refused and Bothwell, not one to cast off the habits of a lifetime, threw down the gauntlet of single combat. There then followed a farcical situation as the first challenger was deemed too low born to cross swords with him, while the second took so long to take off his armour that the armies began to drift away. Mary decided the best course of action was to surrender herself to the Confederate Lords in order that her new husband would go free. The lovers were parted for the final time and Mary watched the only real man of action she had ever known ride off into obscurity. He died years later, rotting with gangrene in a Norwegian prison where he had been consigned for breach of a marriage promise he had made years before. The Queen's fate was imprisonment, abandonment by her son and finally death on the block at Fotheringhay. Whether she thought of her faithful rough-edged Border lord in her final days is unknown.

In June 1567, a number of men were 'put in irins and tormentis' in a bid to find those guilty of Darnley's murder. The testimony of those who, with some assistance from the torturers, implicated Bothwell was accepted, while that of those who did not was rejected. They were all subsequently hanged and quartered all the same. Years later, the Earl of Morton was also implicated and died on the Maiden.

Tradition has it that Bothwell conspired to murder Darnley but there is little evidence to confirm it, for the testimony elicited under torture must, because of its very nature, be ignored. The case seems to confirm the idea that history is written by the victors, for the lords who seized power in the minority of James VI ensured that Bothwell's name was forever tarnished by the events at Kirk o' Field. In reality, it is difficult to see why Bothwell would want to have Darnley killed. There is evidence to suggest that he believed the man was in the final stages of syphilis and not long for this world. Sidelined as he was, he certainly posed no personal threat.

On the other hand, there was still the possibility that the anti-Marian forces could use Darnley as a rallying point and unite against her. Then there was Darnley's claim that James was not his son, which Mary would have seen as an obstruction to future stability. Bothwell may have been so hopelessly in love with the Queen that he would have done anything for her. If she had wanted her weak and mendacious husband out of the way, he was just the fellow to do the job. She certainly appeared grief-stricken and distraught after the killing but within days was at Seton House playing golf with Bothwell, although, in fairness, doctors had decided she needed a change of air and had suggested this. Or were the doctors themselves acting on a suggestion by powerful and dangerous men?

It was said that the plot began in Craigmillar Castle at a meeting led by Bothwell and Huntly. But when all is said and done, there could have been a great deal more said than actually done. Darnley's death may well have been the result of a conspiracy by Bothwell and others, or by the Queen and others, or cooked up by the lords he betrayed. There is also a theory that Darnley himself had the gunpowder placed there to kill the Queen. In trying to escape the blast, he met someone in the garden who meant him harm. His death, then, may have been a case of his misfortune coinciding with an enemy's opportunism.

Rye and Die

The Stuart monarchs were no strangers to plots against their royal persons. Ever since Walter Fitzalan took his first steps towards power as the hereditary High Steward of Scotland, there were those who would have resorted to violent means to remove him from office. The Steward became Stewart and finally, with the arrival of Mary, Stuart. Her life seems to have been one long round of plot and counter-plot. Even her execution was brought about by intrigue, as Elizabeth ordered that the death warrant be concealed among other papers so that she could sign it 'by accident'. James VI suffered in the Ruthven Raid and the Gowrie Conspiracy and, during his reign as James I of England, there was the daddy of them all – the Guy Fawkes Plot. His son, Charles I, was executed by rebels, while under the rule of Charles II and his brother James II other seditious schemes were uncovered and quashed. The Rye House Plot of 1683 was one of these and although it centred on an English farmhouse, the Tolbooth played its part in the events.

Charles II was an ardent fan of horse racing, having made his first visit to Newmarket in 1669. A friend of jockeys and no slouch in the saddle himself, he had Sir Christopher Wren build him a house near the course at Newmarket and twice a year he visited the town to enjoy what was coming to be known as 'the sport of kings'. Fourteen years after that first excursion, his visit was cut short by a calamitous fire that ripped through many Newmarket buildings, including his house. It proved a most fortuitous disaster, for enemies were plotting against him to prevent the possibility that his Roman Catholic brother, James, would succeed him.

One-eyed Richard Rumbold, known as 'Hannibal' to his friends, was a firm Republican and former follower of Oliver Cromwell, reputedly having fought at his side at Dunbar and Worcester. Later claims that Rumbold had actually been one of the masked executioners when Charles I lost his head were denied, although he did admit to being part of the platform guard. Through marriage, he came into ownership of Rye House, situated about 18 miles from London on the road to Newmarket, and in 1683, together with other extremists, he hatched a plan to house 100 armed men in its grounds. The objective was to ambush the King, codenamed 'Blackbird', and his brother, 'Goldfinch', as they returned from the races. Bullets were to be poured into their coaches from all sides as they passed through in the narrow lane. James, Duke of Monmouth – Charles's bastard son – would then be placed on the throne. The change of plan caused by the fire threw the plot into confusion and eventually someone talked, as someone always does. The men behind the plot scattered, including Rumbold, who managed to escape to Holland.

Meanwhile, as further conspirators turned informer to save their own skins, the authorities mopped up their former associates. In Scotland, Robert Ferguson, a minister appropriately nicknamed 'The Plotter', was known to be in Edinburgh. The city gates were all closed and secured to hem him in. However, no sign of the Plotter could be found and it was assumed he had somehow fled the city prior to the shutdown. Ferguson, though, had found a very ingenious hiding place: while most people were desperate to get out of the Tolbooth, he had voluntarily incarcerated himself there. Ferguson had a friend who was at the time under the care of the dark Heart of Midlothian and he used the somewhat liberal visiting hours to sneak in and hide. He managed to conceal himself among the debtors and miscreants of the day until the search for him died down. He then simply walked out and fled to the Continent.

Covenanter Alexander Gordon of Earlstoun had fought at Bothwell Bridge and so was 'put to the horn' – outlawed. He was captured trying to take ship for the Netherlands and imprisoned, first in Newgate in London, then in the Tolbooth. The Rye House Plot was so far-reaching that it became almost fashionable to implicate Whigs, as the Covenanters were known, and Gordon's case was no exception, although there was no firm evidence of his involvement.

The authorities seldom needed such an inconvenient thing as concrete proof but as they had Gordon bang to rights for bearing arms at Bothwell Bridge, it was decided he would hang for that alone. Even though he was condemned, they decided that a bit of torture would be good for his soul and might well yield further information. Permission to go ahead was obtained from Charles II but as the boot was about to be applied, Gordon resisted with such vehemence that his questioners believed he was suffering from some mental aberration. As Dane Love tells us in *Scottish Covenanter Stories*, four physicians diagnosed him as suffering from *alienatio mentis, furore latente laborans*, a mental disorder. They prescribed fresh air, so he was sent first to the Castle and then to the prison on Bass Rock in the Firth of Forth, where the air was so fresh it could shave a minister. Finally, after another spell in the Tolbooth, he was taken to Blackness Castle and in 1689 he was set free, his execution having been called off thanks to the removal of James II from the throne.

Robert Baillie of Jerviswood was the nephew and son-in-law of Archibald Johnston of Warriston, architect of the National Covenant and tormentor of Montrose. Baillie was also an ardent Covenanter and as such was an ideal candidate to be implicated in the plot. Captured and imprisoned in London, loaded down with irons to prevent his escape, he was questioned incessantly, even by the King himself, but either he refused to divulge what information he had or he had none to give. Along with other accused men, he was transported back to Edinburgh, where torture could be applied without compunction. On 14 November 1683, already a sick man, he found himself in the Tolbooth. His wife begged permission to join him in his cell, even offering to be clapped in irons beside him if they feared she would aid escape. Her plea was rejected but when the prisoner's health deteriorated to such an extent that death was thought near, they relented.

Meanwhile, one of the men who had been brought with Baillie from London, William Carstares, was subjected to the thumbkins.

They tightened the screws for an hour and a half, questioning him constantly. The ordeal proved too much for some of the noble lords, who excused themselves, but others were not so squeamish. General Tam Dalyell, if Covenanter literature is to be believed, roared at the prisoner that he would roast him alive if he did not talk. Finally, on being threatened with the boot, Carstares named names, including that of Robert Baillie.

Sir George Mackenzie led the prosecution and hammered away at the sick man's guilt. Baillie told the court that he recognised that the 'sickness now upon me, in all human appearance, will soon prove mortal, and I cannot live many days. I find I am intended for a public sacrifice in my life and estate; and my doom being predetermined, I am only sorry, under such circumstances, that my trial has given the court so much and so long trouble.' He continued to deny any part in the plot against the King and his brother, saying, 'I abhor and detest all thoughts and principles that would lead to touching the life and blood of His Majesty, or of his royal brother, or of any person whatsoever.' He then fixed his eye upon Mackenzie, who had labelled him traitor and would-be assassin. 'My Lord Advocate,' he said, 'I think it strange that you accuse me of such abominable things. When you came to me in the prison, you told me that such things were laid to my charge, but that you did not believe them. Are you convinced in your conscience that I am more guilty now than I was at the interview where you acquitted me of guilt?'

The lawyer, known as Bluidy Mackenzie because of his single-minded determination to convict Covenanters, said, 'I own what you say. My thoughts were then as a private man; but what I say here is by special direction of the Privy Council.' The Lord Advocate then pointed at Sir William Paterson, Clerk of the Justices, and stated, 'He knows my orders.'

Baillie nodded and said, 'Well, my lord, if your lordship has one conscience for yourself and another for the Council, I pray God to forgive you; I do. My lords, I trouble your lordships no further.'

At 9 a.m. on 24 December, the jury found Baillie guilty. The authorities did not wish an execution to mar the holy festivities, so Baillie was to die that very afternoon. His head was to adorn the Netherbow Port, his arms and legs were to be sent to the usual towns. His lands and possessions were forfeit to the Crown and his name tainted forever more.

Two years later, the dreaded royal succession came to pass – an apoplectic stroke seized Charles and he converted to Catholicism on his deathbed. His brother, James, was now King. Plotters lost no time in devising a plan of attack to remove him from the throne. The rebellion would be fought on two fronts: in the West Country of England under king-in-waiting James, Duke of Monmouth; and in Scotland under Archibald Campbell, 9th Earl of Argyll. The earl was already under sentence of death in his homeland for treason, although he denied the charges and had escaped from his cell in Edinburgh Castle dressed as his daughter's servant. 'Hannibal' Rumbold was made a colonel in Argyll's force. The affair was doomed to failure on both sides of the border. The revolt in the West Country was suppressed. There was a bloody battle at Sedgemoor, from which Monmouth fled only to be captured and executed, before the area suffered through the reign of terror known as the Bloody Assizes, when Lord Chief Justice Jeffreys sentenced over two hundred people to be hanged and four times that number to be sent to Barbados.

The rising in Scotland fizzled out before it had properly begun when the Presbyterians could not agree among themselves whether to support it. Argyll found himself surrounded by a superior force and was captured at Inchinnan while trying to escape. He was taken to Edinburgh to face a Privy Council bent on revenge. In memory of the fact that he was one of those who had watched and gloated while Montrose was being taken to his death, he was led up the High Street, bareheaded on an unsaddled horse, by the public hangman. According to Sir Walter Scott, he was kept in the Tolbooth while the Privy Council debated what to do with him, before finally he was taken to die on the Maiden, just as his father had done before him. He was certainly in the New Tolbooth, the council chambers, on the day of his death, having been brought there from his Castle cell. A contemporary record states:

> Argile came in coach to the Toune Counsell, and from that on foot to the scaffold with his hat on, betuixt Mr Annand, Dean of Edinburgh, on his right hand – to whom he gave his paper on the scaffold – and Mr Laurence Charteris, late Professor of Divinity in the college of Edinburgh. He was somewhat appaled at the sight of the Maiden – present death will danton the most resolute courage – therfor he caused bind the napkin on his face ere he approached, and then was led to it.
>
> He soon regained his composure for on the scaffold he is said to have observed that the blade was 'the sweetest maiden he had ever kissed'.

Richard Rumbold, meanwhile, had also been snared. He was captured by a band of Royalists and severely wounded. Taken to Edinburgh, his stay in the Tolbooth would have been very short, for he was tried the following day, so 'that he might not preveen the public execution by his death'. The outcome was unsurprising and the execution was scheduled for that very afternoon, 26 June. On the scaffold, Rumbold delivered an impassioned speech during which, when not drowned out by the beating of drums, he denied being anti-monarchical. However, he did believe that 'Kindly government was best of all where justly executed; I mean, such as it was by our ancient laws – that is, a king, and a legal, free-chosen parliament – the king having, as I conceive, power enough to make him great; the people also as much property as to make them happy; they being, as it were, contracted to one another! And who will deny me that this was not the justly constituted government of our nation? How absurd is it, then, for men of sense to maintain that tho the one party of his contract break all conditions, the other should be obliged to perform their part? No; this error is contrary to the law of God, the law of nations, and the law of reason.'

He went on to say that he died 'this day in defense of the ancient laws and liberties of these nations'. He continued: 'I may say this is a deluded generation, veiled with ignorance, that tho popery and slavery be riding in upon them, do not perceive it; tho I am sure there was no man born marked by God above another, for none comes into the world with a saddle on his back, neither any booted and spurred to ride him.'

He was hanged, drawn and quartered, his heart ripped from his chest while it was still beating and displayed to the bloodthirsty mob on the point of a bayonet. His head was spiked on the West Port, his quarters sent to Glasgow, Stirling, Aberdeen and Perth. Argyll, still awaiting his own death, said, 'Poor Rumbold was a great supporter to me and a brave man and died Christianly.' Sir Walter Scott, in his *Tales of a Grandfather*, records that some form of vengence was meted out when Mark Kerr 'the chief of those who took him', died on his own doorstep at the hands of two men who claimed to be Rumbold's sons. They ripped out his heart 'in imitation of what their father had suffered on the scaffold'.

Argyll's bloodless revolt did have one serious consequence: Covenanter prisoners were cleared out of tolbooths and prisons and transferred to Dunnottar Castle near Stonehaven, where they were crammed into a single vault. If conditions in their former jails had been bad, those here were considerably worse. Scott wrote that they had endured a forced march to the castle, 160 men, women and children, 'rendered bitter by want of food and accommodation as well as by the raillery of the pipers who insulted with ridiculous tunes a set of persons who held their minstrelsy to be sinful'.

The persecution of the Covenanters was nearing an end by this time. James II was not destined to rule the country for long: the Glorious Revolution of 1688 saw him deposed and William, Prince of Orange, proclaimed King. However, there is another story, that of an assassination attempt, to be told regarding the Presbyterian struggle during 'The Killing Times', and for that we must go back to 1668.

James Sharp was a Presbyterian minister from Crail, sent to London on the restoration of the monarchy in 1660 to seek the blessing of King Charles II on the Church of Scotland. Sharp, though, was a man of ambition and he realised that it suited his future best if he turned his coat and joined the ranks of the episcopalians. He returned to Scotland as Archbishop of St Andrews and earned the hatred of his former colleagues. He showed himself to be very much a poacher turned gamekeeper and proved a vocal and ruthless opponent to the growing Covenanter band. After the tragic climax to the Pentland Rising at Rullion Green, he was said to have held back a letter from a king weary of hearing of the death of his subjects, keeping it quiet until a few more Covenanter necks were stretched and heads lost.

On 11 July 1668, a deranged Presbyterian named James Mitchell, who had once shared lodgings with Major Thomas Weir, decided to rid the world of this troublesome priest. As the archbishop sat in a carriage at the head of Blackfriars Wynd in Edinburgh, where he had a home, Mitchell blasted away at him with pistols. The shots missed their intended target but did bring down the Bishop of Orkney, who was at that moment climbing into the coach. Mitchell escaped in the confusion and, although the city gates were closed and no one was allowed to leave without a written passport from the magistrates, avoided capture. Tradition states that he was the first to hide in the Tolbooth until the furore abated – the trick repeated by Robert Ferguson 15 years later and, they say, by a Jacobite gentleman during the 1745 rebellion. According to Sir Daniel Wilson, he 'was quietly taking his ease in "the King's Auld Tolbooth"' while the Redcoats scoured the Highlands.

Six years later, Sharp saw a man staring at him in the streets and recognised the wide-eyed yet hate-filled stare of the assassin. He raised the alarm and James Mitchell was arrested, a loaded pistol found on his person, suggesting that he had planned another attempt on the archbishop's life. On 7 February 1674, Mitchell was imprisoned in the Tolbooth and the keeper warned that no one was to be admitted to 'speak or correspond with him until he be further examined'. During that further examination, the man was promised that his life would be spared if he confessed his crime. Mitchell, a fanatic but perhaps not as certain of his place in heaven as others, agreed to this proposal and was sent to Bass Rock. He was there for four years before he was brought back to Edinburgh at Sharp's behest to be tried before the High Court of Justiciary for his life. The earlier agreement was cited in his defence but one by one officials denied there ever was such a deal. Mitchell's advocate was refused access to official records – a stance sometimes taken even today by the Crown – and the mad preacher was executed in January 1678.

The following year, in May, a gang of 12 Covenanters ambushed Sharp's coach on Magus Muir above St Andrews. He was brutally cut to pieces in front of his daughter. David Hackston was present at the murder but not only did he take no part in the actual killing, he also appealed to his companions to let the archbishop live. Even so, he was there and he ultimately paid the penalty. Wounded and captured at Airds Moss, he suffered an agonising death in Edinburgh on 30 September 1680. Two men, Laurence Hay and Andrew Pitulloch, were also accused of the murder in 1681, although they had not been on Magus Muir at the time. They were held in the Tolbooth before being hanged and headed. Another man, Andrew Guillane, who had indeed been present but, like Hackston, had called for no harm to befall Sharp, was arrested in 1683, chained to the bar in the Tolbooth and executed on the Gallowlee on 13 July. His head and his hands were inexpertly cut off by a drunken hangman and nailed to the Netherbow Port. His body was hung from a pole at the site of the archbishop's murder.

The Age of Treason

The authorities were ever quick to see sedition around them. The Covenanters were often, of course, engaged in treasonous acts. The rioters who took to the streets to protest a wrong were deemed seditious. Even Philip Stanfield was deemed a traitor because he was said to have damned the King. In March 1612, one William Tweedie was whipped and banished from Edinburgh never to return under pain of death for reproaching the King's Council and telling them 'he would not give a scab of his arse for them'. Three years later, a man called Fleming was hanged because he had spread slanders against the King and said he wished he might shoot him dead.

Governments grow nervous when people come together and demand their rights. Politicians much prefer to tell the people what those rights are than have the people decide for themselves. History is rife with attempts by the authorities of the day to combat civil unrest with force – even when that unrest is more vocal than violent.

In 1789, revolution in France gave the British government a serious case of the jitters. Cries of 'Liberty, Equality, Fraternity' were heard on street corners and the men in power grew edgy as they sensed a new era ahead, an era in which they might not have a place. As crowned heads rolled across the Channel, the demand for the rights of man rose in these islands and home-grown royals were understandably concerned for their own necks. Radical leaders began to emerge and the Establishment moved to crush them. In 1792, King George III's birthday was celebrated in Edinburgh by the burning in effigy of Home Secretary Henry Dundas, and a Society of Friends of the People was formed within weeks. This was no body of men issuing a call to arms but rather middle-class liberals, lawyers and artisans voicing a demand for constitutional change. Meanwhile, the powerful landed gentry, who controlled the vote, represented the status quo. Among the Society's members was Glasgow-born advocate Thomas Muir, who vowed 'to live free or die in the French manner'. The firebrand lawyer was arrested and spent some time in the Tolbooth before being brought to trial in a hearing that Lord Cockburn later described as 'one of the cases the memory whereof never perisheth. History cannot let its injustice alone.' Before a jury packed with his opponents, Muir insisted that he was preaching not sedition but parliamentary reform. Lord Justice Clerk Robert Macqueen, Lord Braxfield, countered that to preach such reform was, at a time when blood was high, seditious. Braxfield showed his colours when he told the jury, 'The landed interest alone has a right to be represented. As for the rabble, who have nothing but personal property, what hold has the nation of them?' The judge's reply when told that Christ had been a reformer was also notable. 'Muckle good he made o' that,' he said. 'He was hangit for it.' Tough, unforgiving, authoritarian and coarse but with a savage wit, Braxfield was the template for Robert Louis Stevenson's *Weir of Hermiston*. His handling of the political trials of 1793–4 led Lord Cockburn to call him 'the Jeffreys of Scotland'.

Muir, despite appeals for leniency by the jury, was banished to Botany Bay for fourteen years. Into his short life he packed more adventure than those of ten men. He escaped from the Australian colony, travelled to North and Latin America, lost an eye during an ocean firefight with two British warships and ended his days soon after, advising the revolutionary government in France.

Muir is the best known of the Scottish reformers but there are others whose names are etched on the Martyrs' Monument that thrusts to heaven like an accusing finger in Old Calton cemetery. These men held radical views for their day and may well have expressed them in intemperate language. This made them ripe for being trampled under the feet of the Government and the courts. Muir's motives were never in question, but one man whose name appears on the stone ended his days with his reputation sullied following a claim by a fellow radical that he conspired with the authorities.

The Tolbooth warding book contains the following entry for 14 January 1794:

Maurice Margarot, merchant in Marybone, London and No 10 High Street, presently or lately residing at the Black Bull Inn at the head of Leith Walk. Found guilty of sedition and sentenced to be transported beyond the seas to such place as His Majesty with the advice of the Privy Council shall declare ... that if after being so transported he shall ever return to and be found at large within any part of Great [Britain] during the said 14 years without some lawful cause and be therefore lawfully convicted he shall suffer death as in case of felony without benefit of clergy.

Although born in Devon in 1745, Margarot was hugely influenced by his French father's radical tendencies. He experienced the heady excitement of the French Revolution at first hand and when he returned to England joined the reforming London Corresponding Society, which had been created by Scots shoemaker Thomas Hardy. In January 1792, Margarot wrote that it is 'the duty of every citizen, to keep a watchful eye on the government; that the laws, by being multiplied, do not degenerate into oppression; and that those entrusted with the government do not substitute private interest for public advantage'. He also said 'that in consequence of a partial, unequal, and therefore inadequate representation, together with the corrupt method in which representatives are elected, oppressive laws, unjust laws, restrictions of liberty, and wasting of public money, have ensued'. In these days of 'war' on terror and crime, some of his words have new meaning.

A convention of like-minded radicals was planned for November 1792 in Edinburgh, and Margarot and fellow member Joseph Gerrald were nominated by the London society to attend. The Edinburgh Convention intended to discuss such dangerous notions as annual parliaments and votes for all. Before Margarot and Gerrald arrived, news reached them that Thomas Muir and Thomas Fyshe Palmer had been arrested in Scotland on sedition charges. Undaunted by the obvious intention of the Scottish authorities to stifle reform, they came north and are known to have attended a number of meetings, leading to their arrest in December 1793 along with Society of Friends of the People secretary William Skirving.

Witnesses claimed that they had personally heard Margarot make seditious speeches. Spectators in the gallery, showing their vocal support for the accused, interrupted the trial. Thomas Keddie, an apprentice saddler, 'having given disturbance to the court by indecent noise', was brought before the judge, Lord Braxfield, who told him that he was 'guilty of a gross offence in disturbing and insulting the court'. The court ordered that Keddie be detained in the Tolbooth for two months but he was kept for less than a week before being released by order of the Court of Justiciary. Shoemaker John Mason was also sent to the Tolbooth for making 'indecent noise in one of the galleries' but was liberated within the day. Meanwhile, the court noticed that a witness in the case, lawyer John Wardlow, was in a state of 'gross intoxication' and 'behaving with great indecency'. He was sent to sober up in a Tolbooth cell but was released the same day.

Margarot made a four-hour speech in his own defence, which Lord Braxfield allowed to be heard without interruption. At its end, the judge dismissed the accused's words as 'sedition from beginning to end' and sentenced him to be transported and banished for 14 years. In the Tolbooth records, it is noted that Margarot was transferred to London in a post chaise. In February, he, along with William Skirving, Thomas Muir and Thomas Fyshe Palmer, were all on prison hulks on the Thames awaiting transportation. Palmer, Skirving and Margarot were finally herded onto the *Surprize*, which left Portsmouth on 2 May 1794 to make its way to Botany Bay. En route, a plot to kill the captain, Patrick Campbell, and seize the ship was thwarted. Years later, in a pamphlet, Palmer accused Margarot of turning traitor. An investigation failed to support the claim but the stain of the allegation followed Margarot for the rest of his days.

After an eventful time in Australia, where he was joined by his ever-faithful wife, Margarot was eventually released and he returned to England. He campaigned for convict transportation to be abolished and never lost his reforming zeal. However, Palmer's accusation of collaboration was always there and he was never fully trusted again. Although his health had suffered over the years, he retained his fighting spirit. In a letter written to a like-minded friend two years before his death, he wrote: 'I hear you say your spirit is broken. Believe me, however, you are mistaken in this; it only sleepeth. The storm-beaten mariner does not therefore forsake the sea, but refreshed only awaits a favourable breeze to again unfurl his sails.' He died in London, a pauper, on 11 November 1815. Thirty years later, the Martyrs' Monument was erected. The inscription reads: 'To the memory of Thomas Muir, Thomas Fyshe Palmer, William Skirving, Maurice Margarot and Joseph Gerrald. Erected by the Friends of Parliamentary Reform in England and Scotland.' On another face of the 90-foot obelisk is a quotation from a speech Thomas Muir made on 30 August 1793: 'I have devoted myself to the cause of the people. It is a good cause – it shall ultimately prevail – it shall finally triumph.'

Muir and Margarot may have stopped short of fomenting armed rebellion but the same could not be said of others. In 1794, the so-called Pike Plot was uncovered. John Prebble wrote that it had 'more reality in the authorities' imagination than it had in fact' but it did not stop them from sending one man to his death.

Robert Watt was a merchant who bolstered his income by warning the authorities of treasonable schemes that probably never existed. It may be that he became involved in this half-baked plot in order to profit from the arrests of the ringleaders. If so, his plan was undone when someone tattled the tale first. He, along with David Downie and five other shadowy men in Edinburgh, allegedly talked of procuring arms and taking the fight to the streets. The plan involved inciting the army to mutiny, taking over banks and other institutions and using force of arms to encourage the King to sack his ministers. The plot received its name from the fact that 47 pikes had been manufactured. It strains credibility that this modest armoury could have threatened the stability of the nation. Nevertheless, four erstwhile conspirators turned King's evidence, Watt confessed all and he and Downie were found guilty. Watt's name appears in the Tolbooth warding book, where it is stated that he was executed on 1 October 1794. This note is made against an entry for 16 May regarding a Robert Watt who was warded for a debt owed to James Alexander, merchant in Stirling, of £26 17s. 3d. Further down the page there is an entry on Robert Watt, merchant of Edinburgh, who was 'this day arrested in the Tolbooth until liberate by due course of law in virtue of a warrant of the sheriff . . . accusing him of being guilty of seditious practices'. Beside this is a note regarding David Downie, goldsmith, being arrested for a similar offence, although there is no corresponding entry as to his disposal. He, like Watt, had been sentenced to death and would have died on the Tolbooth scaffold had his sentence not been commuted to transportation. When the news was delivered to him, he fell to his knees and blurted out, 'Glory be to God, and thanks to King! Thanks to him for his goodness! I will pray for him as long as I live.'

Watt's death was barbarous. By the end of the eighteenth century it might be thought that matters of capital punishment had become more civilised. But the man had been found guilty of treason and therefore an example had to be made. He spent the night before his death in a cell in the Castle and was transported to the Tolbooth on a black cart. He sat with his back to the pure white horse pulling the dark hurdle, the black-clad executioner facing him with an axe in his hand. The event was invested with a solemn majesty, as city magistrates, the Town Guard and 200 soldiers marched alongside the cart to the beat of a slow drum. Watt was led to the platform in a grey greatcoat and, curiously, a red nightcap, as if he had been wakened suddenly from sleep to keep his date. He was given a white coat and a cap in exchange before he was hanged and his head lopped off with two strokes of the executioner's axe. The crowd reacted with horror at the sight of the severed head of a traitor being held aloft old-style for all to see.

The zeal for reform did not die. Lord Cockburn would later write:

> These trials sank deep, not merely into the popular mind, but into the minds of all men who thought. It was by these proceedings, more than by any other wrong, that the spirit of discontent justified itself throughout the rest of that age.

In England, there was another ill-conceived plan to kill a king, this time using an air-filled tube and a poisoned arrow. The scheme was quickly dubbed 'the Pop-gun Plot'.

As the cry for Liberty, Equality and Fraternity died in a welter of blood and corruption in France, so the thirst for reform in Britain subsided – but not forever. Just over 20 years later, Scottish justice once again had to deal with radicalism, during the Weavers' Uprising of 1820, which ended in a skirmish and the deaths of three men on the scaffold. By that time, though, the Edinburgh Tolbooth had outlived its usefulness.

CHAPTER ELEVEN

END PIECES

Suspended Sentences

From 1785, the Tolbooth was not only the place felons were held before, during and after trial, it was also the site of public executions. As we have seen, the authorities still stamped down hard on lawbreakers, and from that year until 1816, 37 people were hanged, Robert Watt being also beheaded. The gallows were built on the platform at the west end of the Tolbooth, making it all the easier for the assembled multitude to catch a glimpse of the condemned. The first person to die thus was 'out pensioner' (a former soldier in receipt of a pension) William Mills, on 21 September 1785. He had been incarcerated in the Tolbooth since March, accused, along with his wife and her daughter, of various charges of housebreaking and stealing quantities of cash and 30 frames of glass. The women were 'dismissed out of prison' in August, leaving Mills to face death alone. It was noted at the time that 'the place of execution was improved by the addition of a scaffold for the magistrates and clergy', which added 'a great degree of solemnity to the scene'. The executioner was John High, known to locals as Jock Heich. He was himself a thief, having become the town's hangman the year before in order to escape punishment for stealing hens. He was also a notorious wife beater. He supervised most of the executions at the Tolbooth for the next 30 years, with men and women meeting their deaths for offences ranging from petty theft and horse stealing to treason and murder.

In 1786, John and William Haugh were sentenced to death for the theft of hats, silk and several dozen silver-plated buttons. They were transferred to the Edinburgh jail from Dumfries Tolbooth in January and John met his doom on the platform on 19 April. William managed to put off the day, winning a reprieve subject to His Majesty's pleasure, and was confined in the Tolbooth. However, he failed to understand that the royal will is a fickle thing. On the Sunday before his brother died, he tried to break out of his cell, and then again in May 1787. Patience with his 'atrocious behaviour' ran out and it was ordered that the respite was to cease. On 4 July, he went to his death before the jeering crowd.

And so the roster of death goes on: Walter Ross, executed 19 April 1786 for three counts of theft, including lifting a wallet lined with £25 from the Lord Provost of Glasgow ...

Brothers Charles and James Jamieson, illiterate tinkers who could not tell the valuable bills of exchange from the ordinary letters they stole from Kinross post office. Their mother, Euphan Graham, was also accused but was freed on a not proven verdict ...

Inveterate jailbreaker Peter Young, who, like Billy the Kid a century later, used his thick wrists and small hands to his advantage in slipping free of his manacles and fleeing Perth jail in 1786. Caught again following a break-in, with his wife as an accomplice, he was sentenced to death and incarcerated in Aberdeen prison. She staved off execution by pleading her belly but in any case the pair broke out on 24 October 1787, freeing all the other prisoners in the process. Young was described as a stout young man, pock-marked, of about 22 years of age, with 'a remarkably sharp eye'. By December, he was back in custody and jailed in Edinburgh. The Tolbooth managed to hold him and he died on 2 July 1788 ...

Dundee merchants and bank robbers James Falconer and Peter Bruce, who were jailed at the same time as Deacon Brodie and George

Smith, were lodged in the Edinburgh Tolbooth on 4 and 12 August 1788 respectively. They finally met their end on 24 December. Two co-accused had turned prosecution witnesses but were transported to Botany Bay for another crime. However, they did not escape the rope, for they were hanged en route following a mutiny . . .

In August 1790, William Gadesby, a deserter from the 7th Regiment of Foot, was arrested in connection with 'severall daring robberies' during which 'liedges [were] insulted, beat and abused inn the night time when going about their lawfull affairs'. Town constables, in the process of rounding up the usual suspects, caught him with 'a large stick or cludgeon' and 'an open knife in his pockets'. Sentenced to death, he put off the date by claiming he had further information about who had actually pulled off the Dundee bank heist for which Falconer and Bruce had been hanged. He dangled on 23 February 1791 . . .

That same year, Paisley weaver John Paul and journeyman coachmaker James Stewart were executed after murdering James Smith, Writer to the Signet, for his fourteen-shilling watch as he made his way home to his lodgings. Two other men were accused along with them but may have turned prosecution witnesses, for there is no record of their sentences . . .

In 1813, sixty-year-old Christian, or Christina, Sinclair poisoned her eight-month-old niece with arsenic in the Orkneys. Tried and convicted in Edinburgh, she was carried to the platform in a chair . . .

In 1815, Irishmen Thomas Kelly and Henry O'Neill were found guilty of highway robbery. The crime was then becoming more common in Scotland and so an example had to be made of these two men. They were to die not on the Tolbooth platform but at the site of one of their robberies, then known as Briggs of Braid Road and Braid's Burn, on the high road to Dumfries (nowadays it is the junction of Braid Road and Comiston Terrace). At 1 p.m. on 25 January, the condemned men were led from the Tolbooth and placed in a cart with the hangman. Their escort included police officers, magistrates and priests. In heavy snow, the strange procession made its way to the city limits where the local sheriff joined them and led the march on horseback. The two men were hanged at a point where two square stones set into the roadway now lie. Their bodies were escorted back to Edinburgh and buried in Greyfriars kirkyard.

The last person to die on the Tolbooth platform was robber John Black, on 11 December 1816.

The End

By the nineteenth century, the city was changing fast. It had reached the point where it needed to grow outwards rather than upwards. In addition, some of its more affluent citizens desired clean air, for the term 'Auld Reekie' was more than a nickname – for the city's residents, it was a way of life. In 1766, a contract to design a new town was awarded and the following year construction began. Five years after that, the Robert Adam-designed North Bridge was completed. By 1817, Edinburgh – like Major Weir, Deacon Brodie and their fictional counterpart Jekyll/Hyde – had a double life of new and old, rich and poor, affluent and effluent. The impoverished predominated in the close-knit warren of lands and tenements that formed the city on the hill; the wealthy nestled in the wide streets and spacious squares that covered the former farmland to the north.

The outlook for the tolbooths old and new was bleak. In 1809, the justiciary courts moved to the parliament buildings while the council grew and transplanted itself to custom-built headquarters across the Lawnmarket. In that year, the death knell was sounded for the New Tolbooth. Prison reformer John Howard had visited the Old Tolbooth in 1782 and wrinkled his nose at the conditions. On a second visit in 1787, he was surprised that the dilapidated building had not been replaced by something more modern. The treatment of criminals was changing, albeit slowly, and this impacted on the Old Town jail. Felons were being held for longer before being executed (a punishment that was growing increasingly unpopular, although far from unknown) or transported (which was more common), while sentences of imprisonment were growing in length. In November 1791, Howard's wish was granted when the foundation stone was laid on Calton Hill for a 'new Bridewell', so-called after the old house of correction near the well of St Bride on London's Fleet River.

'It was a piece of undoubted bad taste to give so glorious an eminence to a prison,' wrote Lord Henry Cockburn of the new Edinburgh jail. It would take a quarter of a century before the new totally replaced the old. Towards the end, the High Street prison was used only for debtors, petty offenders and an increasing number of military deserters. The town councillors looked out of their Royal Exchange chambers and decided that for the sake of improvement the 'gloomy and magnificent edifice' of the Tolbooth would have to go. It was past its time and it was blocking the High Street. Lord Cockburn was no fan of the old Heart of Midlothian but he would nonetheless have preferred to see it spared the attentions of the wreckers:

> It was of great age; it once held the Parliament (though how it could I can't conceive); it was incorporated with much curious history; and its outside was picturesque. Neither exposing St Giles', nor widening the street, nor any other such object, ought to have been allowed to demolish so interesting a relic.

The Tolbooth vanished forever in 1817, unmourned by the general public. The stones, the marks of Deacon Brodie's draughts board still upon them, were taken away and used to help create the sewers and drains at Fettes, making that area 'the grave of the Old Tolbooth'. The platform on which felons had been hanged was carried off. The square cage in which the most troublesome prisoners were kept was bought by the councillors of the seaside resort of Portobello to be used as a lock-up house. Sir Walter Scott, who had done so much to etch the building into the collective memory, took the arched doorway, the door and the huge iron lock to be built into his Borders home, Abbotsford. Twelve years later, he noted that 'a tom-tit was pleased to build her nest within the lock'.

The Town Guard was disbanded the same year, a more modern police force taking their place. These old soldiers, still known derisively as the Town Rats, performed their last duty at the Hallow Fair, marching slowly to the martial beat of fife and drum. Sir Walter Scott wrote:

> A spectre may, indeed, here and there be seen of an old grey-headed and grey-bearded Highlander, with war-torn features, but bent double by age, dressed in an old-fashioned cocked hat, and in coat, waistcoat and breeches of muddy-coloured red, bearing in his withered hand an ancient weapon called a Lochaber axe. Such a phantom of former days still creeps, I have been informed, round the statue of Charles II in the Parliament Square, as if the image of a Stuart were the last refuge for any memorial of our ancient manners.

It is fitting that two such ancients, veterans of the Town Guard, were on duty on 15 April 1840 at the laying of the foundations for the Princes Street monument dedicated to the writer. It was a touch Sir Walter would have liked.

Public executions continued to both enthral and horrify the populace. The first man to be hanged before a gawping audience after the sweeping away of the Tolbooth was 23-year-old thief Robert Johnston, on 30 December 1818. The science of hanging might have evolved since the horrors of the dule tree but it was still far from exact, as was proved by this botched dispatch, which prompted a riot that smacked of the old days. The scaffold was erected before the New North Church on the Lawnmarket. Hangman John Simpson had failed to calculate the length of rope accurately, so when the unfortunate felon fell, it did not break his neck. To make matters worse, his feet were touching the ground. He dangled there on his tiptoes, the rope biting into his flesh, until the horrified crowd moved to save him from his agony. The police were overcome by force of numbers and the criminal was cut down. The unconscious Johnston was retrieved from the hands of the mob, bled to revive him and taken back to the scaffold. Even then, things did not go according to plan. As he stood on the platform, the noose again around his neck, Johnston's trousers fell down. The scene might have been laughable if it had not been so grim. While Simpson and his assistant struggled to cover his decency, the man was held upright partly by his feet and partly by the rope around his neck. Then, when Simpson tried to shorten the drop, Johnston was hoisted above the platform and began to slowly throttle. He managed to free one of his hands and clawed at the rope biting into his neck. The crowd grew restive again and cries of 'murder' began to rise in its collective throat. Simpson climbed onto a chair to prise Johnston's fingers free and the hanging progressed. However, the horror was not yet over, for the convicted man's face was left uncovered and the crowd could see his agonies, 'a spectacle which no human eye should ever be compelled to behold', as an onlooker wrote. A napkin was hastily thrown over his face and – finally – Robert Johnston was put out of his misery.

By 1878, public death as deterrent and spectacle had ceased to be popular. From that year, condemned felons met their doom behind the closed doors of Calton Prison, the first man to be executed there being wife-murderer Eugene Marie Chantrelle, in May of that year. Calton Prison was an imposing building but it was gone by 1925 to make way for a new Scottish Office. Only the castellated former governor's house survives, nodding across the serenity of the ancient Calton graveyard to the Martyrs' Monument.

As the centuries passed, the Tolbooth became a faded memory, almost forgotten save for the heart of stones on the pavement near to St Giles'. Few knew or seemed to care that the buildings had played such a prominent role in Scottish history. The Heart of Midlothian now lived only in the words of a revered author long out of fashion with the general reading public.

Then, in 2006, the Tolbooth was back in the news once again. Large parts of the High Street were to be dug up for roadworks and this gave city archaeologists the opportunity to use ground-penetrating radar to identify the foundations of the ancient site. Copper setts were to be laid to mark the location of the buildings.

It is a shame that nothing more substantial exists. It would be fitting if something tangible remained of a building that played such a prominent role in the history and culture of Scotland. They say that ghost sightings are the residue of dramatic events that have soaked into the stones around them and are played back like recordings – what writer Nigel Kneale called 'the stone tapes'. If that is true, what stories might the Tolbooth walls have told? At its windows we might see the gallant Montrose scratching at the glass or Lady Jean Livingston lingering a while to allow the crowd a glimpse of her tragic beauty. Deacon Brodie might yet play his board game on the prison floor and Katharine Nairn forever steal away in her borrowed clothes. The heartbreaking notes of Patrick Ogilvy's plaintive violin might echo through the corridors, accompanied by the screams of agony from tortured souls as they suffer for eternity the boot and thumbscrew. Or perhaps it would simply have been the groans and whimpers of the thousands of debtors and felons, both guilty and innocent, that would have bled into the mortar and rock.

The majority of those prisoners are forgotten to history. Only their names, scribbled in faded ink on yellowing paper, remain as a memorial.

BIBLIOGRAPHY

'Act of the Council Containing Regulations for the Jail of Edinburgh and Conduct of the Jailer' (1810, held in Edinburgh Central Library)

'Address to the Inhabitants of Edinburgh on the Outrage Conducted on 30th December by Amicus Veritatus' (Michael Anderson, Edinburgh, 1819)

Adams, Norman, *Scotland's Chronicles of Blood* (Robert Hale, London, 1996)

Bailey, Brian, *Hangmen of England* (W.H. Allen, London, 1989)

Barr, James, *The Scottish Covenanters* (John Smith & Son, Glasgow, 1946)

Cavendish, Richard, *The Black Arts* (Pan, London, 1972)

Chambers, Robert, *Traditions of Edinburgh* (W. & R. Chambers, Edinburgh, 1967)

— *Domestic Annals of Scotland* (W. & R. Chambers, Edinburgh, 1874)

Cheetham, J. Keith, *On the Trail of Mary Queen of Scots* (Luath, Edinburgh, 1999)

Churchill, Winston S., *This Island Race* (Cassell, London, 1964)

Cockburn, Lord Henry, *Memorials of His Time* (Robert Grant & Son, Edinburgh, 1946)

Crockett, S.R., *The Grey Man* (Jackson & Sproat, Ayr, 1980)

Extracts from the Records of the Old Tolbooth of Edinburgh 1657–1686
(Old Edinburgh Club, 1923)

Falkus, Christopher, *Life and Times of Charles II* (Weidenfeld &
Nicolson, London, 1972)

Fraser, George MacDonald, *The Steel Bonnets* (Pan, London, 1974)

Heppenstall, Rayner, *Tales from the Newgate Calendar* (Constable,
London, 1981)

Horan, Martin, *Scottish Executions, Assassinations and Murders*
(Chambers, Edinburgh, 1990)

Huson, Richard (ed.), *Sixty Famous Trials* (Daily Express, London,
no date)

Lindsay, Maurice (ed.), *Scotland: An Anthology* (Robert Hale,
London, 1974)

Livingstone, Sheila, *Confess and Be Hanged* (Birlinn, Edinburgh,
2000)

Love, Dane, *Scottish Kirkyards* (Robert Hale, London, 1989)

— *Scottish Covenanter Stories* (Neil Wilson, Glasgow, 2000)

— *Ayr Stories* (Fort Publishing, 2000)

MacClure, Victor, *She Stands Accused* (J.B. Lippincott, Philadelphia)

Macgregor, Forbes, *Famous Scots* (Gordon Wright, Edinburgh, 1984)

Miller, Peter, 'The Origin & Early History of the Old Tolbuith of
Edinburgh', in *Proceedings of the Antiquarian Society*, Vol. 20 (1886)

Prebble, John, *The Darien Disaster* (Mainstream Publishing,
Edinburgh, 1978)

— *John Prebble's Scotland* (Penguin, London, 1984)

— *The Lion in the North* (Secker and Warburg, London, 1974)

Robertson, James, *Scottish Ghost Stories* (Warner, London, 1996)

Rosie, George, *Curious Scotland* (Granta, London, 2004)

Roughead, William, *Malice Domestic* (W. Green & Sons, Edinburgh,
1928)

— *Rascals Revived* (Cassell, London, 1940)

— *Twelve Scots Trials* (Mercat Press, Edinburgh, 1995)

Skelton, Douglas, *Deadlier Than the Male* (Black & White, Edinburgh, 2003)

— *Devil's Gallop* (Mainstream Publishing, Edinburgh, 2001)

— *Indian Peter* (Mainstream Publishing, Edinburgh, 2004)

Smellie, Alexander, *Men of the Covenant* (Banner of Truth Trust, London, 1960)

Tod, T.M., *The Scots Black Kalendar* (Munro & Scott, Perth, 1938)

'The Tolbooth of Edinburgh', in *The Architect and Contract Reporter* (1895)

Weaver, Graham, *A to Z of the Occult* (Everest, London, 1975)

Wheatley, Dennis, *The Devil and All His Works* (Hutchinson, London, 1971)

Williams, Ronald, *Montrose: Cavalier in Mourning* (Barrie & Jenkins)

Wilson, Alan J., Brogan, Des, and McGrail, Frank, *Ghostly Tales and Sinister Stories of Old Edinburgh* (Mainstream Publishing, Edinburgh, 1991)

Wilson, Sir Daniel, *Memorials of Edinburgh in the Olden Time* (Adam & Charles Black, Edinburgh, 1891)

Young, Alex F., *The Encyclopaedia of Scottish Executions 1750–1963* (Eric Dobbs Publishing, Edinburgh, 1998)

NATIONAL ARCHIVES OF SCOTLAND RECORDS:

GD406/1/5681

GD406/1/4071

GD406/1/9439

GD220/5/806

GD237/11/101

GD248/52/2

GD124/15/1128

JC27/84

JC49/6

HH11/1-39

ACKNOWLEDGEMENTS

Thanks to all the usual suspects – Elizabeth, Irina, Karin, Katie, Margaret, Eddie, Gary, Mark and Stephen.

Also to the people I work with who held the fort during my absences to write the book: Craig, Jamie, Roddie, Babs, Joyce, Kim and Margaret. I'd better mention Heléna, otherwise a P45 might be forthcoming.

I'm grateful to the staff at the National Archives of Scotland and Edinburgh Central Library. Also to the directors and staff at Mainstream, particularly Bill Campbell for greenlighting the project, Graeme Blaikie for putting up with my 'Tail-End Charlie' tendencies and Claire Rose for being so eagle-eyed and catching my errors. Any that she missed are my fault.